D1564076

Praise for *Washington's Iron Butterfly*

"In my eyes, Bess will always be the person I wanted to be when I grew up."—Lynda Johnson Robb

"A new and fresh look at the inner workings of the Johnson White House from the perspective of the 'Iron Butterfly.' While she was officially social secretary to the First Lady, Bess Abell's political and social skills shaped the success of the East Wing's contributions to that administration." —David S. Ferriero, Archivist of the United States

"Bess Abell was the P. T. Barnum of the White House and Washington in her time. She had the inventive mind to create limitless events big and small and the knowledge and organizational skills to pull them off. This book brings the reader into a storytelling session about her remarkable life through her voice and the voices of those around her."—Larry Temple, special counsel to President Lyndon B. Johnson (1967–1969) and chairman of the Lyndon B. Johnson Foundation

"The story of Bess Abell would have been very different had she been born a generation later. In *Washington's Iron Butterfly*, her story comes alive through her own words and the words of those who knew her. Ably edited by Donald Ritchie and Terry Birdwhistell, two of the best oral historians around, this work allows the reader to feel the emotions, the joys, and the sorrows of a remarkable woman. It is a book that both entertains and instructs—a good read, indeed. The result is a fun, entertaining, and readable book about a very special woman."—James C. Klotter, author of *Henry Clay: The Man Who Would Be President*

"The Katharine Hepburn of Washington in the 1960s, Bess Abell was a force of nature. From a deeply divisive war to luncheons gone horribly wrong, she was able to deftly steer the Johnson family through the tumult of their Washington years. In *Washington's Iron Butterfly* we hear the story from Abell herself and from the members of the Johnson administration who knew her best."—Kate Andersen Brower, CNN contributor and *New York Times* best-selling author of *The Residence*, *First Women*, and *Team of Five*

"Few had intimate access to the Johnson White House like Bess Clements Abell—a young Kentucky woman who took her political savvy as a former governor's daughter from Morganfield to the Potomac. Talented and likable, described as 'feisty and funny' by the editors, she was known to be gracious, but tough as nails when things had to get done. An important read for Kentuckians and anyone who wants an inside view of the Oval Office."—Bill Goodman, executive director of Kentucky Humanities and author of *Beans, Biscuits, Family, and Friends*

"Bess Clements Abell learned from her parents' grace and grit and she used both during her Washington career. She handled difficult situations with calm resolve and demonstrated how to serve and lead. She made her home state of Kentucky proud."—Eli Capilouto, president of the University of Kentucky

"The position of White House social secretary is challenging in even the most tranquil of times. For Bess Abell, who served in the role for Lyndon and Lady Bird Johnson during the 1960s—a time of enormous social change, including some brought about by Johnson's transformative policy itself—the challenges were formidable. Donald Ritchie and Terry Birdwhistell's *Washington's Iron Butterfly: Bess Clements Abell, An Oral History* offers a vivid and entertaining portrait of the inimitable social secretary, whom the Secret Service code-named 'Iron Butterfly' due to her perfect combination of Kentucky grace and unflinching strength."—Mark K. Updegrove, president and CEO of the LBJ Foundation and presidential historian for ABC News

Washington's Iron Butterfly

For our iron butterflies,
Anne and Janice

Contents

Illustrations follow page 124

Foreword

With Bess Abell's passing in October 2020, an event that only deepened the sorrow generated by that annus horribilis, a cruel paradox suggested itself. This woman, robbed of her memory by the most insidious of diseases, had spent most of her eighty-seven years creating memories to be cherished by the family she adored and the countless friends she made to feel like family—not to mention several presidents and vice presidents, or the tens of thousands of White House guests she welcomed as White House Social Secretary. That was her official title, though it hardly did justice to her versatility or brio. Mrs. Johnson came closer to the truth when she pronounced Bess "the greatest showman since P. T. Barnum."

Having eloped with the love of her life in 1955, Mrs. Tyler Abell did her wedding planning belatedly, but on a grand scale. Her efforts to air-condition the ovenlike Shrine of the Immaculate Conception for Luci Baines Johnson's 1966 nuptials came to naught, but she did manage to defuse a potentially embarrassing snafu involving the use of nonunion dressmakers. At least the International Ladies Garment Workers were placated. For Lynda Bird Johnson's East Room wedding to Chuck Robb in December 1967 Bess borrowed four walkie-talkies from the CIA. No friend to the status quo, she proposed to dress the bridesmaids in Christmas red. Emulating her employer's thrift, she figured she could recycle the wedding decorations as part of the seasonal makeover of America's House.

Creativity married to practicality is a rare blend. But then so was Bess herself. Imagine a feminist with a dress code, the love child of Sol Hurok and Auntie Mame. Bess had star quality in her own right. Joined to her utter lack of pretense, this latter quality alone was enough to distinguish her in a town where heads tend to swell under the hot lights of television cameras. On the terrace at Merry-Go-Round Farm no less than in the State Dining Room of the White House, Bess displayed a genius—no other word will do—for making people feel at home. There were no strangers around her dinner table.

Like every great hostess, she elicited the best stories, the shrewdest observations, and the wittiest rejoinders from wallflowers and curmudgeons alike. She gave as well as she got, something I can attest to after interviewing her at multiple presidential libraries as well as the White House Historical Association. A historian friend of mine relishes nature's conversationalists as a breed apart. "He's [or she's] a talker," he'll say, and one knows instinctively the talk is worth listening to. What set Bess apart, besides her flair for narrative and her irrepressible humor, was her singular talent for listening. If any of her guests were less than fascinating, it was through no fault of hers.

Even the gossip around her hearth was edifying, far above the usual Washington speculation over who was in or out and the deconstruction of reputations as ephemeral as the headlines in this morning's *Washington Post*. For years, to cite my own example, I harvested memories of Cissy Patterson, tumultuously Drew Pearson's mother-in-law; and of Tyler Abell's redoubtable mother, Luvie, Pearson's second wife, who was only just dissuaded by Bess from taking her grandsons Dan and Lyndon to join Dr. Benjamin Spock and other Vietnam War protesters picketing the Johnson White House.

These and many more colorful characters enliven the pages that follow. Think of it as the memoir that Bess never got around to writing, in no small measure, one suspects, because her storytelling gifts never overrode her discretion and loyalty to those in the public eye who constituted her second family.

My favorite presidential quote is Lincoln's 1862 admonition that "the occasion is piled high with difficulty, and we must rise with the occasion." That is what the Johnsons, ably assisted by Bess, did in a time of national trauma. That is what Bess herself would be called on to replicate nearly every day she was on the job as White House Social Secretary.

What an extraordinary view of life Bess Abell had, from the Governor's Mansion in Frankfort, Kentucky, to the White House and the vice presidential residence of Walter and Joan Mondale; from the Pedernales to the Potomac as it flowed below the farmhouse Drew Pearson built in 1939 as a weekend getaway. In these conversations Bess shares the view with the rest of us, humanizing events and personalities that might otherwise be confined to a textbook. Betty Ford said it best: "To be remembered with joy has to be a kind of immortality." Is there any other way to remember Bess Abell?

Richard Norton Smith
American historian and presidential scholar

Introduction

Whether in peace or war, the social side of Washington carries on. Formal events take place with great protocol and decorum, and receptions and other informal events help reduce political tensions. Guest lists must be constructed, invitations sent, table seating arranged, entertainment organized, and a myriad of other details accounted for, supervised at the White House by the social secretary.

That post originated during the presidency of Theodore Roosevelt and grew in importance over time. At first social secretaries simply kept track of invitations and acceptances to White House functions. The position gradually expanded into an impresario for entertaining on a grand scale. Managing the social side of the White House became an especially delicate assignment during the administration of Lyndon B. Johnson, set against a backdrop of antiwar demonstrations and urban and racial unrest. That assignment fell to Bess Clements Abell, whose combination of southern graciousness and a firm hand at management earned her the Secret Service handle of "Iron Butterfly."

How Bess Abell coped with and performed her role as the Johnsons' social secretary in this turbulent atmosphere is the underlying theme of this book. The story is told in her own words, drawn from her oral histories, and from the observations of those around her. She often recounted her experiences, but never wrote them down. Whenever anyone urged her to consider writing a memoir, she shrugged and said, "How can I? Everybody has already stolen my best stories." In lieu of an autobiography, her oral accounts recreate her life story.

Born during the Great Depression, Bess Clements was the only child of a well-established, middle-class family in a small western Kentucky town. Her childhood, like those of her small-town friends, revolved around play, school, church, and Saturday matinees. She helped her mother plan social events for the town ladies but also bore witness to the workings of local government though her father's elective offices. At an early age she learned well what social skill and political skill could accomplish when forged into one.

Bess came to understand the political landscape of Washington as well as she did because she learned so much from her father. He had extraordinary political knowledge and insight to share, and many stories to tell. Earle C. Clements's long political career enabled his daughter to expand her world beyond the boundaries of her small town. She accompanied her father to Frankfort as he served in the state legislature and ran political campaigns. Uprooted from her friends and sheltered life, Bess learned to adapt and make the best of it, finding new friends and embracing new experiences.

As she grew older, she realized that her gender came with restrictions. "I am sure that Daddy would have liked to have had a son," she reflected. Perhaps she never appreciated how much she was like her father: smart, charming, attractive, resilient, organized, ambitious, and extremely loyal. Had she been born a boy her father undoubtedly would have groomed her for a political future. As a girl, her path remained uncertain.[1]

Her father's career took the family to Washington, DC, when he served two terms as a member of the US House of Representatives. Elected governor of Kentucky in 1947, he moved them into the Governor's Mansion in Frankfort. After two unhappy years of high school in Frankfort, Bess ultimately convinced her parents to allow her to attend the last two years at the Ward-Belmont School in Nashville. For college, she returned to the Bluegrass State to attend Kentucky's flagship university.

At the University of Kentucky Bess Clements did well academically majoring in the family business, political science, but had not given much thought to where that might lead. She also immersed herself in an active social life, including dating the captain of the football team. She represented Kentucky as the princess to the 1952 Cherry Blossom Festival in Washington.

Bess first met Tyler Abell at the 1950 Kentucky Derby, but they had dates with other people. Four years later, a friend set Bess up on a date with Tyler. She and the aspiring young DC lawyer and stepson of the nationally syndicated political columnist Drew Pearson would eventually elope on New Year's Eve and build a life together, maneuvering through the crosscurrents of power in the nation's capital. Senate Majority Leader Lyndon Johnson and his wife, Lady Bird, hosted a lavish reception for the newlyweds at the Carlton Hotel following their marriage, attended by a who's who of Washington VIPs, which confirmed the couples' status in the nation's capital, where Bess's father served as senator from Kentucky.

Following the birth of her two sons, Dan Tyler and Lyndon, Bess Abell sought outlets for her energy and creativity. She considered law school but ultimately abandoned that path. Her volunteering to help during the presidential campaign of 1960 led to employment with Lady Bird Johnson. She quickly made herself indispensable to the vice president's wife and future first lady. No request was too small or too big for the twenty-eight-year-old assistant, from picking up dry cleaning to planning an elaborate party. All the while Bess honed her already considerable social and political skills.

On November 22, 1963, Bess Abell was at the Johnson ranch in Texas to prepare for the arrival of the Kennedys, who planned to spend the weekend there following their visit to Dallas. Stunned when she learned of the president's assassination, she immediately went into problem-solving mode: How could she and two others on the Johnsons' staff get back to Washington to assist the new president? Everything had changed in an instant, and Bess found herself in the middle of the whirlwind.

Most presidents moved into the White House after a triumphant campaign and a gala inauguration. "The Johnsons moved into the White House after a tragedy in Dallas that killed President Kennedy," Bess noted. "That was something that both the President and Mrs. Johnson were very sensitive to." The Johnson administration began with a state funeral and a somber air that overhung everything, especially the requirements of White House entertaining.

To the surprise of some, Lady Bird Johnson named Bess social secretary, and for the next five years she became an integral part of the Johnson White House. With the skill and charm of an "Iron Butterfly" she tackled small problems and large crises while helping to bring a president perceived as a cowboy out from under the shadow of the Kennedys' Camelot. Through perseverance and creativity, Bess established the Johnson White House to be as glamorous as the president from West Texas would permit.

Bess Abell's memories and stories of campaigning offer a peek behind the curtain of mid-twentieth-century politics from a woman staff member's viewpoint. She operated on the cusp of the modern women's movement as she and press secretary Liz Carpenter assisted Lady Bird Johnson in making women relevant within the Johnson inner circle. It was all done with Bess's unique ability to combine charm, creativity, attention to detail, and political skills.

Her efforts from planning state dinners to choreographing two presidential daughters' weddings took place amid growing opposition to the Vietnam War, which caused protests both outside and inside the White House. Bess managed to cope with protesters and devise ways of avoiding conflict at social events, knowing that any missteps would create front-page news.

Following the Johnson White House years, Bess Abell reprised her White House connections by serving as chief of staff to Joan Mondale, the vice president's wife. In 1982 she also established Bess Abell Enterprises, a public relations and publicity company that specialized in creating imaginative events for clients in the DC area. She remained an acknowledged leader in Washington's social life.

Bess and Tyler Abell developed Merry-Go-Round Farm, Drew Pearson's former farm and summer home, laying out tracts for new homes that would appeal to families who could also board their horses there. Bess employed the same skills she had used at the White House to promote the new development. Still a Kentuckian at heart, Bess made sure that her sons and grandchildren knew about their Kentucky roots. She took each of them to her native state to visit relatives, old family friends, libraries and historical societies, and points of interest where Earle Clements had left his legacy on the commonwealth.

An interviewer once asked Lady Bird Johnson whether Bess resembled Earle Clements in style and matter. The former first lady responded with a smile: "To some extent I would say yes. She did because she could always get me to do a lot of work and yet she went about it very quietly and calmly and she could take no for an answer. But not without making several other attempts to get yes!"[2]

Bess and Tyler Abell established the Earle C. Clements Assistantship in the University of Kentucky Libraries for graduate students in information science, history, political science, or other similar disciplines. Their generosity and the opportunity made it possible for those students to move into professional positions in their academic fields. They also established the Earle C. Clements Memorial Endowment to bring in informative and timely speakers to share their thoughts and insights about the role and actions of government. It is fitting that the Earle C. Clements Collection resides in the University of Kentucky's Special Collections Research Center.

The authors of this volume were fortunate to know Bess Abell as a feisty and funny personality who often reminisced about her childhood in Kentucky, her years at the White House, and many other life experiences. When considering a book about her life and career, we thought it best to let Bess speak for herself as much as possible, along with the reminiscences of her family, friends, and colleagues. At the beginnings of most chapters and at certain intervals throughout the narrative, we were able to add some useful context to Bess's story; our own comments are presented in distinctive type. We also included the questions from different interviewers that elicited their responses, reproduced throughout in italics.

Several oral history collections provided the bulk of the interviews from which we drew: the Lyndon B. Johnson Presidential Library, Austin, Texas, the Louie B. Nunn Center for Oral History at the University of Kentucky, and several of Bess's public appearances preserved in C-SPAN's online archives. Her interviews for the Johnson Library, begun while the president was still in office, are detailed but restrained. Fortunately, she became more candid as she retold many of these accounts over the years. We have blended the stories, with the intent of preserving Bess in her most enlightening and engaging conversational style.

We edited the interviews to preserve every interview's wording and the rhythms of the stories, except when the original phrasing might prove confusing to the reader. We have added some explanatory links in brackets. All of the interviews are cited, and many are available online. When cutting out false starts and extraneous information we have avoided using ellipses and other symbols that might clutter the text and disrupt reading. But we have endeavored to retain the intended meaning of every entry. The cited recordings and transcripts are available for comparison and future research. They ensure the preservation of Bess Clements Abell's unique personality and remarkable career.

1

The Governor's Daughter

Bess Clements Abell's ancestors made their way to Kentucky from Maryland, Virginia, and North Carolina in the early 1800s, eventually settling in Union County in western Kentucky. The Ohio River separates the county from both Indiana and Illinois along its northern and western border. Agriculture and coal mining became the county's primary enterprises.

A historical marker stands near Morganfield, the county seat, noting that a thirty-one-year-old Abraham Lincoln gave his only political speech in his native state there in 1840, in support of Whig presidential candidate William Henry Harrison. Two decades later the county would turn decidedly for the Confederacy. With deep Kentucky roots, when Elizabeth "Bess" Hughes Clements, the Clements' only child, arrived on June 2, 1933, her father, Earle Chester Clements, thought it of utmost importance that his child be born a Kentuckian.

BESS ABELL: I have two birth certificates because at the last minute I was found to be a breech birth and Mother needed a Caesarean. The closest hospital with a surgeon who could do that was across the Ohio River in Indiana, for heaven's sake. Daddy and Mother took the ferry across the Ohio River and then drove on to Evansville, where I was born and issued an Indiana birth certificate. When Daddy got back to Morganfield, he immediately went down to the county clerk's office and said, "Well, guess what? Sara had a little girl last night." So, they just wrote out a Kentucky birth certificate, simple as that. I still have both the Indiana and Kentucky birth certificates.

Years later I decided that I wanted to get a copy of my FBI report through the Freedom of Information Office. Eventually, after three or four years, the FBI report arrived. I was surprised that it was two inches thick and all but a quarter of it had to do with the fact that I have two birth certificates.

I made a mistake. I should have just continued to say that I was born in Morganfield, Kentucky, and there never would have been a problem. But, at some point in my life, it may have been after I was married and was getting a passport, I said that I was born in Indiana because I thought, "This has to be accurate." If I had not done that, there never would have been this problem.

Later, when our second son, Lyndon, was being born, Tyler filled out all the forms including, "Where was your wife born?" He paused, trying to decide whether to say Indiana or Kentucky. Finally, the clerk said, "The last time she said Indiana." So that's the way it was left.[1]

TYLER ABELL: You wondered, what was the FBI doing, that it had to spend dozens, literally dozens, of special agents' time finding out why this woman had two birth certificates? As Bess explained, "Nobody ever asked me."[2]

Bess's father, Earle Clements, came from a family of "substantial, well-liked, town-dwelling farmers" in Morganfield, the county seat. Her mother, Sara Blue, was two years older than Earle. She had graduated from Morganfield High School in 1913, sharing highest academic honors with her cousin Lillie Blue. No valedictorian was named that year because the school would name only one valedictorian, and neither student was willing to accept the honor over the other.[3]

Following a record of academic and athletic achievement in high school, Earle entered the University of Kentucky in the fall of 1915 where he excelled as an "All-Kentucky" center for the Wildcat football team. He left college in December 1916 because his father needed his help on the farm but returned to the university the following spring to take a law course. Earle volunteered for military service in July 1917 at the age of twenty, when the United States entered World War I, and rose to the rank of captain within two years.

Back home in Morganfield after the war, Earle served as deputy sheriff under his father, Aaron Waller (A. W.) Clements, a prominent citizen of Union County who practiced law and had served several terms as both sheriff and county judge. During this time Earle also coached the very successful Morganfield High School football team for several seasons. Following A. W. Clements's death in 1925 following surgery, Earle completed his father's term as sheriff.

He learned about politics from his father, and over time Earle would become a legendary political strategist.

EARLE C. CLEMENTS: My father had an influence on my public life. I doubt that he little anticipated that he would have some effect on me for the future because he had no more idea than I did that I'd ever hold public office.

I rode with Father a good many times when he was a candidate for sheriff or county judge. I remember one time I was riding with him and going up to a man's home out in the county. I thought it was great to hear them talk and see how strong my father was with the Lynn family because Lynn was a good family. I let Father know how pleased I was to know that Mr. Lynn was so strong for him. Father said, "Son, Mr. Lynn is not for me." I said, "Not for you? Why, I thought he said he was." "Oh no, son. Mr. Lynn isn't for me. He gave me great encouragement, but he is not for me. He's for my opponent, who I believe will be second in this race. I think I will win."

I said, "But I don't understand. I just thought that certainly when he said he was for you. . . ." Well, Father said, "There's a difference between being for me and voting for me." I couldn't understand that, but Father explained it to me. He said, "Before I became a candidate, son, Mr. Lynn had promised his vote to my opponent. Now there are thirteen or fourteen members in that family. I'm going to get all of their votes but Mr. Lynn's. See, he's for me, but he's not going to vote for me."[4]

Upon his father's death, Earle served the remainder of his term and subsequently won his own election to a four-year term. From there he went on to serve two terms as county clerk and eight years as county judge, during which time the miles of paved roads in Union County tripled.

Becoming increasingly involved in statewide politics, Earle served two terms in the Kentucky State Senate from 1941 to 1944 before going to the US House of Representatives from 1945 to 1948. Elected governor of Kentucky in 1947, he established a highly regarded progressive record. He won election to the US Senate in 1950. In 1953 Senate Democrats elected him whip, where he served under the leadership of Senator Lyndon B. Johnson until his defeat for reelection in 1956. He remained active in national and Kentucky politics after leaving the Senate, maintaining homes in Kentucky and Washington, DC—although he was always a Kentuckian first.

BESS ABELL: Mother said that she wanted to name me Bess after my grandmother, Bessie Barbour Hughes Blue. But my grandmother did not like her name, and so that is why Mother named me Elizabeth Hughes instead, even though she always called me Bess.

I never knew my grandparents. My father's mother, Sallie Anna Tuley Clements, was still alive when I was born, but she died the next year. I have a photograph of her holding me in the backyard at Morganfield, but I never knew her. My father's father, Aaron Waller Clements, passed away after some surgery in 1925.

Mother's father, James Samuel Blue, had a store in Morganfield, and her mother, Bessie Barbour Hughes Blue, raised plants and seedlings and sold them. Mother was the baby of her father's second set of children. He had three daughters with his first wife, Lou Willis Hughes Blue, who died young. He then married her sister, Bessie, and had three sons and my mother.

Mother stayed at home with Grandmother Blue during the last years of her life. They eventually moved into the Capital Hotel on the corner of Morgan and Main Streets. I remember meeting Mother's brothers, George and David. George was a shoe salesman and lived in Georgia and had no children. I only met her brother David once during a driving trip we made out west when Daddy was governor.

I really loved Daddy's sister, Lucy Clements Scull. She was divorced and lived in Uniontown, Kentucky, but was gay, festive, and fun. I still have a figurine of a little girl that she gave me. Aunt Lucy was a pretty little thing and a good musician who played the piano by ear. I suppose that is the reason that my parents had me take piano lessons for such a long time, hoping that maybe some of her talent had come my way. Alas, it did not. I used to move the hands on the clock around, thinking that it would make my practice time go faster!

Aunt Lucy killed herself [October 23,] 1941, when I was eight years old. One day I was walking home from school, and in the last block before I got home, I tripped and fell. I do not know what happened. All I know is when I jumped up, I said, "Aunt Lucy has died!" I ran home and told Mother, "Aunt Lucy died." She said, "Who told you?" Well, as far as I knew nobody told me, and that was the only time something like that happened to me. Neither of my parents would talk to me about it, but somebody surely told me. Aunt Lucy must have had a lot of sadness because she just walked into the Ohio River and drowned. But she was the relative that I really liked.

Uncle Tuley Clements farmed in Union County. But Uncle Baldwin J. "Binky" Clements was the most interesting uncle. He married Margaret Kagey [in 1911] and had two children.

In 1917 Baldwin Clements was convicted on forgery charges and for stealing money from Union County while serving as a county magistrate. Sentenced to four years in the state penitentiary, he had to repay the county $1,350. Not long after returning home from prison, he left suddenly.

BESS ABELL: One day he just up and vanished. He disappeared into the ether, and nobody knew where he had gone. Margaret eventually remarried a wonderful man, William Jesse Buchanan, who became head of the state prison at Eddyville, and they had two more children.[5]

Binky ended up back in Union County after supposedly being on a merchant ship to China. Mother did not really approve of him until World War II came along and Binky became a forager. Binky was very handy and could find extra sugar and shoe stamps.

We had an army camp, Camp Breckinridge, there in Union County. Binky had a little house that was catty-cornered across from the high school, and it was covered with pretend brick or asphalt shingles that resembled yellow brick and looked just awful! Soldiers' wives and camp followers were coming to town and needed a place to stay. They wanted to spend as much time as they could with their husbands and boyfriends.

Uncle Binky built little tarpaper shacks attached to his house all the way out to the sidewalk and rented them. Mother and Daddy also had three guestrooms in our house, which they rented during the war.

Bess's Mother and Father

Morganfield during Bess's youth was a small community of only about 2,500 people. As the Great Depression began, the Morgan Theater in town presented the first "talkie" and the town's first public library opened. Even during hard times, New Deal programs brought much-needed new school buildings, road improvements, and a remodeled and expanded county courthouse. Also, a Civilian Conservation Corps camp was established just outside Morganfield.

BESS ABELL: Mother graduated from high school and worked for a local lawyer. She decided she wanted to improve herself, so she went to Bowling Green, Kentucky, where she took business courses and learned how to be a better secretary. When she got back home her boss docked her pay by five dollars a week, which she did not understand because she was now better and should be worth a lot more. He said, "No, you inconvenienced me while you were away."

At that point she left and went to work at the bank. That is when she met Daddy, who was two years younger. After I came along, she was acting postmistress in Morganfield.

Mother would have the bridge club over. Those ladies did a lot of entertaining back and forth. I remember making place cards for Mother. They must have been awful, but she let me do it. I glued buttons on construction paper, making tallies for the bridge, and also made place cards. I added faces with hair, hats, and so forth, and it was so funny. Maybe that was the beginning of me being a social secretary!

I also remember Mother with her sisters and neighbors just filling the house full of food, including pecan, chocolate meringue, and lemon meringue pies. The pies were made in individual sizes about three or four inches across.

Several different couples would get together two or three times a summer and have big parties. They would prepare lots of barbecued chicken by digging wood pits in the backyard and start burning it the night before to cook the chicken really slow. You could smell that chicken all over town, and you better be invited.

Later, when Tyler and I had a party he would say, "Well, put together an invitation list." So I would put together a list and it would have all the same people on it. He said, "We just had those people. You have to broaden your horizons." I said, "Well, they are our friends." I had grown up in Morganfield, and when you had a party you invited all the same people. And that happens today when we go back to Morganfield and we have a party. We have the same people. That is just what you do. Basically, I am just a country girl from Kentucky.

What are some of your childhood memories of your father?

BESS ABELL: Two vivid memories are of when my father was county judge. The first is being awakened fairly regularly in the middle of the night for a wedding. Couples would cross over the Ohio River from either Illinois or Indiana and Daddy, the county judge, would marry them. Mother served as a witness. Mother and Daddy told me years later that the fees that Daddy collected from marrying people and waking me up in the middle of the night went into a college fund for me.

The other memory is the 1937 flood, when people were being brought out of Uniontown located on the Ohio River. The town had just been devastated. Daddy brought the Catholic priest and his nurse from Uniontown to come and stay with us.

Years later, I learned that the reason the Catholic priest came to stay with us, even though none of us were Catholics, was that Daddy was the only one that could get him to leave the rectory. The water had risen up so far that the priest and the nurse were stranded on the top floor. The priest would not leave because people that came after him would not agree to take both he and the nurse because they did not think that it was proper.

So Daddy went over to Uniontown and told the priest, "You really have to come with us." The priest replied, "Well Earle, are you going to bring my nurse, Miss Jane?" Daddy said, "Of course." So both of them came and stayed with us. Mother was not terribly happy about Nurse Jane staying with us and the priest.

I remember the priest would sometimes play with me. He would set up a card table in the living room and cover it with a blanket. I would go in there and he would chase me. He was very nice and very, very, very kind to me. Mother told me that the priest suffered from what they called melancholia. Daddy always said that I brought him out of it. I always thought that one of the many interesting things about Daddy was the way he was able to get the Catholic priest out of the flood.

In addition to marrying people, county judges handled both the administrative and judicial functions of the county. Because elected county judges were responsible for everything from trials to roads to welfare, they needed to know how to get things done for their constituents. But the position did not require a law license, and Earle Clements did not have one.

When Daddy came to the United States Senate, he was immediately put on the Judiciary Committee. He told his new colleagues, "Wait a minute, boys, I'm not an attorney!" The other senators asked, "But weren't you a judge in Kentucky?" "Yes, I was a judge, but I was never an attorney." He would have made a good one.

Childhood Memories

BESS ABELL: I lived on South Morgan Street, and all my little friends lived on the same street. Elizabeth Lily lived across the street, and Jimmie Waller, my great friend, was my next-door neighbor. Jane Truitt lived two doors up the street, and Tommy Fortenberry lived between me and Margaret Ford and her sister. So we had our own little group there.

I remember one time that I got so mad about something that I was going to run away from home. I do not know what I packed, probably a peanut butter and jelly sandwich, my pajamas, and my toothbrush. I was sitting on the corner near my house crying, and somebody came along and asked, "Bess, what's the matter?" I said, "I'm running away from home, but I can't cross the street unless somebody's watching me!" I was not very adventurous.

All of our mothers had a different sound to call us home. One mother used a cow bell, and another used a school bell. For me, Mother had a horn that Daddy used when he was coaching football. You would be in the neighborhood and you would hear this toot-toot and knew who needed to go home.

Behind all of us who lived on the west side of Morgan Street was a big vacant lot filled with mint. By midsummer, the mint would be high. We would go out there and play and stomp down the mint so that everybody would have their own fort. I would go out to play and Mother would say, "You can go anywhere but don't go in the vacant lot." So, of course, we would come home stinking of mint. Mother would say, "You've been in that back lot." I would protest, "No, Mother, I haven't been." She quickly added, "But I saw you there. I know you were there." It is said that you cannot lie to mothers because they have eyes in the back of their heads. I believed it.

When I was bad Mother would say, "Go outside and get a switch off of a spirea bush and bring it in here." Well, I would go get a switch, bring it in, and she would switch my legs.

We used to go to the movies on Saturday, and it was always a double feature and always a serial. We would act out the cops-and-robbers movie on the way home. Whoever played the robbers would go behind the houses, and the good people would go in front of the houses. It was a great way to grow up.

MARGARET FORD RUSHING: Morganfield was wonderful. I mean, you knew everybody. I remember we just played all over the neighborhood. Bess was an only child. We were the same age, but she was a year ahead of me in school. There were five of us, and we would go to the movies on Saturday afternoons. We would take five/five, which meant the five of us would sit in the fifth row. They would have on cowboy movies and westerns. We would act them out on the way home. It was a wonderful time.[6]

One time we put on a circus in Bess's backyard on her swing set. We all did one little trick, the same trick. I am sure the only ones there were the adoring parents.

Bess was smart and caring and just fun loving, and she had a lot of friends. She was a wonderful friend. The last time I saw her, she said, "You're my oldest best friend."

BESS ABELL: When I broke a window in Mrs. Shrotes's machine shed it was so sad. Mother made me go tell her that I had broken the window. I am sure she had called Mrs. Shrotes ahead of time and said, "Do not tell Bess that it's all right or that you'll take care of it." Somehow, I got it fixed.

I also remember I had been to the ten-cent store and there was one thing there that I just wanted so badly. They had a whole heap of these little bitty babies, and I wanted one of those so bad. They were probably ten for a penny or something. But I did not have a penny, so I took one, and it just weighed on me.

Sometime later I told Mother what I had done. She said, "Just go right back to that store and tell Mr. So-and-So what you did and that you are never going to do such a thing again." I did and, again, I'm sure Mother had called the man and said, "Don't you tell her it's all right."

Your father was becoming very involved in statewide politics and statewide campaigns. He supported Tom Rhea for governor in 1935. Do you have memories of those campaigns?

BESS ABELL: One time, when I was probably not more than two or three, I was sent home from Sunday school with a note to my parents telling them that I should be spending more time studying the catechism and less time talking about politics. One of the questions in the catechism is, "What did God make? God made everything. Who made me? God made me. What else did God make?" I responded, "God made Mr. Tom Rhea!"

Were your parents very involved with church?

BESS ABELL: No. I mean, everybody believed in God and doing the right thing. But I do not remember Mother or Daddy sitting down and reading the Bible, and we were not steady churchgoers. Maybe it was because Mother and Daddy did not belong to the same church. Both Daddy's church and Mother's church were the two smallest denominations in Morganfield. So when I went to summer Bible school, I would go either to the Methodist church or the Baptist church. I do not ever remember going to the Christian church with Daddy. But I think I do remember him going to the Presbyterian church with Mother.

Being an only child, were you and your father very close?

BESS ABELL: Yes, we were. However, I think he would have enjoyed having a son. He probably wished I were more interested in farming and things, which I wasn't. When Tyler got out of the army and was going to law school, Daddy knew that I was working to help support Tyler, and he did say to me, "Honey, if you want to go to law school, I'll help you." I wasn't interested in going to law school until many years later. And then, by that time, Tyler thought it was ridiculous. It probably was. But I did have three friends who went to law school in their forties.

TYLER ABELL: Bess was definitely a daddy's girl, and her whole life history, I think, is very connected with her father. She looked like her father. She had many of the same characteristics.

Were you very athletic?

BESS ABELL: I was a swimmer, and one time, many years ago, Union County native and former Kentucky congressman John Y. Brown Sr. and Daddy were arguing about which of their children was the better swimmer. We were all in Morganfield for some occasion, and it was nighttime. Johnny [later Kentucky governor John Y. Brown Jr.] was there with his dad. To settle the argument they took Johnny and me out to the local American Legion Hut pool, boosted us over the chain link fence, and had us swim. They must have been into the sauce!

TYLER ABELL: I remember her telling me about how she learned how to swim in the American Legion Hut pool. The Legion Hut was the center of Morganfield's social activity. People had meetings there, and County Judge Clements had arranged for the WPA to build a swimming pool at the Legion Hut. Bess was a very good swimmer, by the way. I don't think her father taught her how to swim. He probably hired somebody who was a good swimmer to teach her. I never remember seeing her father even in a pool, let alone swimming.[7]

How did World War II affect you and your family?

BESS ABELL: I always saved bacon grease. Now I save bacon grease, and I do not know what to do with it! During the war I could not get another tube of Ipana toothpaste until I turned in my used tube. I said I wanted to drink coffee, and Mother said, "I'm not wasting my sugar and cream. You're learning how to drink black coffee."

Daddy had a farm. I have no idea whether the farm made any money or not, but there was always enough food to eat and clothes to wear. Nobody lived high, but I never felt poor.

We had meat because Daddy raised some pigs on the farm. Mother cured hams and bacon on the back porch. There were chickens, and we always had a big garden. She did a lot of canning. So how were we deprived? Well, we did not drive very much. Daddy may have had an extra allotment of gasoline because of the farm.

Mother always said she felt she was rich as cream if she had a country ham in the refrigerator and about a dozen quail in the freezer. She used to love to send people a country ham. If she wanted to really do something nice for somebody, she would send them a country ham. She stopped doing that after she got a note from somebody that said, "Oh, thank you, Sara, for your lovely thought. But you really should know that the ham you sent us arrived all moldy and I had to throw it out." After that, Mother thought,

"I can't send country hams to the uninitiated anymore." I have sent some country hams to people, but I always send them cooked.

When your father went to the state Senate in Frankfort did that seem sort of distant to you at the time?

BESS ABELL: No, because I went along, too. Mother and I were camp followers. She would go up to Frankfort and take a furnished apartment. I would go up and stay three or four months and attend some little school in Frankfort.

Did you have any political involvement in your father's campaigns?

BESS ABELL: Nothing more active really than licking envelopes and taking constituents who were in town around on trips. That was really one of my jobs. Actually, when my father was in the House of Representatives, when I was much younger and long before I could be put behind the wheel of the car to take them on a tour, he would say, "Here is my daughter to take you sight-seeing," at age twelve or whatever.[8]

Where did you live when your father served in the United States House of Representatives between 1945 and 1948?

BESS ABELL: When Daddy first went to Congress, I stayed at home with my mother's half-sister, Camilla. Daddy and Mother lived in an efficiency apartment in Arlington. The next year they got a one-bedroom apartment at 2500 Q Street, NW, and brought me up with them. There was a double bed and a twin bed in the bedroom, and I was there with them.

I remember coming home one hot, hot early spring day, and my mother was standing in the dining area of the apartment, just outside our tiny kitchen, looking out a big window over Rock Creek Park while ironing. She had big tears rolling down her face. I said, "Mother, what's wrong, what's wrong?" She said, "Your father had to get himself elected to Congress for me to learn how to wash and iron." She took the laundry down, and I did this some myself, to the basement where they had washing machines that you put quarters in. And then you go back down and put them in the dryer and so forth. She was not used to that.

At that point, Tyler and I lived five blocks apart. He went to school at Saint Albans, and I walked up the street to Jackson Junior High School. It was hard when I moved from Union County to Jackson Junior High School because they wanted to put me back a grade. I do not know why, but it was tough for me to keep up. I developed this rash on my hands.

My happiest times were Saturdays when Daddy would take me to the office with him. We would go down early in the morning and have breakfast in the Longworth Building cafeteria. Then I would go to the office with him and open mail, staple things, or cut out paper dolls. I loved that.

Then, because I did know Washington, they would put me in a car with constituents and have me take them around and show them places. That was when you could drive to the Lincoln Memorial and park there on the circle, and park next to the Capitol building if you wanted to.

We were in Washington during the tail end of World War II, and one summer evening they turned the lights back on the monuments and the US Capitol. I had never seen that before. We were down in that open area between Union Station and the Senate office building, and they had the lights go on the US Capitol and Union Station and the fountain there. And then to drive back home down the Mall towards the Washington Monument and drive around the Lincoln Memorial. You cannot imagine how thrilling that was.

I was thirteen when Daddy ran for governor. My participation in the campaign, I remember, was sometimes going along, sitting around, and being very proud of my dad. All these people wanted to pay attention to him.

Earle C. Clements won election as governor of Kentucky and was inaugurated on December 9, 1947. He used Bess's Bible for the swearing in. Bess recalled that it was when her father became governor that he first warned her about the dangers of thinking they were special.[9]

BESS ABELL: When he was inaugurated as governor it had really gone to my head. Daddy was really worried about his little girl getting too big for her britches. So after the inaugural ball that night, which was at the capitol and was quite splendid, there was a knock on my bedroom door. It was the first night Mother and Daddy and I had spent in the Governor's Mansion, and I said, "Yes, yes, who is it?" "Bess, it's your Daddy. I'd like to come and talk with you and have you tell me about your day." Oh, I couldn't wait to tell him what a big deal I was. How much I loved sitting on the front row hearing my dad give that great speech. And then riding in a car in the parade with my name, Bess Clements, on both sides of the convertible. I said, "Oh Daddy, it was just so wonderful." He said, "Well, come over here and tell me about it." So I proceeded to tell Daddy what a big hit I was and how everyone wanted to dance with me at the ball.

Then Daddy said, "Bring me that globe over there and sit it here in front of us." He started turning the globe around, and he turned to me and said, "Find India." And I said, "Oh, India is right here," as I pointed to it on the globe. He then said, "Okay, find England," and I did. He asked me to find a couple more geography lessons, and I passed all those. Then he said, "Find Kentucky." I said, "Well, Kentucky on the globe is very small, but the Mississippi River is here and the Ohio River here, so Kentucky would be about here," as I pointed to the globe again. Daddy said, "See, Kentucky is not very big, and you didn't have anything to do with getting me here!" That is a lesson that stuck with me in red letters always.[10]

JANE DYER ARNOLD: After the inauguration, I went with Bess towards the mansion for her first trip. Of course she was just a young girl, fourteen years old, and was so excited over the whole thing. But she was anxious to get to the mansion because she needed to get to the restroom. When we got there, all the help was trying to get the mansion in order for the new governor coming in, and they were still running the electric cleaners and all. But Bess had a big armload of chrysanthemums and every step that she took the chrysanthemums were scattering, so they followed us all the way up the steps to the bathroom. And while we were there, Bess showed me each layer of clothing that she had on; that this was the first time that she'd ever had everything all brand new at one time.[11]

BESS ABELL: My parents did something wonderful. They let me give a house party at the Governor's Mansion, and I invited my friends from Morganfield and Madisonville. I used to spend some summers in Madisonville with Mary Whip Cox. She was my good friend. And then I had a summer beau there whose name is Dickey Pollock.
   Mary Whip, Dickey, and my friends from Morganfield all came up for several days, and we had a big party. We had a big dance in the ballroom. It was quite jolly and really made a difference. Everybody stayed there in the mansion. I guess the boys were stacked like cordwood up on the third floor. And all of us girls were luxurious in the various guest rooms and my room around on the second floor. I loved living in the Governor's Mansion. But you did feel like you were somewhat on display.

MARGARET FORD RUSHING: When her daddy became governor, she had a house party. I have pictures of it. Another friend and I got to spend two weeks in the Governor's Mansion. It was really fun. I was so impressed.[12]

BESS ABELL: There were always people in the Governor's Mansion. It was exciting around the Kentucky Derby when they had the big Derby breakfast. There would be horsemen and a few movie stars. I mean, nothing in comparison to what it is today. I remember my mother trying to get beaten biscuits made in the shape of a horseshoe. I do not think that worked, but I remember her trying to do that. Once you make it in the shape of a horseshoe, it is hard to split and have it hold together. The kitchen was full of country ham and biscuits, and I remember my father being up early in the morning, or maybe he started it the day before, making the mint syrup for the juleps.

A lot of furniture and things were gone from the Governor's Mansion when we moved in, and Mother was very conscious of wanting to leave a fully furnished house when she left. She was also very conscious of not wanting to say anything bad about anybody who lived there before. People wanted her to say, "Wasn't it terrible that Mrs. [Ida Lee] Willis [wife of Governor Simeon Willis] painted the gold leaf mirrors white?" "Well," Mother said, "I think these mirrors are beautiful. I don't know why Mrs. Willis painted them white, but she may have done it because they didn't have enough money to repair the gold leaf on them. I don't know. And maybe furniture was missing from those rooms because it was missing when the Willises moved in and they moved in with their own furniture."

Mrs. Willis was very conscious about fine things. I met her, but I never knew her. But I do know her daughter, Sarah "Sally" Willis Meigs, and Sally's mother would never have run off with furniture. One of the other things that Mother wanted was to have enough silver julep cups in the mansion, and she added to them periodically. Another thing that Mother did was place out in the governor's mansion big bowls heaped full of matchbooks with a photo of the mansion on the cover.

What was high school like in Frankfort as the governor's daughter?

BESS ABELL: I had always liked school. I am sure I was usually the teacher's pet because of my parents. The only time when I came apart at school was when I went to Frankfort. Daddy's inauguration was at the beginning of December. I left Morganfield, where I knew everybody and where I guess the year before maybe I had been president of my class.

I came up to Frankfort and attended the preinaugural parties. I was hauled around to those because I was an only child. Various ladies, being very nice to me, would come up and say, "Oh, you're going to be at Frankfort High, and I think you're going to be in the same class with my daughter. She's a member of such and such sorority." I thought, "Oh, sororities. I didn't know that was coming." She added, "I hope maybe you will join my daughter's sorority." And then somebody else would come up and replay the same thing. I thought, "Oh, sororities, oh." I thought, "I hope maybe after I meet some of those girls, they'll ask me to join their sorority. That sounds like fun."

I arrived at school the day after the inauguration and was handed two envelopes inviting me to join the two sororities. Well, I was just killed. I did not know any of the girls and they did not know me. So, I thought, "This is crazy, I don't want to be here. People ask me to do things only because I live in that big house on the hill. This is awful." It is hard to describe how miserable I was. I did not know people with whom I thought I could be friends. Maybe they did not want to be friends with me because they thought I was stuck up. I was always suspicious of people that made an effort to be friends with me. It was terrible.

Then there was an evil man who was school principal. He called me into his office the first week that I was there. He had this awful attitude and said, "I know about girls like you. You think you can throw your weight around because your father is governor." Big bug-eyed me, always wanting to please, thought, "Who is this man?" I was under the gun, and I spent a lot of time in detention.

It was my sophomore year when I really, really, really wanted to go to the state basketball tournament in Louisville. Mother knew how miserable I was, so she arranged to take me and three of my friends. We took a suite at the Seelbach Hotel in Louisville, and we were there for a week. After that, I spent the rest of the year in detention for missing all those unexcused classes. I hated it. I really do not remember anything pleasant about it. You could go to detention and do your homework like a study hall. It was really fine, because I did not have any friends anyway!

Bess spent her last two years of high school at Ward-Belmont School in Nashville, Tennessee, which offered four years of high school and a two-year junior college program. Her many activities included having membership in the Penta Tau Social Club, being class cheerleader, and serving as president of the High School Council. She also participated in The Roundtable, which promoted interest in world affairs and other governments. She graduated in 1951, the same year Ward-Belmont closed, eventually becoming Belmont College.

BESS ABELL: I begged and pleaded with my parents to send me away to school, which was very difficult for them because they could not afford it. But they knew how unhappy I was. And they finally did, at some considerable expense to them. I do not know what the governor's salary was then, but it was less than $10,000 a year.

I do not remember what boarding school cost then, but it was certainly a lot more than living at home and going to Frankfort High School. My roommate at Ward-Belmont was Lucy Ward, who was from Georgetown, Kentucky. She was a very, very, very nice girl. And my suitemates were two girls from Texas.

What kind of adjustment was it for you to change schools?

BESS ABELL: Well, I was wreathed in smiles. I guess a state trooper had driven Mother and me down from Frankfort to Nashville. Then, when Mother was getting in the car leaving, I was surrounded by crying girls and thrilled parents! But here was little Bess Clements just wreathed in smiles, and Mother was crying. I remember saying to Mother, "Would you feel better if I were sad?" She said, "Yes." But I was so happy to be there with new faces. I loved it.

My big sister at Ward-Belmont was Joan Weingarten. Her roommate was another girl from Houston. The two of them were great friends with Suzanne Cohen. There were three girls from Houston. It was my first experience with some really attractive Jewish girls. I used to go with them frequently on Sunday to brunch instead of going to church because, since they were Jewish, they were supposed to have been to the synagogue on Friday night or Saturday morning. I do not know if they did or not. I think I did go to synagogue with them once.

How were the classes at Ward-Belmont?

BESS ABELL: I liked the classes. I liked mathematics, loved geometry, and was crazy about chemistry. I thought I should study chemistry in college. But then I found that it was a rip-off. In order to get one credit in chemistry, you had to go to school for something like six hours and take all these labs, and they did not count. I thought, "I'm not going there." I did not like it that much! So, I stuck with the other stuff. I had a wonderful English teacher, Miss Billie Kuykendall.

I had arranged to get the *Louisville Courier-Journal* sent to me. Then, for a time, it stopped coming. I must have called somebody in Daddy's office, maybe Cattie Lou Miller, and said, "I'm not getting the newspaper." She told me, "Don't worry about it, I'll find out what happened." Well, I learned years later that they stopped it because Daddy was getting so much abuse from the teachers who said that "he knows that the schools in Kentucky aren't any good because he even sent his daughter away to school." Mother and Daddy did not want me to know that. They were really good to me. More so than I deserved.

Did you meet any boys in Nashville?

BESS ABELL: No boys that I remember. There were a lot of dances and parties back and forth with boys' schools. A couple of times we went to dances at Sewanee [The University of the South]. We had clubs and club-houses on the campus and had our own little dances. Of course, the person that I liked best there was my Morganfield next-door neighbor, Jimmie Waller, who I suppose I always must have had a crush on. I was just crazy about him.

Did your father's political career spark your interest in politics?

BESS ABELL: Oh sure, and it is still there. Maybe if I had lived in Kentucky I might have run for office. More than once Tyler said, "The best people in the world come from Union County. We ought to buy a farm in Union County." I knew this guy named Charlie, who had been a classmate of mine in grammar school. When I knew him, he was just a poor farm boy, but a nice boy. Anyway, he has done really well. He bought a lot of land and was a great horseman and a really good horse trainer. We bought a couple of horses from him. He had some property for sale, but I just said, "No, I can't do it."

How did you go about deciding where to go to college?

BESS ABELL: Mother thought that maybe I should go to Smith College or to an Ivy League school. I do not remember that I applied. I certainly do not remember being accepted. I wanted to go to the University of Kentucky because that was where my beau, John Griggs [from Union County], was and that was where I ended up. He was my great, great love, and we were going to get married. But Mother and Father told me, "Nobody in our family has ever graduated from college. It's very important to us that you graduate before you get married." I speeded up things to finish school in three years so I could get married with my parents' approval. John was from Grove Center in Union County, captain of the football team, and a big deal. He was just lots of fun, and I loved being with the captain of the football team.

Sue Wetherby [daughter of Kentucky governor Lawrence Wetherby] and I were roommates our sophomore year at the university. We lived in the attic of the Kappa Alpha Theta house with five other girls. She had the top bunk, and I had the bottom bunk. She dated UK quarterback Vito "Babe" Parilli, so we were having lots of fun.

I was chosen to represent Kentucky as a Cherry Blossom Princess [1952] in Washington, DC. It was great fun, and we had all these great parties. Perle Mesta taught us how to curtsy, and I had new clothes. We also got to pick out various handsome bachelor military officers to squire us around. It was fun.

Daddy asked me one time, "What do you think John [Griggs] is going to do this summer?" I said, "I think he's going to be selling Bibles in Alaska." And he said, "Why don't you get him to come up and spend some time with us." I said, "Oh, that would be great," because I was crazy about him. So John came to Washington, but he kept getting tossed into situations where he was not comfortable. I know that Daddy did that on purpose, I just know he did. I know he was thinking, "I want you to see, little girl, whether you really want to tie your love to this? Are you sure and positive certain about this?"

It finally focused into my thick head what happened, and I tried to talk to Daddy about it. Either he no longer remembered it, or he had just decided it was something he was never going to discuss. Anyway, Daddy did the right thing. I do not think Daddy ever did anything that was not the right thing. But I am sure that this whole thing was just something that he arranged. But he was always very nice to John, and he and John were devoted to each other. Daddy would sometimes call John to say, "I'm flying into Lexington. Could you pick me up at the airport?" John was standing on the steps of the Baptist church when we arrived there with Daddy's casket. He just stepped in there, this big strong guy, and got that casket up the steps.

John ended up marrying a girl I had introduced him to. But he was just the best guy and the most fun. I was crazy about John, and we stayed in touch forever.

TYLER ABELL: Although the town was small, there were a lot of citizens there who did fairly well. And Bess, remarkably, stayed in close touch with all of them her entire life. There was one boy that she was eventually engaged to, named John Griggs. He was captain of the UK football team when they were both at the University of Kentucky. There's another guy named Jimmie Waller, J. K. Waller, whose father had founded the bank and who was a brilliant, just amazing guy and a leader of the community for years. Joe Bell's father was managing editor for the local newspaper, the *Union County Advocate*. Her father and she were so much alike: they both kept track of people, remembered people, remembered also some details about people that most of us would normally forget. She was always reporting to me different things that happened in her early days.

Bess was at Ward-Belmont when she and I met because I was a guest of her roommate, Elizabeth "Cissy" Collings, at the Kentucky Derby in 1950, when Middleground won the Derby. Bess has never let me forget that I remember Middleground, and I remember her boyfriend's fancy Oldsmobile—he was the son of the car dealer in Louisville, Charlie Dishman. But I really didn't remember Bess. I was too honest in admitting that I didn't remember her, but four years later, when a friend said she wanted to fix her up with Tyler Abell, Bess said, "Oh, Tyler Abell, I remember Tyler Abell." We'd only met at the Kentucky Derby, and I was paying all my attention to the horses and to Cissy. But anyway, we did remeet in 1954, and we had a good time on the first date. And we kept dating, although I was dating other girls at the same time, and she was dating other boys. It developed, as those things tend to do.

Bess accelerated her graduation from UK so she could graduate the same year that John Griggs did. But not too long before graduation, she told John that the engagement was off. By that time, I think she had decided that there was a life somewhere beyond Morganfield and that she could be part of that. And, of course, she did.[13]

2

The Johnson Orbit

From the start of their marriage, Bess and Tyler found their lives swept into the orbit of Lyndon and Lady Bird Johnson. They enjoyed close connections thanks to the friendship Bess's parents had developed with the Johnsons and to her father's role as the majority leader's reliable whip in the Senate. Other links developed more by accident, as unintended consequences of the young couple's New Year's Eve elopement in 1955 and Bess's search for something to do while her husband was away campaigning in 1960.

BESS ABELL: My first connection with Lyndon Johnson was because of my father. My father was in the Senate from Kentucky. I guess my first real awareness that I remember is when Daddy was assistant Democratic leader and Mr. Johnson was then the majority leader. He and Daddy were very close and were very good friends, and Mrs. Johnson was always very nice to my mother. I remember such things as hamburgers in the backyard of the Johnsons' house when Lynda and Luci were small and I was in college. And then I remember a couple of times when Mrs. Johnson and Lynda and Luci and Mother and I used to go over to Bethany Beach and things like that. It was a close personal friendship, definitely on the basis of the men; I think less so with Mrs. Johnson and my mother.

I worked for my father when he was executive director of the Democratic Senate Campaign Committee, which was 1957 and 1958. My father's office at that time was the same office that he had had as majority whip of the Senate, and the majority leader's office—I've forgotten the number on the door, the numbers have long since been changed—was on the gallery floor. You could walk out our door and down the corridor directly into the majority leader's office. So at that time Daddy worked closely with Mr. Johnson, and I was just very much on the fringes, but an enormous admirer. Tyler also had this feeling. And then in 1960 Tyler quit his job to go to work for the Johnson campaign. He had great and enormous respect and admiration for him. Those were the marvelous days of Johnson running the Congress, and I don't guess there will ever be anything like it again.

What was it like to watch him operate?

BESS ABELL: A great deal of awe. He and [Senate Republican leader] Bill Knowland worked so well together, with a great deal of honesty and understanding and appreciation, one for the other, of their problems. There were none of these sessions that ran needlessly into the middle of the night. When they were ready to take a vote on a measure, both of them generally knew how the chips were going to fall. They'd be ready for the vote, and I guess there weren't very many surprises because the tally had been taken before; they knew where their people were.[1]

Bess's father recalled the origins of his relationship with Lyndon Johnson.

EARLE C. CLEMENTS: We became great friends. I guess the first time that I recall, if I was picking out a single time, he and I went down to the [Kentucky] Derby together while I was in the House, along with Clint Anderson, Dick Russell, maybe one or two others. After I was elected governor in 1947, that group of folks was down there nearly every year at the Derby while I was governor and I really got to know him. That was really the closest association I had with him. I really had a closer association with him, oh, slightly in the House, but even more when I was governor. Then the friendship just kind of grew from there.[2]

Lady Bird Johnson confirmed the social as well as political closeness between her family and the Clementses.

LADY BIRD JOHNSON: I knew them from early days—at least early Senate days—and watched Bess grow up. I was in their home a good many times in Washington, which was a lovely apartment, a sort of a small version of their home in Morganfield. It was sort of a custom to go there on Sunday and have lunch with them. There was always Kentucky ham, and I would have been disappointed if there hadn't been! It was absolutely delicious. He and Lyndon—their conversation would pretty soon start off on a business nature and would make good listening in any case. But likely there would be just the four or five of us, and Bess was often out following her own young life.

I remember that Bess's mother, who was one of these gentle Southern ladies, would ask Bess to help Lynda smooth her way a little bit. We went to the beach one day, spent the day, Mrs. Clements and Bess, who must at that time have been eight or ten years older than Lynda, and Lynda was kind of an awkward eleven in this year, and Luci eight. Mrs. Clements was helpful and nice to my children, as she was to everybody. I could see that Bess was a very bright, capable young woman. I did not foresee at that time that she would one day be my right arm, but all of that was to come in the future.[3]

Did Mrs. Clements seem to enjoy being a political wife in Washington?

LADY BIRD JOHNSON: I think she enjoyed her husband and her daughter and handled her job competently. I would not say it was something that she sought, or it was not particularly her thing. She was just a lovely, kind person. I remember one time, I forget just what it was, but I think maybe my daughter, Lynda, had an impacted wisdom tooth, and I was at home helping Lyndon in the campaign—just the sort of thing that I had to do. I called back and she took Lynda to the doctor. She was just so kind to her and tended to her all day long. Another time Lynda was thirteen or fourteen and another little girl came up from Texas to see her. Mrs. Clements packed a good picnic lunch, and we all went to the beach together. It was her treat, and it was very sweet.[4]

LYNDA JOHNSON ROBB: Her mother was the gentlest woman, at least to me. She was the archetype of a Southern lady. She was able to do things, but she made no attempt to outshine her husband. And she was like cotton candy. She was soft and gracious and treated us children like we were grown-ups, or at least young adults.[5]

An Impromptu Elopement

Tyler Abell reconstructed the spontaneous sequence of events that led to his and Bess's impromptu wedding and the Johnsons' elaborate reception for them.

TYLER ABELL: Bess and I fell very deeply in love in the late summer of 1954 and then had a rather torrid romance through the winter. I invited her to be my date to go to a rather famous New Year's Eve party. It was given every year at the Burning Tree Club, which normally excluded women. There were no women allowed in the Burning Tree Club, then and now. But every New Year's Eve, the father of one of my very good friends, Bobby Alvord, would have a New Year's Eve party. I escorted Bess to the party, and Bess and I both drank bourbon in those days, a good Kentucky drink. Naturally, New Year's Eve being what it is, we had a little bit too much bourbon. Not so much that I was stumbling around, but we were having a really happy time and we were in the locker room. A bunch of us were standing around in a circle playing drinking games and singing songs.

Somebody said, "You know? You two ought to get married." We just sort of looked at each other and thought, "Well, maybe we should get married." In the spirit of the occasion, we said, "Let's go." By this time it was probably about 1:00 in the morning. A caravan set out from the Burning Tree Club and slowly but surely, the cars began to drop off. Because the first place everybody thought of was Elkton, Maryland. That was the famous place that everybody had heard about that you could go there and get married on a moment's notice. But they didn't marry you anymore. They said, "Maybe you should go to Virginia." We set out to Virginia and on the way, Bess decided that she wanted to get some other clothes. She stopped at her apartment, got out of her evening gown and put on a pair of Bermuda shorts and a few other things. Because we'd said, "Well, we'll go get married and then we'll go to Florida, and have a vacation, honeymoon." I was still in my tuxedo, and I figured I could always buy a toothbrush if I needed one, buy some clothes if I needed them. I think I did stop long enough to pick up a bathing suit, on the notion that I was going to Florida.

We got all the way through Virginia without finding a place to get married and on into North Carolina. We finally found a place near Elizabeth City called Hertford, North Carolina. By this time, it was broad daylight and probably about noon when we finally found a justice of the peace to marry us. We'd been arrested once for speeding. For years I still had that speeding ticket. But the cop didn't take us in. He just said, "Well, I'll take you to the station if you want to argue about it. But if you don't argue about it, you can pay the $25 right here." Twenty-five dollars was an awful lot of money, but I fortunately had $25, paid him, and we went on.

By this time, we'd had quite a few hours without anything to drink and we were thinking much more clearly. After we finally said our "I do"s, we thought Florida is a long way away, and I was scheduled to go into the army on the fifth of January. So getting to Florida and getting back and going into the army sounded like we were squeezing too much in. So we headed home.

Bess stopped to call home and tell them where she was. When she got back in the car, she was very glum because her father had talked to her in a way that he later apologized for. He was very sorry about the things that he said. I called my home, and my stepfather, Drew Pearson, answered the phone. I told him what I'd done, and he said, "Oh, Tyler. You've married a wonderful girl. That's great." So I came back and reported that, and we were very happy about his comment.

When we finally got to Bess's home it was starting to get dark, and her father was out front, pacing up and down the sidewalk on Woodley Road.

He just came over and hugged her and told her how sorry he was for what he had said. He shook my hand, and we were all very chastened. I said that, although we were happily married, I knew that Bess wanted to be with her parents and so I would go home and sleep at my house, which I did.

The next day, we reunited and decided that Bess and I would get married at a church. There was some question about what church, naturally, that's the bride's prerogative. But when they couldn't decide what church they wanted to be married in or didn't know the minister very well, I said, "Well, I know a church that I do not go to very often, but I know the minister very well and his name is Cookie Anshutz [the Reverend John R. Anshutz]." To this day, I cannot tell you what his real first name is, but Dr. Anshutz was a very good Episcopalian minister and a very nice guy. He said he would be glad to perform the wedding that afternoon.

There could not be an official wedding, but he said, "I will bless the marriage. Do you have the marriage license from North Carolina?" We said, "Yes, here it is." And he said, "Well, I will bless the marriage and then we will all sign the book. Nobody in the church will know that it was not a real wedding, but it is just as good as a real wedding. It is blessing the wedding that you've already had." Bess and I always remembered that and thought that this guy was really brilliant. Without batting an eye, or having to think too hard, he just solved everybody's problem because Bess's father was certainly someone we wanted to please. His daughter getting married without having a real wedding would have been very troubling for him. The same went for my mother. My poor mother had gone to her niece's wedding in Cleveland, Ohio, while her only child was running off eloping, and so she was devastated.[6]

The wedding ceremony was held in the Christ Episcopal Church in Washington, DC, in front of a dozen witnesses on January 2, 1955, at 4:30 p.m. Tyler recalled, "Everybody who meant anything was there. Drew was my best man, and Bess's father gave the bride away. Mary Hays was bridesmaid." A *Louisville Courier-Journal* article the following day did not mention the elopement but noted that "the ceremony . . . was arranged on a few hours' notice because the bridegroom is entering the Army Wednesday."[7]

TYLER ABELL: Bess's mother was unable to find a wedding cake, but she had found some little petits fours. She put the petit fours on a plate, and we cut one of the petit fours in two and had a few people for a wedding reception at the Clements' apartment.[8]

A highlight of the two families' relationship was the wedding reception that Lyndon and Lady Bird Johnson threw in March 1955 for the newly married Bess and Tyler Abell.

TYLER ABELL: Months later, when I got out of the army briefly for my first leave, Bess's father's good friend, Lyndon Johnson, gave us a wedding reception. He had told Bess's father almost as soon as he was told that Bess had eloped, "Well, I want to give Bess a wedding reception." We had a really terrific party in the Carlton Hotel Ballroom. It was a big party. The Johnsons had a lot of guests there. Bess and I had a lot of guests. Some of her Kentucky friends came, and some of my college pals came. A majority of the Senate was there. The Senate adjourned early that afternoon so that everybody could go to the majority leader's party. Bess was a beautiful bride and just shimmered. She was saying hello to everybody, and everybody was congratulating her.

I was in the army at that time, and my contact with Mr. Johnson did not really flower until much later. I had one other slight contact with him in 1956, when I took some leave from the army to attend the Democratic National Convention in Chicago. Senator Johnson had recovered remarkably well from his heart attack, but still there were very, very few politicians outside of the state of Texas who took his candidacy for the presidency that year very seriously. I remember at that time going up to Senator Johnson's suite in the Hilton Hotel and really being amazed myself at the fact that anybody was taking Johnson very seriously. My stepfather, Drew Pearson, for whom I had worked before entering the army, was a longtime friend of Mr. Johnson's, but they frequently fought, usually over petty things. My stepfather enjoyed referring to his friend as "Landslide Lyndon," and Mr. Johnson was unable to see the humor in this type of thing.[9]

BESS ABELL: It was rather a backward sort of marriage. First, we eloped just four days before Tyler went in the service. When he finished his basic training, I joined him and then we went on our honeymoon. When we came back to Washington Mr. Johnson gave us a reception. It was absolutely marvelous. I felt very special that day because the Senate adjourned early.

There were a large, large number of the Senate there and a number of people from the Pentagon. My husband, who had finished about two and a half months of basic training, was standing there in the receiving line. He had never seen anybody with more than maybe one gold bar on his shoulder, and coming down the line was a three-star general who was making the apologies to Tyler. He was so sorry that General [Matthew] Ridgway [the Army's chief of staff] couldn't be there. Tyler just was panicked when he saw this man coming down the line because he didn't know whether he was supposed to salute or faint into the potted palm.[10]

The *Washington Post* reported: "The bride, who's tall and blonde, is the former Bess Clements, whose parents, Senator and Mrs. Earle Clements, are close friends of Senator and Mrs. Johnson. Senator Clements—former Kentucky Governor—and Mrs. Clements were in the receiving line with Senator and Mrs. Johnson and the suntanned honeymooning couple, who've been in Nassau and Florida and now must head back to Camp Gordon in Augusta, Georgia. Not far away from the receiving line in the early part of the afternoon were Tyler's mother, Mrs. Drew Pearson, and columnist Drew Pearson, his stepfather. Texas and Kentucky were out in force for their two members of the Upper House. . . . Every other guest it seemed was a Senator or a Senator's wife."[11]

When she and Tyler eloped, did that surprise you?

LADY BIRD JOHNSON: No, not particularly. I mean, I didn't know them all that intimately. But I think they were independent young people and I presume they didn't want to go through the long folderol of—whatever the reason, they did elope.

So you gave a party for four hundred people for them.

LADY BIRD JOHNSON: Yes. To introduce them to the whole bunch of people that they already knew, but to sort of give a special stamp to saying this is a new marriage starting among two families that matter in this town, and we care about both of them.[12]

LYNDA JOHNSON ROBB: The first thing that I really remember was when I heard about Tyler and Bess running away on New Year's Eve and getting married! That's the most exciting thing I've ever heard. You know, that only happens in movies. You mean people really run away and get married on New Year's Day? Oh, how exciting.[13]

"Nobody thought it would last," Bess later reminisced about her elopement. "But we had to be as sure and determined as people who go through a big wedding. We went from town to town looking for an open town hall or a justice of the peace."[14]

Earle Clements's Political Fate

Did you see much of LBJ in the interval between 1956 and 1960?

TYLER ABELL: No, I don't think I saw him at all during that time. If I did, it certainly was very casual. In 1956, my father-in-law ran for reelection to the Senate and was defeated by a very, very narrow margin. He was quite disappointed and quite despondent. He would not have been defeated but for an incredible series of circumstances. Eisenhower had carried the state of Kentucky by over a hundred thousand votes, and my father-in-law had lost by a mere two or three thousand votes. If any one of a number of things had not gone wrong, he would have been reelected. In other words, if Eisenhower had not run, obviously he would have been reelected. If Stevenson had not come out against atomic testing, which was a very unpopular stand in Kentucky, he would have been reelected. If Stevenson had not come out against the draft, he would have been reelected. The Kentucky mountaineers take their military service and defense of country quite seriously. If the then governor of Kentucky, a Democrat by the name of [A. B.] "Happy" Chandler, had not been an arch foe of Earle Clements, he would have been reelected. And so on down the line. If Stevenson had done any one of a number of things right during that campaign, Earle Clements would have been reelected.[15]

LADY BIRD JOHNSON: I noticed the toll that it took on him. I mean the worn, tired look he got and, well, it interested me to see that it was not only Lyndon who reacted that way to the job. It was the caliber job that really could drain whoever tackled it. Oh, Lyndon loved it, no doubt about it. That was his cup of tea, the Senate majority leadership, but you really had to struggle and so did Senator Clements. Later on Lyndon felt regret that Senator Clements's loyal and strong efforts for the party, for the job, for Lyndon did keep his nose to the grindstone so much that he did not go home to Kentucky enough during that period of time. Because the next year he was up for reelection, and you will recall that was in 1956 when President Eisenhower was just so popular, and Adlai Stevenson was not at all a favorite in Kentucky. So General Eisenhower did carry in with him Clements's opponent, and he lost the Senate race. Perhaps nothing could have made any difference, but maybe if he had gone home over and over and over and made himself felt from one end of the state to the other in '55, maybe if he had been less of a whip and more of just a senator from Kentucky it might have helped.[16]

As Secretary to the Democratic Majority, Bobby Baker was Lyndon Johnson's right-hand man, which gave him insight into Senator Johnson's indebtedness to his whip.

BOBBY BAKER: Senator Earle Clements was able to protect Texas and Senator Lyndon Johnson from the liberals because he was unusually liberal for being a senator from Kentucky. He had great support with the American labor movement, who were very powerful with the liberal Democrats. So anytime we had a massive fire, Senator Clements could put that fire out. He committed political suicide when he was whip. Senator Johnson was very strong for amending the Social Security Act, and Senator Clements, knowing he had a tough reelection coming up with Thruston Morton, had made a deal with the medical society in Kentucky that he was going to vote against the Social Security plan.

When it came down that his vote was the difference for Senator Johnson to be a winner or a loser, [Clements] was more loyal to his commitment to Senator Johnson than he was to his commitment in Kentucky. As a consequence, he lost his seat. His daughter, Bess, is a dear, dear friend of mine. Anytime I'm in Washington we visit and renew our ties. But Senator Clements knew the Senate better than any Democrat I've ever known. He knew how to put out the liberal fires, and he was more helpful to Senator Johnson as leader as any senator I knew.[17]

TYLER ABELL: In the midst of my father-in-law's despondency I think Senator Johnson showed both his warmth and sometimes his lack of feeling, both at the same time. He announced, without consulting my father-in-law, that he was making my father-in-law executive director of the Senate Campaign Committee. I think unquestionably it was a very wise choice. My father-in-law was really responsible for the class of 1958; the incredible group of senators who were elected that year gave the Democrats an overwhelming majority in the Senate. But at the same time, although it was a very wise decision on Johnson's part and although the job turned out beautifully for my father-in-law, my father-in-law was very disturbed at the fact that Johnson hadn't mentioned this to him before he announced it publicly.[18]

Neal P. Gillen, who served as a campaign advance man for both Lyndon Johnson and later Edmund Muskie, got to know Earle Clements and evaluated his importance to Johnson.

NEAL P. GILLEN: Bess's father was a consummate politician, a great politician. She was his secretary when he was head of the Democratic

Senatorial Campaign Committee, which is a very important job. Raising money was very important to Lyndon Johnson. Lyndon Johnson derived all his power in the House of Representatives as a young congressman due to the fact he was able to get Texans, mainly through the Brown brothers, of Brown-Root construction, to contribute, make large contributions to the Democratic Campaign Committee in the House. As a young congressman, he was making sure that his colleagues were getting money for their campaigns that they couldn't raise themselves. And in turn, they owed him, and that's a great reason for his rise to power. The fact that he gave Senator Clements that appointment when he was the majority leader to raise money for the Senate so he could maintain his position as majority leader was very, very important to him. So Bess, as his secretary, knew what was coming in, and Johnson decided who got it. So yeah, she understood politics very, very well, very well.[19]

TYLER ABELL: After the election of 1958, my father-in-law continued on the campaign committee and resigned sometime during 1959. During the year 1959 it was clear to everybody that Johnson would be a major contender for the Democratic nomination in 1960, and my father-in-law was one of Johnson's many friends and associates who attempted to counsel him and attempted to have him follow a pattern which would lead to the nomination. I don't suppose that any of us will ever know why Johnson didn't follow a lot of the good advice that was given him.

I went to work for the Citizens for Johnson for President Committee sometime in May 1960. This was a frenetic effort to put together some semblance of an organization which would collect delegates, have delegate votes committed, and go in to the Los Angeles convention with a sufficient show of strength to stop Kennedy on the first ballot, which then presumably would lock up the convention long enough for Johnson to do his marvelous job, which he can do, of persuading individuals, and the convention would slowly bend over to him.[20]

The 1960 Presidential Campaign

Despite the efforts of Johnson's supporters, Senator John F. Kennedy won his party's presidential nomination on the first ballot at the Democratic National Convention in Los Angeles in 1960. He surprised everyone by selecting Lyndon Johnson as his vice presidential running mate, and Johnson added to that surprise by accepting. He thus sacrificed one of the most powerful positions in Washington, Senate majority leader, for one of the least powerful. Both Tyler and Bess volunteered to work in the campaign, just after the birth of their second son, whom they named Lyndon.

TYLER ABELL: Bess had our second child, Lyndon, in June of 1960 just before the convention. In September of 1960 she decided it was time to go back to work. She had worked for her daddy in 1956, 1957, and 1958, during the time that he was executive director of the campaign committee. She had left that job almost on Election Day, which was the fifth of November 1958, and our first child, Danny, was born on the fifteenth of November. After the second child she decided it was time to go back to work, and she went to work at the Democratic National Committee in the speech-writing department.[21]

BESS ABELL: After the election, Mrs. Johnson called me in and said that she had a present for the baby. The reason his name is Lyndon is because when his brother was born, Senator Johnson called me in the hospital and said, "I hear you had a boy." I said, "Yes, sir." He said, "What did you name him?" I said, "We named him Dan Tyler Abell." He said, "Too bad. Too bad. If you had named him Lyndon, I would have given him a heifer calf." So Tyler and I started thinking about that and we said, "Hmm, well, we're going to have seven or eight children, and that sounds like a good name." So the next baby was Lyndon, and then I did not have any more.

Did he get his calf?

BESS ABELL: Well, after the President was in the White House and I worked there, he was always coming around with a little pad or sometimes a cocktail napkin and his ballpoint pen. He would say, "I think this would be a good brand for Lyndon's calf, what do you think about it?" I would say, "Mr. President, you know a lot more about brands than I do. That has the L and the A that looks fine to me." But I told Lyndon, "I guess the cow died, because it doesn't seem like she had anymore calves."[22]

TYLER ABELL: I had just resigned from working for a federal judge when Lyndon was born, and I'd started working for Senator Johnson, who was then trying to be president. Bess was, of course, very much for that, but she got lonely with me being away all the time. I was campaigning as an advance man, doing an awful lot of travel. Bess was home with two children, and she got tired of it. She would say, "I want to talk to some adults."

So she volunteered to work for the Democratic National Committee. Her father was also working on the presidential campaign to elect Kennedy president and Johnson vice president.[23]

BESS ABELL: I came to the Johnsons' house because my husband had lied to me. When we got married, he told me that he was going to build his life not around politics like my father had, not like his stepfather had, but around his hobbies and his family. Suddenly, I looked up during the campaign in 1960 and where was he? He was nowhere. He was off traveling. He was doing advance trips for Senator Lyndon Johnson, who was then on the ticket with Senator Kennedy. I couldn't talk to anybody about anything over the age of eighteen months. I thought, I'll go down to the Democratic National Committee and see if they'll take on a volunteer.

They assigned me to the Lyndon Johnson speech-writing office. I was not a speech writer, I was a typist. It was a useless office because Johnson only gave one speech during the whole campaign—and he gave it *over*, and *over*, and *over* again. But there was mail that was coming into the DNC for Senator Kennedy, Senator Johnson, Mrs. Kennedy, and Mrs. Johnson. Sometimes the mail would come in for the Johnson girls, Lynda and Luci. People were handling the mail for the Kennedys, and they were handling the mail for Senator Johnson, but nobody was doing anything with Mrs. Johnson's mail. I thought, I can do that. That's easy. I was used to handling mail in a congressional office where the mail comes in today and you answer it today. So I just went down and ordered some little blue stationery with their Thirtieth Place address on it and I answered the letters, signed Lady Bird Johnson, stamped the envelopes, and put them in the mail.[24]

What kind of letters would she get?

BESS ABELL: The sort of thing that she generally got when she was in the White House. "Would you send me something for a parcel post sale?" "What's your favorite recipe for my recipe book?" "How do you raise your daughters?" That was always the hardest one. But we would stumble around and find a recipe and answer, whatever.[25]

But it was easy. I was reading interviews that she was giving, and she would answer questions about how she felt about her husband running for vice president, so I would answer in her words. People would ask for something for a parcel post sale for their church, and I would send some campaign buttons and bumper stickers. It was easy, and I just did that.[26]

The Inaugural Committee

On Election Day, 1960, Kennedy and Johnson eked out a narrow victory over Republicans Richard Nixon and Henry Cabot Lodge Jr. Crucial to their election was carrying Texas and much of the South, confirming the wisdom of putting Johnson on the ticket. Work then began on planning the inauguration for January 20, 1961.

TYLER ABELL: Bess was mad at me because I'd promised that after the election, I would take her for a vacation, but instead of a vacation I said, "No, I want to work on the Inaugural Committee." She came down and worked on the Inaugural Committee too, and neither of us were getting paid for that.[27]

BESS ABELL: I just wanted to [work at something] because Tyler was traveling so much, and I've never been much of a volunteer type for the Ladies' Hospital Board. I hadn't worked between the births of my two children. Tyler then went down to work at the Inaugural Committee and the Parade Committee, and he said, "Come and be my secretary," so I went down there as his secretary, really thinking this would end in January.[28]

TYLER ABELL: But one day, she got a call, and I was sitting across from her in this little room where we were all huddled. She put the phone down and said, "Well, that was Mrs. Johnson. She asked me to come and have lunch with her. I think maybe she wants to hire me." And that's exactly what happened. Mrs. Johnson decided she needed a secretary now that she was the wife of the vice president. Bess decided that she needed a part-time job, and a friend of mine had already asked me if I would come and work for him at the post office department. So that's where we started life more on less on Inauguration Day. She was Mrs. Johnson's part-time secretary. I had what I thought was a magnificently high-paying job at the post office department. I think I got $9,000 a year. And that was the start of a rather spectacular political career for Bess.[29]

BESS ABELL: I was working at the Inaugural Committee when Mrs. Johnson called me one day. She was looking for an address of somebody. I gave her the address, and then I asked her what I think is probably a really stupid question. I said, "How has your life changed since the senator's now a candidate for vice president?" She said, "Oh, I don't know what I'm going to do. I can't keep up with the mail. I just can't keep up with the mail. I don't know what I'm going to do." And I thought, "Well, Bess Abell, that is a little job for you. You know you can do that."

I said, "Well, gee, if I could come out and help you a couple of afternoons a week, I'd be delighted to." Then I started thinking about it and I talked to Tyler about it, and I said, "This is really the thing for me. I did that for a couple of weeks during the campaign with no great effort, and it's something that I rather enjoy, and it will get me out of the house a couple of afternoons a week." So I'd just finished typing a letter to Mrs. Johnson, saying I'd like to do it and I thought I could. I was really literally taking it out of my typewriter down at the Inaugural Committee, and she called me and asked me to have lunch with her. I met her a day or so later, Mrs. Johnson and Liz Carpenter and myself, and she asked me if I would come to work for her and do that in what both of us envisioned would be a part-time job and one that grew like Topsy.[30]

3

A Part-Time Job

"This was originally planned to be a part-time job," Bess Abell mused in 1966 about going to work for the vice president's wife, "but I have been waiting for things to quiet down since the 1961 Inauguration, and they never have."[1] Lady Bird Johnson expressed similar surprise that Bess's role in her life had expanded so dramatically.

Mrs. Johnson in 1976 was asked how she came to hire Bess.

LADY BIRD JOHNSON: Oh, gosh, I'm so glad I did! She came with me, I guess, in January of 1961 and was with me in those two years and nine months thereabouts. I think perhaps it was partly Lyndon. Liz Carpenter may have had a few words to say about it. It just seemed to be a good thing to do because she had the right blend of quiet competence and aggressive persistence, and creative talents too—the last in marked degree.[2]

Many people who knew them called Lady Bird Johnson her husband's North Star.

BESS ABELL: Well, that is a lovely comment. She was an anchor for him as well as something to follow. I did recently run across some notes that she had done in shorthand while she was listening to, I guess, a Johnson press conference from the East Room. She had been watching it on television, and she had made these notes about how he should look into the camera, and how his pauses were good but how his pauses could be improved, and words to emphasize. They were not critical comments. They were things that she thought would improve his presentation.

I didn't know Mrs. Johnson when people talked about her as being this shy, fragile person. I knew her after she had been in speech classes with Hester Beall Provensen, and she knew how to mark her speech cards. She knew how to emphasize certain sections and how to look at an audience. Sometimes you would just walk into her room when I was coming over to work with her on perhaps a guest list or White House entertainment, and I would walk into her bedroom where her desk was, and she would stand up and start talking to me. It would be kind of a momentary shock because before I realized what she was doing, she was using me as the audience to practice her speech cards!

Mrs. Johnson is a person who I don't think in her whole life was ever bored because she had this deep curiosity about everything and everybody. Whether it was learning about a new plant and what would make it grow, or whether it was a new person, or whether she was seeing you and she hadn't seen you in a while. She was interested in what you were doing, what you were interested in. She just viewed life as a rich experience. I sometimes thought of that line in the play *Auntie Mame*, where Auntie Mame says that "Life is a banquet and most poor fools are just starving to death." Well, Mrs. Johnson was never starving to death. When you were around her you were never starving to death either, because she brought you into the excitement of what she was interested in, and what she was doing, and new things that she was exploring.[3]

What was it like to be the vice president's wife? How did it change your life in terms of the staff you had and various other things?

LADY BIRD JOHNSON: It didn't change my life. I had the same staff I had had at 4921 Thirtieth Place except that I added a gardener and I got myself a secretary. Bess Abell was a secretary for all purposes: social, business, typewriter, everything. She was absolutely a jewel.[4]

TYLER ABELL: Mrs. Johnson called, I think in December of 1960, and Bess started working right away. It started out that the hours would be 9:30 a.m. to 5:00 p.m. five days a week. Before the tour in the White House was over, Bess was working from about 9:30 a.m. until 2 a.m., sometimes seven days a week.[5]

Bess and Liz

Liz Carpenter, a Texas reporter who, with her husband Les, ran a Washington news service, handled press relations for Lady Bird Johnson during the 1960 campaign. She and Bess would become close allies on the Johnson staff.

LIZ CARPENTER: I went to Chicago to the [1960] Republican convention, and I was there when Mrs. Johnson called me and I'll never forget the words, "Lyndon and I've been talking about it. We've got a campaign ahead, and I'm going to need someone to be traveling with me and helping me. We wondered if you will share the great adventure of our lives?" I guess it was the line that changed my mind.

BESS ABELL: Liz was on the staff during the campaign but, you see, Liz was going back to work with Les in the Carpenter News Bureau. She went back there before she joined the vice president's staff the second time around. So really it was just me. Before that Grace Tully, who had worked for Mr. Johnson as majority leader and who had been FDR's secretary, had handled a great big chunk of Mrs. Johnson's mail.[6]

Liz is a force of nature, and uproariously funny. Mrs. Johnson appreciated that, and so did the president. I guess when he was vice president, first she went to work for him. She was in his office on the Hill, and then he'd get mad at her and send her out to the house. So we always kept her office going there next to me. Then sometimes he'd want her to come back and be in the office of the vice president. Then he'd get mad at her and send her packing. But I love her.[7]

Liz Carpenter traveled with the Johnsons during the 1960 campaign and then after the election joined their staff.

LIZ CARPENTER: Well, I rested. I slept. I helped Mrs. Johnson do an awful lot of letters and thank-yous for everybody that had been in the campaign. In the meantime, Lyndon Johnson was saying to me he hoped that I would keep on working with them. He wasn't making any serious overtures, and I wanted to go back to the newspaper business, I thought. But you'd been swept up, caught up. So the next April he called me back and he told me that he wanted me to work for him. He was going on a trip to Senegal, and by then I had sand in my shoes.

I was back working with Les. So he urged me to go, and I went on the plane with the vice president on this first trip. I helped work out Mrs. Johnson's schedule, which he kept latching onto and tying in with us, because it was a good schedule. It was going out and seeing the country, going into a little fishing village, and going into the marketplace. He was thrilled with the trip, I think. So then he asked me if I wanted to come work for him and be his executive assistant. Bill Moyers was leaving about this time, and so I did.[8]

TYLER ABELL: Liz Carpenter was writing speeches and working with Mrs. Johnson in the 1960 campaign on a strictly volunteer basis. At that time Liz was an active newspaperwoman, but she had known Mrs. Johnson for years and years. She got to know Bess as a very competent secretary in the speech-writing department and recommended to Mrs. Johnson that she hire Bess. That was really the way it got started.[9]

White House curator James R. Ketchum and Shirley James, who later served as Mrs. Johnson's executive secretary, worked closely with both Bess and Liz Carpenter.

JAMES R. KETCHUM: They worked hand and glove. I saw them as a team. They had their differences of opinion, but they resolved them. Everybody had their ideas, and they shared them, and there was plenty of thanks to go around. Liz was Texas Guinan [a brassy nightclub singer during the Prohibition Era] and Bess was Lauren Bacall [the sultry and svelte movie star]. Bess knew how things could get done and get done both in style and with grace and with a happy participant at her beck and call. She just knew people. If you had a good tale, both of them enjoyed it. But Bess was always especially interested in what the human sense was up to in a person. She always could come back with, "Well, let me tell you how this particular person handled this about a similar situation." She processed all these things and had a lineup which she could bring front and center. I don't think there was any problem that she could not come up with two or three solutions. Mrs. Johnson would say many times, "Bess, use your best judgment."[10]

What were Liz and Bess like together?

SHIRLEY JAMES: Best buddies. Harry Middleton [director of the LBJ Library] always said he never could understand how two such strong women, who worked so closely together, got along so well. But they did. They had a beautiful friendship and loved and respected each other.

How were they different?

SHIRLEY JAMES: Oh good Lord, let me count the ways! Liz was just a whirlwind. Someone, it might have been Liz, described Bess as "an iron fist in a velvet glove." Liz was always in a panic about something, and Bess was the calm one. But they got along so well and just respected and admired each other and truly loved each other. There's just no comparison. Bess was the calm and steady one.[11]

LYNDA JOHNSON ROBB: From our standpoint, it could not have had a better twosome. Liz was kind of pushy and "my way or the highway." I loved Liz, but sometimes she commanded rather than asked. Bess knew she got a lot more with sugar that she got with a stick. She would try to tease me into doing something or making me think that I was really needed, as opposed to Liz, who kind of commanded me to do things. Liz catered to the press. She was wonderful, and she's probably one of the best press secretaries that they've ever had. Nobody got as much good press as Mother. If Daddy had only gotten a third of good press as Mother! Of course, Mother was twice as much fun to be with, and Daddy wasn't in any way. So I can't give Liz all the credit, she was working with someone better. But they were a great twosome, and Bess could go behind Liz and take the sharp edge off sometimes.[12]

LUCI BAINES JOHNSON: It was real clear to me that sometimes, although I might resent the power and influence that Bess and Liz might have on my mother's time, the only reason they were there, they were trying to help her be the best that she could be. And what help would I be giving to either of my parents to resent or conflict? You knew you couldn't afford to do that. That might be an adolescent yearning, but you never, ever felt like Bess or Liz were doing stuff because of their egos. It was all to help my mother and father be the best that they could be.[13]

LADY BIRD JOHNSON: Liz was just as much my friend and my fellow worker as she was Lyndon's. She was strong enough, and tough enough, to stand up to Lyndon, and he was honest enough, and realistic enough, to know that she had so much to offer, even if she was sometimes abrasive. Even if she sometimes wanted him to do something that he was just too exhausted to do, or that didn't come natural for him to do. He usually did it, and he might roar at her, but he always loved her and admired her, and me too. And very much laughed with her.[14]

Personal Secretary

Bess served as Mrs. Johnson's secretary and also the general "household fix-it" person. She recalled middle-of-the night calls from the vice president: "Bess, the air conditioner isn't working," or "Bess, the water in the pool is too hot." These prompted her to keep a list of repairmen handy for any emergency.[15]

What did you find your duties consisting of after you got into it?
BESS ABELL: Everything from cutting flowers in the backyard and arranging them on the table to getting the clothes from the cleaners, to paying the bills, to writing the letters, keeping track of appointments.

Had the Johnsons moved into The Elms house when you began working for them?

BESS ABELL: No, they were in the house out on Thirtieth Place, the house that they had bought a number of years ago. I had a little office up on the third floor in what had once been the children's playroom. Actually when I first got there, I operated out of Mrs. Johnson's dressing room, which was terribly unsatisfactory, because you'd come in to work in the morning and there would be last night's stockings on your typewriter. I'm sure it was equally unsatisfactory for Mrs. Johnson. She would be dressing to go out in the evening, and she'd find paper clips and envelopes where she wanted to sit down and put on her makeup. So as soon as they were off on a trip, I think to Southeast Asia, I moved everything up and took over a mostly unused children's playroom in the attic. They lived three places when he was vice president. They lived in the house that they had bought when he was in the House of Representatives, right across the street from J. Edgar Hoover. That area of Washington, I think, is called Forest Hills. So then they did do entertaining through that spring and summer, but I really wasn't involved in that because Mrs. Johnson would plan the menu with Zephyr Wright, who was their cook for many, many years, and an absolutely great, great lady.

They bought Mrs. Perle Mesta's house, a grand, lovely house. In between times, they rented a very nice, gracious apartment at the Wardman Park Hotel, on Woodley Road. I had an office there in a hotel room next door to their apartment. But when they got to The Elms, there was much more entertaining. I wrote the invitations, answered the telephone, wrote the checks, and did the mail. For wedding presents and birthday presents and so forth, they liked to send silver cigarette boxes. In those days, everybody smoked. They had silver Senate seals on the top of the box. The vice president or Mrs. Johnson would write out, "To So and So, with great appreciation, Lyndon and Lady Bird Johnson," and then the engraver would take that and transfer that to the silver box. We needed some vice-presidential seals, and so the vice president said, "Oh, well, I'm going to get my friend in Mexico to get those seals for me in Taxco, because they'll be much, much cheaper there." So I was waiting. We had all those boxes, beautifully engraved, ready to send out for wedding presents, birthdays, and so forth. The seals didn't come and didn't come and didn't come. And then suddenly this box arrived, and I was thrilled. I unwrapped them and they were beautiful, just beautiful. Around the outside it said, "Vice President de los Estados Unidos de América." I always thought that was the beginning of LBJ saying, "We're going to buy American!"

What did Lady Bird Johnson do as the wife of a vice president?

BESS ABELL: She did a lot of pinch-hitting for her husband, and for Mrs. Kennedy. With small children and one thing and another, and I think a whole different type of personality, there were a lot of things that Mrs. Kennedy just didn't feel that she wanted to do. Mrs. Johnson would fall heir to a number of those. Letitia "Tish" Baldridge on Mrs. Kennedy's staff would call me or call Mrs. Johnson and say, "Can Mrs. Johnson come down to the White House tomorrow and pose for a picture with the muscular dystrophy child?" The invitations do go up. They go up much less in the case of the Johnsons, moving from majority leader to vice president, than they would for Spiro Agnew moving from governor of Maryland to vice president of the United States, so that she had had a taste of the world of embassy and congressional and lobbyist and White House entertaining before that. But instead of being invited to three White House dinners a year, the Kennedys invited the Johnsons to every official dinner they had.[16]

Legendarily, Mrs. Johnson was also a very good businesswoman.

BESS ABELL: She was. She took the money that was left to her—I think it was out of her mother's estate—and invested it in the radio station in Austin. I didn't do anything about that except get the financial reports that would come in every couple of weeks, and they would be there on her desk and she would be paying attention to them. She would call Mr. J. C. Kellam, who was the manager of the radio station there. So there was real interest. Actually, I was on the payroll of their television station when Mr. Johnson was vice president. I don't know what I did for that TV station, except a couple of times I stayed in the apartment in Austin. The station had a great apartment in the KTBC Building at Tenth and Congress. The apartment on the top floor had a big deck. You could go out there and feel as if you could reach out and touch the Texas Capitol Dome.[17]

TYLER ABELL: What started out as a part-time job for Bess worked really well, but it wasn't too long before Bess showed her true colors and decided that she wanted to do more things with the Johnson family. At some point, she told Mrs. Johnson, "The next time the vice president goes on a trip, I would like to go. I believe I can be helpful." Mrs. Johnson agreed that it would be wonderful to have her on the trip, but Mrs. Johnson, who always looked at the other person's problems, said, "But I thought you wanted to work part-time?" And Bess said, "Well, I do want to take good care of my kids, but I would like to go on some trips." So she went on the next trip. But Bess made working for the wife of the vice president into a really valuable job because she could do everything. Anything that she couldn't do, she very quickly learned how to do. And the vice president and Mrs. Johnson both relied on her very heavily for all kinds of things.[18]

LUCI BAINES JOHNSON: Mother relied on Bess's judgment. She just thought she was sound. Daddy relied on Mother's judgment—just thought she was sound. Having Bess around was invaluable to Mother because Mother knew her first job was to try to help my Daddy be the best that he could be. And believe me, when you're talking about doing that for Lyndon Johnson, you need to be doing a lot of work. My father trusted my mother to tell him the truth even when she knew darn well it might be hard for him to hear. Not a soul on earth likes to be told there's spinach in their teeth. But Daddy knew he needed to hear that. Mother knew she needed to do that. And Bess kind of helped make sure that there was always water in the well, so to speak, and did that very steadily, reliably, and calmly.[19]

LBJ and JFK

Did you see much of Mr. Johnson in those years when he was vice president?
BESS ABELL: Yes. I saw him, not like a secretary in his office or a staff member there, but he would be at the house when I would get there in the morning generally because he would do some work from the bedroom. He would never come home at night before I left, except when they moved over to The Elms and were doing more entertaining there. I guess I saw more of him there.

During those years of the vice presidency, was Mr. Johnson unhappy?
BESS ABELL: I would say frustrated. He did not complain per se. I remember very well his saying more than once, "I've got one friend at the White House—the president." I was not paranoid at all, but I felt that even with the very few people that I knew on the White House staff, that they sort of looked down on you because you worked for Johnson.

The only way that I came in contact with it was on a social basis. And by a social basis, I don't mean not being invited to the party—I mean when you were there. It wasn't not wanting to have anything to do with you, it was not wanting to "waste my time with you," was the feeling that came to me.

But one interesting story was told to me by my assistant at the White House, Barbara Keehn, who had worked at the White House with Tish Baldridge. She said that President Kennedy always insisted that the Johnsons be invited to every state dinner that was held. When Tish would send the guest list over to President Kennedy frequently the Johnson name would be left off, and it would always come back in Kennedy's handwriting with Johnson's name on it. She said the list would come from the State Department and Tish really wouldn't do too much with it. She would add a few names at the bottom, suggestions of staff members, etc., and then send it over to the president. And neither Kennedy's name nor Johnson's name was ever on the list when it came from the State Department.

She didn't feel that Tish did it by design, but apparently it slipped her mind, and then when President Kennedy was going over the list the day before the dinner, he realized that the Johnsons weren't on it. He called her and said, "Why can't they come?" She said, "I don't know, I'll have to check," and she realized they weren't invited. That was one of the few times that Barbara said that President Kennedy had really gotten very angry with Tish. I do vaguely remember someone calling from the White House Social Office and saying a mistake was made and they hoped the Johnsons could come.[20]

What was the relationship between President Kennedy and his vice president?
BESS ABELL: Well, I don't know. The only time I ever saw them together was at The Elms when the Johnsons were asked to give the party after the gala. Probably it was some big Democratic fund-raising event with stars and so forth. They were convivial and friendly, and Kennedy was wonderful. He did this little soft shoe and singing some Irish whoop-de-doos with—I think—Gene Kelly. They rolled up the rugs in the living room, and it was quite a festive night. But that's the only time that I ever saw the two of them in an informal situation, and it was lovely.[21]

Tyler Abell recalled that Gene Kelly took the vice president by the arm and led him to the middle of the room where he suggested they sing a song together. Johnson's jaw dropped, and he fled back to the side of the room. Kelly then called on President Kennedy, and they performed a duet of "When Irish Eyes Are Smiling."[22]

BESS ABELL: The Kennedys had a series of lovely, informal dinner dances, smaller groups. I don't know how many people; maybe fifty or sixty. The Johnsons were always invited to those. Mrs. Kennedy, I think, liked to dance with LBJ. He was a good dancer. And also, she wanted the chandelier out of the vice president's office in the Capitol that apparently LBJ had the say-so over. That is what's in the White House Treaty Room now.[23]

*During the years of the vice presidency, did you get the impression that Mr. John-
son was under a kind of unnatural restraint in that office?*

TYLER ABELL: No question. I never talked to him about it personally. I
talked to members of his staff, and he would talk to Bess about it. I think
you'll get a better insight on those years from her than from an awful lot of
people because she was in the house all the time. But there would be days
there when he was just terribly despondent and felt that all the Kennedy
people were out to get him. And there was a lot of justification for it, obviously. He would give them some very good advice, and they would just
ignore it.

*Did this kind of thing extend to social Washington, that is, people not directly
associated with the White House or the government?*

TYLER ABELL: No, social Washington viewed him as the vice president,
a guy that many of them knew because he had been here longer than John
F. Kennedy had been here. He had not only been here longer than Kennedy,
but he had gotten to know an awful lot of people in social Washington that
Kennedy did not really know, did not really waste any time about and did
not care about. So in social Washington there wasn't any problem. And on
the Hill, there wasn't any problem, because he had his old friends down
there. My view is the problem was strictly the guys on the inside in the
White House. They felt a little bit cocky, and it was a product, I think, of
their immaturity. They had beaten Johnson, they had beaten the most
powerful man in the Democratic Party, and they probably just were not
smart enough to realize, as Jack Kennedy realized, that after beating him
the next step was to profit by his experience and knowledge.[24]

November 22, 1963

*November 22 and the beginning of the Johnson presidency, you were at the ranch
that day.*

BESS ABELL: We were all so excited about having the President and
Mrs. Kennedy visit the ranch, and the Johnsons wanted everything to be
just perfect for President and Mrs. Kennedy—a wonderful, relaxing time
and introduce them to some of the flavor of Texas. But the whole place was
in an uproar. Mrs. Johnson had brought down the staff that worked with
her at The Elms to be there at the ranch. The place was crawling with Signal Corps putting telephones in everywhere so that the president and his
staff would not be separated from world leaders or if they wanted to call
Caroline or John-John and chat on the phone. The Secret Service was

everywhere. Walter Jetton, the barbecue king from Fort Worth, was down by the river organizing his cooking pits, tables, and chairs all on the beautiful grounds underneath the live oak trees along the edge of the Pedernales River.[25]

TYLER ABELL: Bess tells the story about how just as the vice president and Mrs. Johnson were leaving, Johnson said, "Now, whatever you do, just be sure that I don't bring the president in the back door," because that was the door he always went in and out of. There was a little carport outside the back door with a golf cart there, and he would walk out the back door, get in the golf cart, and go wherever he felt like going.[26]

BESS ABELL: We had planned some local entertainment to give the President and Mrs. Kennedy the flavor of this part of Texas, and they were some goofy acts. One was a sheepdog act, where a monkey rides a sheepdog and herds some sheep into a little corral. Then there was a cowboy who was to shoot a cigarette out of a pretty lady's mouth. At that point, we thought, "Well, we better get the Secret Service down here and be sure that's going to be okay." So somebody from the Secret Service came down, and he said, "Well, now, let's see. Where are we doing those," and so forth. Then he said, "That's okay. We just don't want any surprises."

Helen Williams, who was on Mrs. Johnson's staff in Washington and was in Texas for this event, came running down the ranch road, and I'm really not sure what she said. She must have said, "The president's been shot," but I thought what I heard at that moment was, "Mr. Johnson's been shot." I don't know what she said, but at that point we all began running to the house.

The nerve center at that point was the kitchen because the kitchen had a big refrigerator and a big freezer, and on top of it were three TV sets tuned to the three networks. There was also a remote switch between channels, although [we were] getting most of our news from Walter Cronkite, because the Signal Corps had pulled out the ranch phones and had not yet gotten the other phone operational. That was pre–cell phones. Our news was coming from television.

Standing there in the kitchen, I noticed all the pots of cream soup, which we had been told was President Kennedy's favorite food. We had tasted all the soups and decided that corn soup was the best. And then there were pecan pies, lots of pecan pies, and lots and lots of homemade bread piled high. Wonderful aromas amidst sad, sad faces.

And what to do, what to do? We have no president. We have no Mrs. Kennedy coming. We need to get Helen and Gene Williams, who worked for the Johnsons in Washington, and me, at least the three of us, back to Washington. I made a reservation for the three of us from Love Field in Dallas into Washington Dulles. But then how to get to Dallas in time to catch the plane? I called J. C. Kellam and asked him if he could send the television station's little airplane out to pick us up at the ranch and take us to Dallas. He said, "I can't do that unless the vice president or Mrs. Johnson tells me to do that."

Somehow, I stiffened my backbone, and I said, "Mr. Kellam, you have to send the plane for us. We have vice president and Mrs. Johnson's clothes here. We have to bring those back to Washington, and I don't know that they care about me, but I know that they want Helen and Gene back at the house." So he did, and we landed at Love Field.

As I was walking through the airport, who should I see but my husband's stepfather. Drew Pearson was down there to give a lecture in Austin, but the event had been canceled. So we landed at Dulles in the middle of the night, and miraculously, there was a White House car there to meet us. I do not know who arranged for that, but it was wonderful. I lived in the same neighborhood at that point as the Johnsons did, and we took Helen and Gene first to the Elms. There were photographers and police and lights and people on the street there. The White House car drove through the mob, left Helen, Gene, and a mountain of luggage, then drove me home. I was back early the next morning.

To tell you the kind of person Mrs. Johnson is, when I arrived at the house, I went into their lovely den room with this beautiful soft green paneling on the walls, and there was Mrs. Johnson. She said, "Oh, Bess, you've been through. . . ." I thought, you know, where does that come from? Where does that come from, that she's thinking about me? But that is what she does. She thinks about other people.[27]

Mrs. Johnson moved into the White House at a difficult time. Most presidents move into the White House after a triumphant campaign and a huge inaugural and parade. The Johnsons moved into the White House after a tragedy in Dallas that killed President Kennedy. That was something that both the President and Mrs. Johnson were very sensitive to. I remember Mrs. Johnson saying, "If Lyndon could pull down all the stars in the sky and make a necklace for Jackie, he would make it happen." She was constantly asked when she would be moving into the White House. She said, "There's not a lot of things I can do for Mrs. Kennedy, but at least I can serve her convenience."

So there were a couple of weeks before they could move into the White House. Mrs. Kennedy asked if she could continue running the nursery school for the little ones. The Johnsons said, "Please continue that, absolutely, for as long as it's convenient for you." That was the start. So they moved into a house that was covered in black crepe, on the chandeliers and out on the columns on the portico. It was not the way that one would choose to move into that beautiful house.[28]

That weekend and those first few days, and the whole process of moving into the White House, obviously your life was turned upside down, as well. What was that like?

BESS ABELL: Well, everybody wanted to do something. It was such a horrible, horrible, awful situation, and everybody wanted to do something. So many of Mrs. Johnson's friends, her friend's wives, Senate wives, congressional wives, just showed up at the house. The mail was arriving by truckloads. My office was on the third floor, and Liz had a little office there as well. There were a couple of little guest rooms there where Marie Fehmer, the vice president's secretary, was staying and maybe somebody else too.

But there were two other large rooms up there, and we set up a big operation there. Bethine Church, whose husband was Senator Frank Church from Idaho, Lindy Boggs, whose husband was Hale Boggs, who was the Whip of the House, and good, good friends from New Orleans. Abigail McCarthy [Mrs. Eugene McCarthy] was there handling mail. Betty Fulbright [Mrs. William Fulbright] was also there. Anyway, just lots of good friends, and they knew the names of people, so they opened the mail, stapled the mail, and put them in piles of what was to be answered by whom.

Then people who had worked for Johnson in the past, like Ashton Gonella, who had been one of his secretaries in the Senate and had gone to work for Esther Peterson, vice chairman of the President's Commission on the Status of Women. Ashton later came back to oversee the mail operation and then went from that to being Mrs. Johnson's personal secretary in the White House. It was an incredible team effort. A lot of people coming and working together. It was a time everybody wanted to do something. You just wanted to do something.

The man who ran the place where I took my cleaning just showed up at our house and dropped off our cleaning and said, "I know you don't have time to do this." And then a good friend of Mrs. Johnson's, she must have done this for lots of people on the staff, but she brought us Thanksgiving dinner. I still have the platter. I tried to return the platter to her, and she said, "No, no, no. Keep the platter." It comes out on many occasions, and I think lovingly of Lillie Lou Rietzke.

How was the transition from one social secretary to the next?

BESS ABELL: Mrs. Kennedy took her social staff with her, including Nancy Tuckerman and Pam Turnure, who was the press secretary. I'm not sure whether there was anybody else. The office that answered Mrs. Kennedy's mail stayed and started answering Mrs. Johnson's mail. The two assistants in the Social Office, Barbara Keehn and Bette Hogue, did not go with Mrs. Kennedy. They stayed and were there when I arrived.

Was that awkward at all, working with people who had been Kennedy people or who had been Mrs. Kennedy's staff?

BESS ABELL: It wasn't at all for me. I had some limited conversation with Barbara ahead of time, though I had never met her and did not know Bette at all. Barbara, alas, has gone to that great social office in the sky, but Bette is still around. I see her every once in a while at things at the National Archives. She comes to LBJ events.[29]

Bess told Tyler that she wanted the social secretary job. She said she had gotten to know Mrs. Kennedy's social secretary, Tish Baldridge, and thought that was the job for her. She talked with Mrs. Johnson about it before they moved to the White House. After Bess became social secretary, the *Washington Post* reported: "For the past three years, Bess Abell, 30, has been personal secretary to Lady Bird Johnson. She has helped with the LBJ brand of hospitality at The Elms, the Spring Valley home of then Vice President and Mrs. Johnson. She has marshaled some of the finest American theatrical and musical talent to appear at the Vice President's parties. She is expected to be just as resourceful and gracious at the White House when she assists the new first lady at functions for visiting heads of state."[30]

4

White House Social Secretary

When Lady Bird Johnson met with White House chief usher J. B. West after becoming first lady, she introduced him to Bess Abell, who would be her social secretary, and Liz Carpenter, her press secretary. "Little did I realize how important a role these two very dissimilar women, Liz and Bess, would play at the White House scheme of things," West reflected. So intent had he been on orienting Mrs. Johnson that he barely took notice of her "two lieutenants." But he soon recognized his error. "Her generals (I'd thought of them as lieutenants at first) managed the corporation. Liz was in charge of the public First Lady; Bess the White House First Lady."[1]

Official mourning for President Kennedy ended on December 23, 1963. On that day, Bess telephoned West, telling him: "Hold on to your hat. President Johnson has just invited all of Congress over to the White House this afternoon. They announced it from the rostrum in Congress. What can we do?" she implored. "How many and what time?" West replied. "Nearly a thousand," she told him. The White House staff went into immediate action, taking down the black mourning crepe, hanging Christmas decorations, and preparing food. The guests included nearly every senator and representative, along with many of their families. The reception served as a symbolic celebration to reassure members of Congress of the government's continuity. President Johnson also felt confident that the event made all those who attended feel part of what the administration was trying to accomplish.[2]

"Gone is the black mourning crepe that swathed the great crystal chandeliers in the State Room and draped the high doorways," Lady Bird Johnson recorded in her diary. "The flags, at half-mast this long month, now rise—and with them my spirits," she wrote. "I have put my small wardrobe of black dresses, worn every day since that day in November, in the back of the closet and put on my Christmas red."[3]

When that open house came together miraculously in just a few hours, Bess Abell expressed her amazement at the willing response of government agencies and private companies to a White House request. "Mr. West, I never realized what power went along with the title 'Social Secretary of the White House,'" she said. "You ask for something and it's delivered immediately, if not sooner!" From then on, he noted, "Bess never hesitated to use that power."[4]

BESS ABELL: I was shot with luck to work with the Johnsons, because I loved them. There were tough times, but there were wonderful times. I think most First Ladies probably spend a lot of time on the food that was going to be served the prime minister or the queen ahead of time to make sure that it was right. When Mrs. Johnson was asked what were her goals, and what did she think that she would be concentrating on so far as food, and decor, and flowers, she said, "I've had to worry about those things for thirty some-odd years. Now I have all these wonderful people here in this house. They do that, and I can concentrate on the guest lists and doing things for people." And that's what she did.

Before a large or small occasion, she would study the guest list and go over who was going to be there, and think about introducing various people to each other, but also making that brief experience of guests when they go through a receiving line a meaningful moment, having something to say to that guest. Perhaps it was an author about his book. One of the things that she did with authors was have them autograph their books to be placed in the White House library. It made the book more wonderful for the White House library, and also for the author. But with people going through the receiving lines she would say, "Now, I want you to meet so-and-so." Or she would tell them that she wanted them to see some object that was in the White House that might have come from their state or that they might have some special tie with.[5]

What was the relationship between Mrs. Johnson and Mrs. Kennedy at that time? Did Mrs. Johnson do anything special for Mrs. Kennedy?

BESS ABELL: She did all that she could do and not near as much as she yearned to do and wished she could do. One thing that both Mrs. Johnson and her husband tried to convey to Mrs. Kennedy was "we want you to stay here as long as you want to. Don't leave this house one minute sooner than you want to. Don't feel rushed about anything." Caroline had a kindergarten and John had a little nursery group there, and Mrs. Johnson said, "I know that that's on your mind, and please continue to have it here as long as you want."

Mrs. Kennedy asked Mrs. Johnson to come down to the White House several days before they moved in to show her around the house. She had sent—and I imagine this was probably Mrs. Kennedy's idea—J. B. West, who was the chief usher at the White House out to see Mrs. Johnson with photographs of the rooms and floor plans of the rooms. Of course Mrs. Johnson had been in the White House any number of times, but when you go in a house to a reception or you go in a house on a tour with some constituents, it's an entirely different feeling than thinking, "this is the house I'm going to live in for a year."[6]

James R. Jones served in the Johnson administration, eventually becoming the president's appointment secretary, a modest title for a post that actually functioned as chief of staff. In that role he oversaw Bess's budget.

JAMES R. JONES: Bess had a hard act to follow because Kennedy's social secretary had captured the press and had really good relationships with the media. They put on good programs that advanced President Kennedy's plans, what he wanted to accomplish. So Bess had a difficult—I mean, everybody in Johnson's sphere had a difficult act to follow, whether it was from the president on down. But I never heard her complain or say how unfair it was or anything like that. She put her programs together—and oftentimes, they entailed money or budget—and would say why and what it was going to do. Oftentimes, she did that with the president. My sense was that what she did was not something that the president had expertise in, but he totally trusted her. When she recommended ideas, it was not that he questioned whether it was right or wrong. It was informative as opposed to trying to be convincing.[7]

The White House as a Home

What's it like to move into the White House as a home?

BESS ABELL: When Mrs. Johnson came back after Mrs. Kennedy had so nicely asked her to come down and walk through the rooms with her, she came back saying how much she hated to leave The Elms; that it was a much more comfortable place to live in than the White House was going to be. And that's true. The White House, for all its space and all its rooms, is not what you would ever call a family home. Another thing that Mrs. Johnson always felt, a room isn't a room if it has more than one door. What was really their sort of family sitting room and where they would be if they had only six, eight, or ten guests, was the west sitting hall in which you had doors into the kitchen, into the dining room, into Mrs. Johnson's bedroom, into Mrs. Johnson's dressing room, then the wide, double doors into the long hall. So it was rather like being in Grand Central Station.

If I had been meeting with Mrs. Johnson in her bedroom, where she did most of her work at her desk and the sofa by the fireplace there, we might run into the lunch hour. If the president had Secretary [Dean] Rusk and Dick Helms from CIA and Clark Clifford or [Robert] McNamara there for a luncheon meeting, they would be seated out in the west hallway. I would either have to go out and walk through them or else go out through the president's closets and into his bedroom, and then out into the hallway.

Did they get to take many personal things with them, furniture and pictures?

BESS ABELL: All the furniture in Mrs. Johnson's bedroom was hers, with a couple of exceptions. All the furniture in her little dressing room—I call it a dressing room—it was an area of closets and a desk and a sofa and a small fireplace. All of that was hers. They brought a number of paintings with them, which hung primarily in their own bedrooms. Then the furniture in Lynda and Luci's rooms was their furniture. She had a couple of French lamps that she had in the Yellow Oval Room, but other than that, that's just about all.[8]

One Saturday I came in to work with Mrs. Johnson on some guest lists and some entertainments. It was a lovely summer day, and we were sitting out on the Truman balcony. She looked at me and said, "You just look very tired and very haggard. What is happening that you just seem so exhausted?" I said, "Oh, Mrs. Johnson, we moved into this new house and I just don't think that I'll ever get finished." She said, "Well, of course not, dear, you never get finished with a house. You never get finished until you move out." And that is so true, and it's something I've reminded myself of often and also reminded friends of mine when they get in that same shape, "Well of course not, you'll never be finished with your house, not till the day you move out."[9]

Dressing for Work at the White House

Did Mr. Johnson take a direct interest in Mrs. Johnson's wardrobe?

BESS ABELL: Absolutely. No saddle blanket fabrics, which are thick, woolly things. He likes the things that show the shape of your figure, if you have one to show. He does that not just with his wife, but with his daughters. He does it with his secretaries and with anybody who will sit still and listen. I always knew when he liked something I wore, and I knew when he didn't like it too.

I suppose a woman in that position must have to worry about her choice of clothing?

BESS ABELL: In the last few years I used to work with Mrs. Johnson on her clothes. She would buy twice a year for spring and summer and fall and winter. We would go up to a suite at a hotel in New York, and then a number of the designers would come to her and bring clothes that they thought that she was interested in, and swatches of other fabric. Her daytime clothes she really didn't worry too much about. If Mary Jones down the block had the same thing in four different colors, that really wasn't a concern. But her evening dresses, she really wanted to be one-of-a-kind.

She didn't feel like that in the beginning. But one night when she was planning to wear a lovely green dress with a gold-embroidered jacket on it, I was downstairs as the guests were coming in, and her dress walked in on Kay Graham—Mrs. Philip Graham of the *Washington Post*. I ran upstairs and said, "You may want to change." It's an embarrassment to the guest. I really always tried to have my evening dresses different from everybody else's. I no longer feel like that now. But I always felt that some guest who had really knocked themselves out getting this pretty dress to wear to the White House dinner did not want to walk in and see the hired help wearing the same dress.

She liked two lady designers who were very accommodating, Mollie Parnis and Adele Simpson. She wore a number of other clothes, but she found that she had great difficulty in, translating from a sketch and a swatch of fabric into a finished product. She found it much easier to try on the sample size, and she could generally get into them, to tell if "this is for me." To try it on, walk around in it, and think to herself, "Can I get on and off a helicopter in this dress? Can I get in and out of an automobile and still look like a lady?" Then, of course, we would go back to New York for the fittings, and when they were pinning up the skirt hem, she would always move a chair over in front of the mirror and sit down and see if she could sit down and not need to reach for a scarf or a program or an enormous handbag to cover her knees. She was very conscious of how things moved and how they photographed.

Rarely ever did she buy anything, as most women do, that just hung in her closet. She didn't buy something for a specific occasion and wear it once and put it away. She would decide before the season began, "I need two new dresses and coats. I need three dresses and jackets. I need two afternoon dresses that I can have my picture taken with the ladies' auxiliary or the 4-H girls. And I need four new evening dresses." Then that would be the guideline that we would go by.

She had some dresses that the president was not really wild about, but generally it was after the fact. She would bring something down to show him and ask, "Do you like it?" If he was turned off by it, she would not get it.[10]

LYNDA JOHNSON ROBB: Bess had flair. I don't care what she was wearing, she always looked better in it than anybody else did. And she would know how to tie a scarf! I never could understand how Bess knew how to tie scarves and make an outfit look entirely different, beautiful, take a piece of something and put it with something else and make it into an entirely different outfit. She could have been a fashion model, anywhere. She just had style. And I had no style. First, I couldn't care less. I inherited that from my mother. If Bess was really honest about Mother, she would say that, too.[11]

NEAL P. GILLEN: I can tell you about Bess and fashion. Abe Schrader was a prominent leader in the garment industry. President Johnson visited there during the 1964 campaign. Abe was a beguiling figure. He was short and compact, very well dressed, and he had this Polish accent which was charming. He spoke the King's English but sort of in a funny way. He spoke many languages, given where he was brought up. His father was a lumber merchant in an area of Poland that was controlled from time to time by the Germans, Russians, or the Poles. As a result, the people from this area were multilingual.

When President Johnson visited Abe's showroom on Seventh Avenue, Abe led Johnson into the cutting room and showed Johnson how to cut fabric. Johnson was more interested in the models. Abe showed Johnson how a dress came to creation. Abe took the president into his small office, where off to the side was a rack of dresses hanging.

Mrs. Johnson was along on the trip, but she was sort of in the background with Bess. Abe explained to the president, "These are the most expensive dresses in the world, Mr. President, the most expensive." And Johnson said, "Well, why are they the most expensive?" Abe replied, "Because this is the only one made. I couldn't sell them, and it cost much to make it." He explained that when the buyers come in, a model would wear the dress, and they'd say, "Oh, yeah. I'll take 200 of those." "But sometimes," Abe explained, "they don't like it." So the dress comes back here.

Johnson was intrigued by that. Following that visit, the president had Bess call Abe Schrader.

Abe was a wise and generous man. Mrs. Johnson traveled to New York with Bess and visited Abe's showroom and purchased dresses at wholesale prices. Abe wanted to give them to her, but she insisted on paying. Abe outfitted her, and I think he outfitted Lynda Bird. Abe got invited to the White House through Bess at the president's request. He became a strong supporter of the president. He was a very happy man, very generous man, politically, after that also.[12]

In her diary, Lady Bird Johnson noted one of the shopping trips: "I made a few more tentative choices, being very parsimonious according to Bess' way of thinking. She and Helen [Williams] both look at me with mild reproval and assure me that I will, indeed, need everything that I am getting, and several more in addition that I maintain I cannot afford."[13]

Setting up Shop

Social secretaries had operated within the White House since the era of Theodore Roosevelt. The first were simply secretaries for social occasions, who located addresses for invitations, kept lists of who accepted, and provided the press with a social calendar. Under Jacqueline Kennedy, Letitia "Tish" Baldridge became the first social secretary to take charge of programming events for the East Room, although she often found that Mrs. Kennedy had her own ideas. By contrast, J. B. West observed that "Bess Abell directed everything. She was in on everything for the Johnsons' private parties as well as for official entertaining. She dreamed up the decorations, she told the chef how to cook, told the housekeeper what needed to be cleaned and where the ashtrays should be placed."[14]

Was it just assumed that you would stay on with Mrs. Johnson?

BESS ABELL: Well, it was assumed that I would stay on with her. What was not assumed was that I would be the social secretary. I did some thinking about this myself and talked to Tyler about it, I think probably before Mrs. Johnson or the president had given it any thought. I knew that Liz would be at that point going to the White House in all likelihood on Mrs. Johnson's staff unless she went on the president's press staff. A lot of people had thought that she would have been given an appointment to

President Kennedy in his press office, so there were a lot of people who assumed that she would be going into Johnson's press staff. But I think that she really always very much wanted to work with Mrs. Johnson.

After I decided in my own mind, and got the okay from Tyler, that I really did want to be the social secretary, I talked to Liz about it. I told her, "I don't know what Mrs. Johnson's and the president's plans are, but this is what I want to do. Don't let anybody tell them I can't do it because I've got small children and I don't want that extra responsibility. I do." Then I talked with Mrs. Johnson about it. I think she probably considered maybe asking Tish Baldridge to come back, I don't know. I do not know who else she considered. I'm sure that both the President and Mrs. Johnson were a little bit nervous about whether or not I could handle it.

I don't suppose there is such a thing as having prior experience for that kind of job.

BESS ABELL: No, I don't think so. You get all kinds of letters, once you're in that job, from girls in high school and college saying, "I want to grow up to be the White House social secretary. What do I do?"

I did a lot of the same things during the vice presidential years, even more so when we moved out to The Elms when they started doing more entertaining, so that I had had a tiny flavor of what a social secretary does, only I did it myself instead of having a staff to help. If you wanted flowers for the table, then I went down to the florist and bought them and came back and arranged them. If you wanted the invitations to be sent, I looked up the addresses and wrote the invitations and licked the envelopes and met the guests at the front door and hired the butlers and ordered the liquor and wrote the place cards.

Did you also assemble a staff to help you as social secretary?

BESS ABELL: I really walked into a staff that was there pretty much. There were two girls who had worked for Tish Baldridge and then had worked for Nancy Tuckerman [White House social secretary during the Kennedy administration], and one of them was an enormous help and the other one, I would say, was less interested in working and less interested in the White House and less interested in any job. I don't think her feeling was about Lyndon Johnson; I think her feeling was about "I really only want to work part-time." After that we had another girl who came in and worked with us in the office. But it was working with the social correspondence office, which handled all of Mrs. Johnson's mail and all of the girls' mail, and that took an enormous amount of time in the beginning, trying to get them to write like Mrs. Johnson would, trying to get them to write like I did, like Liz did. No matter how hard I worked during the most difficult period, the hardest time of all was the beginning because we were new, but also because nobody understood how we did things, and the mail was just a crushing, crushing blow.

Initially, most of the mail received by the White House was favorable and sympathetic.

BESS ABELL: I really don't remember any crank letters. You get complimentary letters from nuts too, they're not always just ugly letters from nuts. The crank letters come in phases anyway. The White House operators will tell you that—you're going to think I'm putting you on, but they really do come with phases of the moon.

There are a class of letters that are just called PRS, Protective Research Section, and they go over there. Also, there are some nutty telephone calls that you'll get that sometimes you can send over to PRS. Somebody will call, and heaven knows how they would end up with the White House Social Office, but they would be calling because somebody was sending brainwaves in, killing them, or giving them migraine headaches.

You try and give individual attention to all the mail of course, but you can also give individual attention with a form letter. You know, how many different ways can you say, "Thank you for asking for my recipe, here it is." You just develop a way of saying it, and then out it goes. How many different kinds of letters can you write enclosing an autograph?

How do you separate out the letters that the Johnsons would want personal attention to from old friends and family?

BESS ABELL: I had a little card file, which was of great help to the people who were opening up Mrs. Johnson's mail, which were names and addresses and a salutation on it. Also, I had put on them things like "has two sons, Billy and Joe," where I happened to know it. I had done that in December of 1960. I was in the hospital for two days, and before I went in, I went by to see Grace Tully [the last personal secretary of President Franklin D. Roosevelt] and packed up tons and tons of Mrs. Johnson's correspondence and had gone through it and had taken down names and addresses and put those on card files. Then I just tried to keep it up to date with people that she would write to, people that she was on a first name basis with. So they took that file, the man who opened the mail, and he would look up every one of those names in there, and if it was somebody in that box, he would write FF [friends file] on it. In the beginning those would generally come into my desk or come into Liz's desk.[15]

Setting up her own office in the East Wing, Bess quickly made contact with James R. Ketchum, the White House curator, who became a trusted ally.

JAMES R. KETCHUM: My first recollections of Bess would be on one of the first days that she started at the White House. Our office, let me explain, was in the very center of the ground floor, across from the diplomatic reception room, which was the family entrance when they would be arriving by automobile. There were double doors out into the hall. These doors opened up, and there was Liz, talking more than I was talking, and Bess, who was laughing all the way. Within minutes, I was laughing until the tears were falling. I don't know what exactly we were discussing, but that was my first meeting with Bess and Liz. It was not long after that we had a mutual admiration society. It was the happiest association with both those good people, and with Bess, you became family. But what she was able to do and the kind of stamp that she could put on 1600 Pennsylvania Avenue was just amazing. I could not say enough about what she taught me and everyone else on that staff.[16]

Marta Dunetz, who worked as Liz Carpenter's assistant, recalled a special quality that contributed to Bess Abell's accomplishments at the White House.

MARTA DUNETZ: One impression of Bess that I always have had is that she—although I know Kentucky is not in the Deep South—she had southern charm, that ability to say things and do things in a way that is so delicate and soft; and yet, on the other side, kind of determined, knowing how to do it. But not coming off harsh. I guess it's used in a slightly different context but, when used with Bess, like the steel magnolia. The combination of the southern charm, the wonderfulness of that embrace with an efficiency and an ability and a degree of organization. Someone without that softness could be harsh or could be overpowering. I look at some of that through the prism of today's politics and not being political at all, but it's hard for women in politics—I don't mean Bess was running for office, but she was working in a public sector. You want to come off as efficient and competent and good, but you don't want to turn people off by being officious or overbearing.

What Bess did for the weddings, or what she did for the state dinners, somewhere there would be more detail about the specifics of what she did, but more important is how she did it; how she got along with people; how she created not only success but a happy atmosphere to success. She dealt with people like the White House florists, and the calligraphers, and the social correspondents, they're there, administration in and out. They're not political, but they do their jobs. They take pride in their jobs. Bess created such happy feelings with them. She had her standards. She wanted a certain thing, but she asked you for it and appreciated it and expressed her appreciation. She didn't take people for granted. She respected what they did and made sure they knew that she was appreciative of what they had done even though it was their job to do it. So the description iron butterfly is fabulous.[17]

A Working Mother

As a working mother with two young sons, Bess still had to balance work and family, which had its challenges and stressful moments.

LYNDON ABELL: Mother was, of course, working for the Johnson administration in the White House. One of her perks was that she got a limo to pick her up and take her to work, which was not very far. The driver was Fred Jefferson, who for some reason we just called Jeff, presumably because he wanted us to call him that.

A lot of times I got tossed off the bus that took me to school for causing trouble. So when that happened, instead of being punished, I got picked up by a White House limo. Fred Jefferson would drive me to the White House and drop me off by the East Wing, and I would scamper through the gate and go in the doors of the East Wing and hang out at the White House for a few hours before it was time to go home. Very different time back then, of course.

I remember one time getting out of the car and running through the gate. A Marine who did not know who I was saw this little kid scurrying through the gate, and he just reached down with his big Marine hand and grabbed me by the scruff of the neck and lifted me up. I was sort of, what's going on here? Another Marine at the entrance to the East Wing called out to this fellow and said, "That's okay, that's just Lyndon. He's all right." The Marine set me back down and I, somewhat quizzically, ran on up to the door and they let me inside. I had the right name, Lyndon!

It was a very different time in the 1960s, even though there were protests and things like that. But I had a tremendous amount of access to run around the White House. I remember just leaving the office area and wandering around the hallways of the White House. That was just a more normal thing back then. I think if anybody did that today they would be horrified. I would go down and talk to the drivers. They would be talking about football, and I liked football. I would also hang out near my mom's office in the East Wing where her assistants worked. I would do some homework or, you know, goof around with their stuff.

When I was probably four there was a "bring your kids to work day" at the White House. I got up and went to work with my mom. Later she was doing something, and my dad was taking me around the White House. President Johnson popped up and he was with former President Harry Truman, who had come to consult with him on some things. President Johnson said, "Hey, Tyler, let's get a picture with Lyndon and two presidents. So they took a couple of pictures and then my dad said, "Well, can I get my picture in there?" President Johnson said, "No." I think Dad still feels a little resentful![18]

DAN ABELL: I remember going with Mother to her White House office on occasion and meeting the various people that she worked with, like Liz Carpenter. I have this image in my mind of a wide-open office with lots of different people working and it being exciting. Mother worked with a number of Marines on detail to the White House. They were always in their dress uniforms, which were quite dramatic and made an impression on me.

There is the story of me at the White House Christmas party when, evidently, I went up to the president and tugged on his pant leg and said, "Mr. President?" I was trying to get his attention, and Dad was just a little too far away to do anything quickly about it.

Finally, the president turns around and looks down at this kid who is pulling on his pants, and I said, "Merry Christmas, Mr. President." And then he lit up and beamed and said, "Oh, Merry Christmas." Dad wiped his brow and said, "Okay, that went better than I expected!" I feel like Mom did something right bringing me up and teaching me about how to behave.

It was kind of a big deal that Mother worked in the White House. But I never felt that it made me special. Mother made clear that just because you have the opportunity to walk around the halls of the White House you are not any better than anybody else.[19]

LYNDON ABELL: We were the only people that I knew growing up that had a phone with two lines on it. It was very exotic. The phone had buttons on it for one line and another line. The second line, when you picked it up, there was about a three-second pause and then one of the White House receptionists answered. It was a direct connection to the White House. So I was told if I needed to reach my mom, press that button, and lift up the phone.

I know that at some point Mother told me how guilty she felt about not being around. But I remember her calling when she had to be at work late. She would ask someone to cover for her for a few minutes during a state dinner or something, and she would duck away and call Danny and me. She read us stories from a series of books called *Old Mother West Wind*. I think maybe she had them when she was a kid.[20]

DAN ABELL: A childhood memory I have is Mother read to Lyndon and me in the evening before bed. The stories I most remember her reading were the *Old Mother West Wind* stories. Thornton Burgess was an excellent writer of children's stories, a conservationist, and he wrote stories about Old Mother West Wind, Jimmy Skunk, Reddy Fox, and Grandfather Frog. They were just wonderful stories that children could listen to and also take away a little something about what is important about our natural world.

Mother would read them to us with drama. When Grandfather Frog spoke, she would make her voice a little more deep and that sort of thing. They were just wonderful, and we would be really into it.[21]

LYNDON ABELL: One of the things Mother had in common with her father was that they were both good cooks. She really was a good cook and that balanced with her hard job and long hours. It was pretty common that she would come home after a long day and put everybody to work organizing dinner. So my brother and I learned to be competent in the kitchen early on. She was very creative in the kitchen and was not opposed to following recipes, but she was quite good at looking in the refrigerator and taking the ingredients that she had and turning it into something quite good.[22]

DAN ABELL: Luvie Pearson, Dad's mother, was very much against the Vietnam War. I remember seeing images of the Vietnam War on television when Mom and Dad would watch the news. So Granny took Lyndon and me down to one of the protests at the White House, and Mom was not happy about that. Of course, she heard about it later and asked, "What if the President and Mrs. Johnson had seen her two boys out there protesting?"[23]

MARTA DUNETZ: There's Bess. She has a husband. She has children. She has a demanding career. She is doing it all. There were certainly others who did that, but as a young person just getting out of college, it showed me that a woman could do it all. And when you think back to that time, women were not front and center. We didn't have women on the Supreme Court. We didn't have women in the Cabinet necessarily. Except for Margaret Chase Smith, we didn't have women in the Senate. You certainly had certain women that popped up like Bess popped up, but they were not as numerous as they are today. I look at Bess more as a role model for women at a time when she came along that she was more the exception than the rule.

Now, Liz Carpenter would be the same. She had a career before the White House. She had children. She had a husband. She did it all too. They were great, great role models. And I would say Lady Bird Johnson had a job too. Her full-time job had been supporting her husband. We worked in a generally female environment in that East Wing—although the florists and the calligraphers were men, and we had the military down the hall. But when you look at that operation of Liz's and Bess's, and you include the social correspondence office, they were all women. For the most part, the rest of the White House then was all male. I'm hard-pressed to think of a woman in the West Wing back then. Can you? I can't.[24]

Entertaining at the Johnson White House

White House usher J. B. West marveled that for every occasion except formal state dinners, Bess's invitations came "in every color, every style of printing. For the after-dinner entertainment, the printed programs were mighty fancy, as in a regular theater. Some were covered in red velour, some in green silk, and some contained cartoons or drawings." She also set themes for the parties with appropriate decorations. In planning these affairs, he was on the phone with Bess many times a day, "for Bess was indeed the White House social director."[25]

Bess's chief limitation was the image of Lyndon Johnson as a Texas cowboy that made him a figure of derision among Washington's elite "Georgetown set."

BESS ABELL: I think that a lot of them were terribly disappointed that the president didn't walk into the White House with boots and spurs and a ten-gallon hat.

I'm sure it kept the president from doing a lot of things that he might otherwise have done. It kept me from doing things in the way of entertainment at the White House that I would have loved to have done. I would have loved to have had a square dance, American folk dancing, in the East Room for a visitor from abroad, but I just did not feel that we could get away with it.

What could you gain by it? You would amuse and delight a hundred and forty guests and a visitor from one country abroad by having an

American square dance, American folk dance, in the East Room. They would love it if you had the right guest of honor. But it is the sort of thing that a lot of columnists around the country would pick up and the sort of thing that would stay with you. Although I have a feeling that all of us on the inside of the White House took it all perhaps more seriously than we should have. While I was there I tried to always be able to step back twenty-five yards and look at it and say, "Is that really as important as it seems?" Sometimes I felt that I had not stepped back quite far enough.

We only served Texas barbecue on the White House lawn once, and that was for a White House staff party that we had the last year. I told the president, "You know, all these people that worked for you here, they are not going to feel like they really worked for you if they don't have any Texas barbeque. So we did have a Texas barbeque, and it was a great, great success. Everybody said, "Why haven't we been doing this for five years!"[26]

In 1967 the Johnsons held a country fair on the White House lawn for children of members of Congress, Cabinet members, and other government employees. In September 1968 the country fair was put on again for underprivileged children and extended for another day so that White House staff and their children could attend.

BESS ABELL: The president told me, "You know, people appreciate what you do for their kids more than what you do for them, so think of something that would be fun to do for the kids too." Then as I was leaving I thought, "The country fair." So we had a carnival on the South Lawn with a merry-go-round, a Ferris wheel, fortune-teller tents, and all kinds of games and hot dogs.[27]

We had baseball players from Baltimore who came in and ran a tent that you could knock down bottles and so forth. As I was working on getting the props for the carnival I called this place in New York where we ordered a lot of props, and I said, "I have two fortune-teller tents and I need two crystal balls." And this guy I was talking to said, "Where do you want me to send the crystal balls?" I said, "Send them to the White House." He said, "Lady, I'll send them, but you've got to tell the president they don't really work!" But the country fairs were a great success.[28]

When you are social secretary, do the parties fall into types?
BESS ABELL: They do fall into types, absolutely. There are the state dinners that are the most formal occasions that are given at the White House. Those are to honor the president's high-ranking visitors from

abroad, the prime ministers, the kings, and the presidents who come to this country on a state visit, an official visit, or a working visit. Then there are the receptions and teas. Those could be for everything from the officers of the DAR to three thousand Democratic women who are in town for a Democratic women's conference. Mrs. Johnson had a number of teas for the kind and generous people who had given furnishings and paintings to the White House collection. Then there were also the teas and receptions for young people like 4-H kids from out of town.

Did you try to have a certain number of parties a week?

BESS ABELL: No, there would be occasionally a week that would go by, even when the President and Mrs. Johnson were in town, with maybe only one or two parties; then the next week you might run an average of three a day. On average, for the whole five years that the Johnsons were there, there would probably be a party and a half a day. When I say a party and a half a day, I'm just speaking of a function. One party might be the reception for three thousand ladies. Another might be three ambassadors' wives for tea; another party might be four thousand foreign students; and another might be a state dinner for a hundred and forty guests.

There are a whole lot more ideas generated than you can possibly use. The president moved into that house and repeatedly said to groups he met with either socially or business-wise, "This is your house, and I just have a short-term lease here." The Johnsons really felt that. They wanted to share that house and its history with as many people as they could, and I must say the rate of entertaining in the White House seemed to go up much more rapidly than our population explosion.

In looking back on the records, not just during the Johnson administration, but since the end of World War II, I went over the figures with the White House housekeeper one day. The number of people entertained in the White House doubled about every three years. That doesn't make so much difference when you're doubling from one hundred to two hundred, but when you're doubling from ten thousand to twenty thousand to forty thousand, it's a significant increase.

Did President Johnson ever originate an idea for a party or some kind of entertainment?

BESS ABELL: All the time! Always, whether it was an informal gathering for a Sunday night supper when he would tell his wife to call some friends in to dinner, or whether it was a luncheon planned the day before for three prime ministers who were in this country at the United Nations, which was quite a feat in itself. They were not all prime ministers. There was the foreign minister of Great Britain, Mr. [George] Brown; and I think [Aldo] Moro of Italy, and Prime Minister [Jens Otto] Krag of Denmark. I seem to recollect it had something to do with NATO.

But the president called me about two or three in the afternoon and he said, "Would it be possible to do this?" My attitude in working with President Johnson was always that anything is possible, it's just that some things are more difficult than others. We knew it was possible, but we didn't always know quite how possible. So he said, "Well, make up a guest list, do the grocery shopping, send me a suggested guest list. I will be back in touch with you and let you know whether or not we're going ahead with it." In the meantime he was trying to reach the people. My office went to work on developing a guest list.

This was in the afternoon before the luncheon the next day. We just told everybody around the office that if they had plans for that evening, they'd better cancel them. As I was typing a page of the list in my typewriter, my secretary would take it and make a clean copy and make a carbon for the people who would do the invitations and the place cards down the hall in the Social Entertainments Office. In effect, we had the place cards done before the guests were invited. I think I finally got the okay about five or six o'clock to go ahead and invite some people, but he said, "We don't know if these people are going to be able to come definitely. We think they're going to be able to come."

I had the girls who made telephone calls issue invitations, which Emily Post will tell you you're not supposed to do from the White House. But Emily Post doesn't know that we have to work with the possible. They called the people who were in government, people who were in the State Department, and people who were in the agencies and invited them. They just said, "The president wants you—or your boss—to come for lunch tomorrow at one o'clock, southwest gate." I said, "Don't tell them who it's for or anything."

The next morning we were flooded with calls from people who had accepted the invitation and then they thought, "Well, what's it for?" Fortunately, by that time we were able to tell them that it was in honor of the four foreign guests. But it worked out very well. I have forgotten what the chef had, but I know that he had to reach some of the wholesalers at home that night and say, "What do you have for me tomorrow morning?" so that we could plan the menu.

Did that kind of thing happen often?

BESS ABELL: Not nearly as often as people think. Of course, Johnson was always the person to make the spur of the moment trip or to have the spur of the moment entertainment. I would guess that maybe a tenth of our entertaining or less was done on short notice. Some of it was because of an idea that came to the president or an idea that was presented to him that he bought, and time was short, and we just moved ahead with it.

A lot of it was also because of the world situation, this Jet Age diplomacy we live in. I suppose twenty or thirty years ago when people crossed the Atlantic more often in boats than in airplanes that plans were made further ahead of time and they were more relaxed. But now you can get to Washington from any capital in the world in something like sixteen or eighteen hours. Some of our state functions were planned with as little as ten days' notice. But even when we had six months' notice we would move up almost to the wire with the invitations out, and the place cards written, and the food ordered, and then the visitor from abroad would not be able to come.

LYNDA JOHNSON ROBB: "Poor Bess." That was a phrase I heard often. "Poor Bess," Mother would say. Daddy would change things and invite people that had not been invited before.[29]

Because of last-minute changes did you ever have to disinvite someone?

BESS ABELL: Oh yes. Once we actually canceled a state dinner. What do you do with the ladies who talked their husbands into spending a couple of hundred dollars for their new dress? You try and invite them again. I think before President Johnson's administration was out, we had backtracked on all those people and included them in one dinner or another.

Were you able to enjoy the parties?

BESS ABELL: Some of them I really enjoyed quite a lot, but I really did not enjoy them until it was about time to wind them up because you were always thinking about all those little details, all those little things that go into rolling up the ball of wax.

Occasionally I was lucky enough to be a guest, and then you get to eat dinner, but I never went hungry in my days in the White House. We always had a dinner in the Navy mess for the social aides and then for the women on my staff and Liz Carpenter's staff who were there and helped out at the dinner, shepherded press around, and so forth. I do not know whether they still do that or not.

The dinners were served French service, which meant there was always an extra portion on every platter that goes to the table. So if there are ten people at the table, the platter is presented with eleven portions on it. So if you hang out in the family dining room, which during a state dinner is turned into a pantry, and it was possible to get the extra portions that had not been needed that evening. President Johnson would show up with extra people who were not on the list and who we did not have seats for, and I would look at the list to see who I could disinvite and ask them to have dinner with me in the family dining room. Those people always thought they had the best time because they were backstage, and it was really quite cozy.[30]

LYNDA JOHNSON ROBB: The social aides loved Bess. If they held a state dinner, that meant the social aides had to be there before because they had to hobnob. If they had enough people who in the end did not get to come to the party or the dinner, or if they had just four social aides for the night, Bess would feed them. I had to come down and make an entrance and entertain people too. That was part of my job, to go around and make everybody feel at home because frequently I knew the people and the social aides did not know them. But then I was not invited to the dinner. So there I am, all dressed up, and there they are, all dressed up. Sometimes Bess would say, "We'll set up a table for you to eat."

I remember one time, we ate in the library of the White House with the same food they were having upstairs, but maybe not as big portions. Bess went out of her way to make the social aides feel comfortable, feel like they were not just somebody standing around. They had to be there early, and Bess would tell them what they were supposed to do. Then, when the guests would go into dinner, the social aides had nothing to do except twiddle their thumbs and would not have had anything to eat. Sometimes they might go to the White House mess. But Bess made sure they got something to drink and eat. She was just thinking about these guys, who were not married, did not have anybody to go home to and feed them late that night. So, everybody loved Bess.[31]

BRIAN LAMB: I was single. I had heard somewhere that there must be this thing called a social aide. I did not know what you called them. I called a friend of mine who worked for Senator Birch Bayh of Indiana. She said, "Call commander XYZ at this number and tell him you're interested in being a social aide. I've called him, and he's expecting your call." We set up an appointment, and I went over to the Bureau of Personnel and he interviewed me. The next thing I knew I was sent to Bess Abell's office in the White House. I did not know her. I didn't know who she was, but I knew she was a social secretary. She interviewed me. And then a short time later, she asked me if I would come be a social aide, and that's how it started.

She was a fascinating person to meet. She was nicer to people like me than she had to be. As you know, White Houses can be rather egocentric. The one thing that I never, ever saw about Bess Abell was any ego. She was young. She was only thirty-three when I went there. And she explained what it was. I was all kind of big eyes on all this. I had no idea what I was getting into. She told me that I would be one of twenty-five, that it was a collateral duty. My office at the Pentagon had to agree to this. But when they would call, no matter what it was—and they were flexible, but no matter what it was, they wanted me to come to the White House for that event. We would work everything from a breakfast in the morning to a lunch to a dinner to a state dinner. I would do two or three events a week.

If I saw somebody, I would go up, introduce myself, ask them if I could help them in any way, and tell them where to go. When people walk in the White House, they're not regulars. They are wide-eyed. They're looking around, "What do I do next?" It was just so simple to say, "The reception is in there. Go and take a seat," or "Get something to eat, get a drink," and tell them what the rest of the day or evening was going to look like.[32]

BESS ABELL: The whole thing about entertaining at the White House is to make your guests welcome, to make them feel as much at home as possible, which is not always easy to do in the first house of the land. Entertaining there is always going to be different from anyplace else, no matter who the president is. You can't walk into that house without remembering all the presidents and their families who lived there before.[33]

During state dinners, Bess and chief usher J. B. West sat in the family dining room, as West recalled, "eating the same food, having the same food, having the same service as the other guests, and joking with each other about being the 'official taster,' and wondering who would get poisoned first." At one state luncheon for the Queen of Greece, the butler who served the president came running in to tell them, "The president says not to serve any more meat. He says it's rotten!"[34]

BESS ABELL: When I got to the president, he pointed to his plate and said, "I cut into this meat and look what came out!" I told him that the dish was Tournedos Rossini and what he thought was rotten was foie gras. He was of course more interested in his guests, and he leaned over the table, spreading his arms and saying, "Everything's okay. It's all right." I made a quick exit back to the family dining room.

Two days later he called me from the Oval Office and, before he could speak, I told him I was sorry about the lunch and that it would never be put on a White House menu again. "That's good," he responded. "But I'm glad you had it this once, otherwise last night in New York at the Waldorf Astoria I would have told 800 people their meat was rotten."[35]

If someone were about to become social secretary in the White House and asked your advice, what would you tell them?

BESS ABELL: I would say enjoy it. It is the best job in the White House, next to being First Lady. You get to have your fingers in everything, and you get to know everybody in the White House. Some of them you get to know at their best, and some of them you get to know at their worst.[36]

5

White House Impresario

Beyond handling the traditional duties of guest lists, calendar, and correspondence, "Bess was the impresario of the Johnson White House," wrote chief usher J. B. West. "We called her Sol Hurok [one of the world's foremost impresarios]." She recruited the artists, designed the programs, named the dishes on the menu, selected gifts for state visitors, decorated the staterooms, coached the military social aides, and "acted as assistant hostess at all the parties, introducing guests, and starting conversations, choreographing the crowds from one room to another." Her instruction sheets served as scenarios for the staff to follow. "Because the gregarious Johnsons used all the house all the time, combining official business with entertaining," the usher recorded, "Bess was on duty all the time."[1]

How do you go about making up a guest list?

BESS ABELL: Depending upon the type of party, many of your guest lists are ready-made. If you are entertaining the officers of the American Bar Association, that is predetermined by somebody else; if you're having a reception for the White House Fellows, that's predetermined: you have the White House Fellows. If you are having a dinner for a head of state, some of that is predetermined. We set up some guidelines for ourselves to work within. I just arbitrarily said, after thinking that this is probably the fairest number for the foreign visitor and for us, that "we will have ten members of your official party."

Some visitors from abroad come with three people; others have a tendency to come with thirty people. But when they are told that only ten members of their official party can come to the White House that cuts down on the number of people that they bring with them, which is really good for everybody. It is good for the logistics people planning the moves, and it is good for the people entertaining them at other places that they go.

The people that were always invited were the vice president, the secretary of state, and if the secretary of state were not there, we would always have the assistant secretary from the State Department. We would always have the chief of protocol and his wife; we would always have the under-secretary of state who was responsible for that particular area. If it was the president of Colombia, it would be the assistant secretary for Latin American Affairs. We would always have of course the ambassador from their country to ours; we would always have our ambassador from our country to theirs. And then from there it was free, but it did fall into categories. We would always try and invite two additional cabinet members above and beyond the secretary of state. The secretary of the treasury was most often invited because these people very frequently had money problems.

If it was a country that was very interested in improving their agriculture, we would try and have the secretary of agriculture, so that we would have a couple of cabinet members, and we tried to rotate it so that the same secretary did not come every single time, but that each one of them were given an opportunity to meet the foreign visitors. The same thing was done with members of Congress. We would invite ten or twelve members of the House and Senate but try to rotate those. In the business community and in the banking community we would attempt to have the people who had business in those countries.

Did you get help in finding out that kind of information?

BESS ABELL: I guess the first person who really touched this guest list, who began the model of it, who began working with it, would be the desk officer from the country. The list that came to me was really only as good as the imagination and ingenuity of that desk officer. It was hard for me to get over to the desk officer that, "I know that you want to have [Dean] Rusk and you want to have [Douglas] Dillon or [Henry] Fowler or Joe Barr, and that you want to have [Senators] Mansfield and Dirksen and [Bourke] Hicken-looper and [William] Fulbright. But don't you realize that these are the people who every country wants to have and out of the last six dinners, they've just been here three times, and we want to have other people? We want to reach around and have somebody else on the Foreign Relations Committee, somebody else in the Democratic leadership." So that a lot of the names that would come from the State Department were the same on every single guest list, and it was up to my office to try and weed those out and not invite Senator John Sherman Cooper to eight dinners in a row.

Then the guest lists also went beyond that to include private citizens, entertainers, and such.

BESS ABELL: We tried to introduce this visitor from abroad to a wide variety of Americans. He might, in standing in that receiving line, meet going down it a man who had been a missionary in his country twelve or twenty years before. He might meet a young man and his wife who had served there in the Peace Corps. Or he might meet a man who had been there working with his highway department on developing an effective road system.

A lot of this comes from the really good desk officers, but also a lot of them do not take it seriously. Everybody who was invited obviously did not have something to do with that country. Mrs. Johnson on her trips or the president on his trips would meet a teacher or mayor and would come back from the trip and say, "Invite Susie Glutch to the next dinner that seems appropriate for her." People who would serve on special commissions for the president for the good of the country and not for the per diem involved, the president would frequently try to say, "Thank you. I appreciate what you did for me," by having them to a dinner in the White House. They would invite some staff members from the White House. They would invite some entertainers, and these might have been entertainers who had gone on the campaign trail for the president in 1964, or they might have been entertainers who had volunteered to do it in 1968. Or they might be an entertainer who was in the news, hopefully favorably for one reason or another. Or it might be Charlton Heston invited to the dinner for the prime minister of Australia because he had spent six months in Australia touring in a play.[2]

Bess's secretary, Carol Carlyle, recalled that they were always making lists.

CAROL CARLYLE: We'd have to build an invitation list. We'd start out with the Congress or with whatever political leaders. We put down our thoughts on who we thought should be there. Then it would go to the first lady, she would add or subtract. Then it would go to the president and then he would add or subtract. After that point, when it was agreed upon who would be invited, then it would go to the Secret Service for clearance. Then once everything was final, then it would go to the calligrapher's office for whatever type of invitation we needed. Whether we were running a carnival or a state dinner, our minds were also five events down the road. I can just remember always building invitation lists. These were always in progress. Bess would run in the office. She'd been over to the West Wing or up in the house, and she'd come back and say, "Oh, by the way, add so and so to the March 15th event." We had these rosters going all the time. You didn't focus on one thing and then it ended and then you started up on the next thing. It was always in progress. We were working on the next one and three other events down the road while we were doing the event in front of us.[3]

TYLER ABELL: A good party starts with a good guest list. As social secretary, Bess would take the guest list that the State Department sent over to be the guests that should be invited to the White House for a state dinner. I remember her reading through a guest list like that and saying, "Those guys in the State Department have absolutely no imagination. They're all the same: assistant secretaries and deputy assistant secretaries, or this, that, and the other. We want somebody who's going to spark up the party." So she would think of good guests who would be the type of people that the foreign visitor might enjoy.[4]

Were some of the guests selected for political purposes, as past or maybe future campaign contributors?

BESS ABELL: Oh sure, absolutely. The governors and mayors were never overlooked. We never could have enough of them, but the president would almost always invite one or two governors to a dinner. Governors, depending upon the time of the year, find it very hard to get away for something like this. They've got colossal legislative programs. But he did frequently issue the invitations to them. When they could come, he frequently would invite them to be overnight guests at the White House so that he could see more of them than just a howdy and a handshake in a receiving line.[5]

And, of course, we had to have people who had given money to the Democratic Party.

I would call Cliff Carter over at the Democratic Committee and would say, "Give me the names of six couples for this dinner." And he would always send me thirty. I would say, "Cliff, look, these big givers see each other at the big Democratic dinners. They don't want to come to the White House and see each other. They want to see the vice president, and the cabinet members, and the movie stars." So we finally got that scaled down. It was like putting together a jigsaw puzzle.[6]

Did the president see the guest list and have final authority over it?

BESS ABELL: Yes, he always saw the list. The first person who touches the guest list is the desk officer. From there it goes to the office of the chief of protocol. They would gather up [information] from various other places. The cultural affairs office would know that Charlton Heston had been in Australia for six months, or they would know that Peter Nero had given a concert for the king of Thailand, and so those names would come over.

One of my hardest battles with these people was to say, "I'm very dumb. I don't know who Charlton Heston is. If you write him down on that guest list, you have to tell me who he is and why the president ought to invite him." It was a never-ending battle because everybody assumed that I was smarter than I was, or they thought if I didn't know who he was that the president would know who he was, but the president was a busy man and he might not know who he is either, or he certainly would not likely know that he had just given a concert for the prime minister, and they got along very well and he ought to come back. So then the chief of protocol approves that list, and then it comes to my office. I would go over it and primarily at this point scratch people off, the people who had just been, and the people I just knew that there was not going to be room to have. At the same time, or previous to this, we would have called Mike Manatos, who was administrative assistant for congressional relations for the Senate, and we would have called the person who was responsible for the House side. They would send us the number of names that we requested of Senate members and House members, and also with a sentence: "Mr. President, or Mrs. Johnson, you will want to have this man because—"

Then I would get press names from Liz Carpenter and from George Christian [LBJ's press secretary, 1966–1969]. I would almost always go over all these bits and pieces of paper with the man in the National Security Council who was responsible for that area and ask his advice. You know, "Here are eighteen businessmen. Who are the three really musts? What are they? Who's first, second, third, and fourth priority on them?" So that when we got the list finished and the president added twenty names to it we would know that we had to cut and we wouldn't have to make all those calls over again.

Did the president generally accept most of the lists as they were shaped by all of this process?

BESS ABELL: I would say most of them, yes, because by the time the list got to him—I had the advantage of having worked with them before. You know, you can't always zip yourself up in somebody else's skin and know how they think, but I tried to present a list to him that was, one, balanced, and two, not so heavy in numbers that he would have to cut it. Frequently I would get a list back from him that would have eight people added on it, and I would say to the president and Mrs. Johnson when I sent them the list, "Here it is. It numbers two hundred. We should cut twenty people from it before we can safely send out the invitations." The president might add twenty more and say, "You cut it."

Did you have to worry about people with whom the president might be temporarily angry?

BESS ABELL: Well, yes. Occasionally he would send me a memo that said, "Have Joe Blow to the very next state dinner," and I would put Joe Blow's name on the list for the very next state dinner, and then he would scratch him out and say, "Don't ever invite him." I would think that I was living in some other world. In one of those cases, I was very distressed about it because I just could not understand why he was so angry with this man. He didn't say, "Don't ever invite him," but he had scratched through it sort of like that [heavily marked through], and everybody else that he had scratched out just had a nice little line through it. So with fear and trepidation, a couple of days later I asked Mrs. Johnson, "Is there a problem?" She laughed and said, "No, he was at dinner with us the night before."[7]

You mention it being a hot ticket—everyone wanted to come. What would people do to try to get invited to something like that?

BESS ABELL: They send the social secretary presents. They sometimes will call the Social Office and say, "I'm sure that my invitation has gone astray. Can you tell me the time and the address of the event?" For Princess Margaret, there was a woman who wrote and said she should be invited because ever since Princess Margaret had been born, she had kept a scrapbook on her. After the event, we sent her some things for her scrapbook.[8]

Seating the Guests

BESS ABELL: President Johnson thought that an empty place in the State Dining Room was a waste. "Think of all the people I could have filled that seat with!" Sometimes he did try and fit more people into the house than it would hold. He was also very good at expanding the party at the last minute. If you were having a dinner for the prime minister of Ireland, he wanted to have all of his Irish friends come, and he wanted to have all the parents of the Irish people on his staff come. And he did the same thing if the Italian prime minister was coming. One time the tables were set and people were beginning to arrive. The president got off the elevator with some Italian staff member's family, who I guess had come for the arrival ceremony. He came up to me and said, "I've invited them for the dinner." I thought, "Well, I just have to disinvite somebody." He knew it would work out somehow, but he really did not want to see any empty seats.[9]

For seating arrangements, do you really have to follow a rigid protocol scheme, and do people get upset if you don't?

BESS ABELL: Very seldom do people get upset. Of course I'm not sure that they would come and tell me if they did. I had one lady who was the wife of a senator, a very lovely lady whom I had known for a long, long time. She was a very close friend of the President and Mrs. Johnson and I had seated her next to the guest of honor with another gentleman on her right. She stormed up to me just as the receiving line was breaking up and as the president was walking down the hall with his guest of honor. I thought it was really very unlike her. She said, "Bess, I won't sit where you've put me tonight!" I was a little bit aghast. I said, "Well, then, why did you come?" She said, "I won't sit next to that man." I thought she was talking about the visiting president, and I was about ready to have heart failure. I said, "What is the problem?" Bear in mind that here the man comes down the hall. She said, "Not him, that other man I'm sitting next to." I couldn't even remember who it was. Her husband had just been through a campaign and had been defeated for the Senate. She added, "He contributed thousands of dollars to my husband's opponent," and I understood how she felt. But I just said, "Now look, they're coming down the hall. What do you want to do? Do you want to get sick and drop out? I can move you someplace else, but somebody will want to know why. Why don't you be a good sport about it?" And she was. I told her that I would remember and never invite them at the same time.

We also, with guests, ended up with a man and his new wife and his ex-wife at the same party. Once, when Roberta Peters [an American opera singer] was a guest, my entertainment program fell apart at the last minute, and I had to put something together again on short notice. And who did I call on? I called on Bob Merrill. He and a group of madrigal singers from the University of Maryland sang a series of Christmas carols at one of the prettiest state dinners we ever had. But there in the audience was his ex-wife, Roberta Peters.

Did you deliberately try to have an atmosphere of informality at the parties? I believe you generally used the small round tables rather than the more formal long tables.

BESS ABELL: There is a hard and fast protocol list. But we solved that problem and what I think is a colossal problem for the enjoyment of your guests, which is that long, long table where everybody who has a title sits at the center of the table and everybody who is without title but equally interesting, if not more so, sits down at the far ends of the table. The whole thing about entertaining is to make your guests welcome, to make them feel as much at home as possible, which is not always easy to do in the first house of the land. Entertaining there is always going to be different from any-place else, no matter who the president is. You cannot walk into that house without remembering that thirty-five presidents and their families have lived there before. But by the use of the round tables I think that we got the best of both worlds. Each table—say the tables hold ten guests—would have a host or a hostess or sometimes both, and for those people you pull from your rank! Cabinet members, State Department people, congression-al people. And then you let them sit next to a movie star or a businessman, and everybody enjoys it more because everybody feels like they've been a part of the evening.

Did President and Mrs. Johnson enjoy the social occasions, or make an effort to appear to enjoy them?

BESS ABELL: I think that they almost always enjoyed them, some of them they enjoyed a lot more than others. Occasionally for a state dinner we would have a long head table, where we would seat about twenty peo-ple, and then we would have twelve round tables for ten. But at that head table you really have to use your rank there, because one movie star does not understand why the other one was there and he wasn't; or one busi-nessman does not understand why that businessman outranked him. So you are stuck with using your rank there. I asked Mrs. Johnson once, what difference it made to her in the enjoyment of an evening to sit at a long for-mal table or a small round table. She said that when she had a really mar-velous guest of honor, like a prime minister that she loved talking to, that she much, much preferred the round table because he could become more a part of the conversation of the whole table. But she said where she had a man who was really difficult to talk with, difficult to converse with, difficult to entertain, that it really did not make that much difference because it was such a struggle, whether she was at the small round table, that she spent all of her time with him and not that much time talking across the table. I think the president always enjoyed the round tables more.[10]

The Secret Service can be helpful to you if you don't get mad at them and say that they're getting in your way about things, if you can make them part of your group. The military is fabulous. They provided all these hand-some, sharp military officers who greeted guests, danced with ladies, and we did a lot of dancing. President Johnson, as I've said, was a good dancer and enjoyed dancing and liked all the show tunes, especially when "Hello, Dolly!" became "Hello, Lyndon!"

Tell me about the Johnsons as hosts.

BESS ABELL: They loved people. They loved to share the beauty and the history and the excitement of being a guest at the White House. And I loved Mrs. Johnson when she would be going over a guest list, say a state dinner list the afternoon of the event. She would go over the list, look down it, and say, "Oh, look, Miss Sara Jones has never been to the White House before. She's probably never even been to Washington before." Then she would pick up and call a friend of hers. It might be a Senate wife. It might be her good friend Katie Louchheim. She would call this person, and she would say, "Now, Sara Jones is going to be at the dinner tonight, and she has never been to the White House before, and she won't know a soul, and you know everybody. So will you make a point of looking her up and be sure that she meets some interesting people?" That did two things. Say it was Katie Louchheim—it gave Katie something to look forward to, gave her a job to do at the dinner, gave her an excuse to take Sara Jones up to meet the vice president and meet the movie star who was there and so forth.

The other thing she would do, as she was going down the list, she would say, "Now, do I remember something about this man?" I said, "Yes, ma'am. He's a pincher." Do you know what that means? It means that he'll be at his seat at the table and he reaches over to the lady next to him and pinches her on the leg or the fanny. I don't know why some people seem to get their jollies doing that, but apparently there are, so we called them pinchers. And so she said, "Well, have you called this?" I said, "Well, I have a man seated next to him on one side and I have understanding Hazel Brawley on the other side of him, and I've already warned Hazel Brawley about him." I do remember one time in a situation like that calling somebody and she said, "You must think I'm a good sport because you sat him next to me before. Find somebody else!"[11]

Recruiting the Entertainers

Bess Abell "counted dullness as the original sin," judged presidential aide Jack Valenti. "If you were invited to an evening in the State Dining Room or East Room, then, by God, you weren't going to be starched with tedium. She worked at her job, although it was impossible to search out any signs of nervousness. She just simply went about her tasks with no minute wasted, pursuing every void until it was filled."[12] J. B. West, having been an usher at the White House since 1941, had never seen anything like Bess's entertainments: "From

Shakespeare to musical comedy to ballet to American Indian dancers, Bess Abell began to put on a really big show after dinner."

For these performances, the little red velvet stage previously used in the East Room proved inadequate. "Can't we expand the stage?" Bess asked, and when West shook his head and explained their budgetary situation, she responded, "What we need is an angel!" She contacted Rebekah Harkness, who agreed to fund a Broadway designer—Jo Mielziner—to create something larger that fit the East Room decor.[13]

Did the President and Mrs. Johnson have any particular taste along the lines of entertainment?

BESS ABELL: They preferred musical comedy. Remember that entertainment at a state dinner is secondary to anything else that happens that night. It begins about ten-thirty at night after a day when President and Mrs. Johnson and their guests have gotten up early, spent a full day at the office, had a drink or two drinks before dinner, a four-course meal, and three wines. So it is not the time to give a serious concert. I always tried to explain to each of the artists, whether it was an opera singer or a musical comedy star or a violinist, "This is the timing. This is what your audience has done that day. Therefore, make it on the light side." Our programs never ran longer than half an hour, generally from fifteen to twenty-five minutes, not because we were trying to short-change the artists but because we wanted the guests to go away wishing for more and not saying to themselves, "If that program had been one aria shorter it would have been better." We wanted them to leave wanting more.[14]

Was there a different climate entertaining at the Ranch than at the White House?

BESS ABELL: It sure was different, because where else could we have a big barbecue in December for Chancellor [Ludwig] Erhard? We thought maybe we could use the gymnasium in nearby Stonewall, Texas. When we visited the gymnasium, there was a man over in the corner sweeping up some things. I went over and asked, "I wonder if I could see the principal?" He said, "That's me." So I asked him whether or not we could use the gymnasium for President Johnson to welcome Chancellor Erhard, and he said, "Oh yes." So it's amazing what having a few hay bales, bandanas, red kerosene lanterns, and a lot of saddles and ropes around, while Van Cliburn played the piano, would do to the Stonewall gymnasium! It was very incongruous, but it all seemed to be very happy, and it was a good visit all around.

Were there entertainers who were particularly memorable, either because they were wonderful or temperamental or whatever?

BESS ABELL: There were lots of memorable ones. I remember one evening Sarah Vaughan, the great Black jazz singer, came to sing for the prime minister of Japan. I think it was Prime Minister [Eisaku] Satō of Japan. She just did a great program. A little bit later in the evening, it may have been the president was looking for Sarah, and I went looking for her and I found her down in this area that we let her use as a dressing room for that evening, which I think was the housekeeper's office. She was just sobbing. I said, "Miss Vaughan, what's wrong? What can I do for you?"

She said, "This is just the most wonderful, most fabulous night of my life. It's just the most wonderful night of my life." I said, "Why are you crying?" She said, "Well, the first time I came to Washington, I couldn't even get a hotel room and tonight I danced with the president." I still get chills when I tell that story or think about it, but such a time in our life, the changes that have gone through. I mean, my children, much less my grandchildren, cannot imagine some great entertainer not being able to get a hotel room because she was Black.[15]

LYNDON ABELL: Because Bess was social secretary performers sometimes visited our house after the White House event. I recall a story I was told because I am sure I was asleep when it happened. Leonard Bernstein and the Kingston Trio, which was a pretty eclectic grouping, somehow ended up after things at our house. My mom scrambled up some eggs. The Kingston Trio guys thought that they were on pretty solid footing saying negative things about the Beatles. Leonard Bernstein listened to them say the Beatles music was no good, and he responded that essentially the Beatles' music was a whole lot better than the crap that the Kingston Trio played. So maybe things were a little tense at that moment.

Phil Ramone was a very famous music producer who passed away recently and who I never had the pleasure of meeting. He produced almost everybody. He also did sound for several White House events. My mother was having some problem with our stereo and she asked him, "Since you are here in town anyway is there any chance you could take a look and tell me what is wrong?" He did and told my mom, "The speakers were blown so I left you two speakers." She said, "Oh, just send me a bill and I will be happy to pay." He said, "No, I took care of it." Mother said, "No, no, I can't do that. You were so kind to look at them, please just send me a bill." So he sent a bill for KLH Studio Monitors that had some exorbitant price tag at the time, and she had to pay the bill. I still have those speakers today and they are quite good![16]

Expecting the Unexpected

Despite all of Bess's planning, there were often unexpected developments, from uninvited guests to inclement weather. The most elegant event of her tenure, Bess recalled, was a dinner for Britain's Princess Margaret in 1966. "We got a little carried away with all the copy about it ahead of time as the party of the year," Bess recalled. "It was, but in an unexpected way." Newspaper reporter Ann Wood noted that "Christina Ford [Mrs. Henry Ford II] danced so vigorously that her dress slipped halfway off her chest. The wackiest White House dinner was given for the White House Council on the Arts; it went off despite a snowstorm that delayed guests for varying times up and down the East Coast, thus creating a progressive dinner." Reporter Wood went on to note, "It takes a certain presence of mind and confidence to ask the president of the US to move over so a place may be set for a latecomer next to him, and Bess Abell has done that. It takes respect for power and enjoyment of the trappings of power—without being cowed by them. A sense of humor helps, too."[17]

You had a rather distinguished party crasher in South Carolina senator Strom Thurmond.

BESS ABELL: He didn't crash, he was always invited. But he always had Miss Peach Blossom or Miss Watermelon Queen that he would show up with who was not on the guest list. Well, it was not my role to make Senator Thurmond mad. The president had enough problems with Senator Thurmond without my getting crossways with the Watermelon Queen. So they came in.

People smoke less and drink a lot less now, which brings us to Joan Crawford.

BESS ABELL: Every time I was seating a White House dinner, there would be one table that I would think, "Gosh, if I was a guest at the dinner tonight, that's where I'd like to sit." This dinner, I thought I would like to be at the table with Joan Crawford, Don Hewitt, Joe Califano, and Cathy Douglas, who was the brand-new bride of Supreme Court Justice Bill Douglas. Well, Joan Crawford arrived with her own flask of vodka. We did serve a lot of drinks, but she apparently didn't think there were going to be enough. Anyway, the dinner was served, and in Joan Crawford's defense, I should say, we weren't smart enough to know that we had also invited her ex-husband. They passed notes back and forth during the dinner.

Cathy Douglas was just a lovely person, but she was new to Washington, and she was new to a party like this. The finger bowls came, and when the finger bowl comes, there's the dessert dish. On top of the dessert dish is a lovely little doily, and on top of that is the finger bowl which has a little water in it and probably a leaf of scented geranium, maybe a little sweetheart rose or something, and also the dessert fork and the dessert spoon. What one is supposed to do is move the fork and the spoon to either side of the dessert plate and then take the doily and the finger bowl and put it up ahead of the fork.

Cathy did not know that. She would have figured it out, but Miss Crawford wasn't going to wait for that. She stood up and said, "This is what you're supposed to do." And she moved Cathy's silverware and finger bowl. She said, "You'll learn to do that in the future."

I remember standing there in the doorway of the Blue Room as people were leaving, and Don Hewitt came up to me there in the doorway and he said, "You sure do know how to seat a dinner."[18]

In her memoir *Ruffles and Flourishes*, Liz Carpenter noted that Bess had grown up in Kentucky politics, "as unpredictable and uncertain as the racetrack," experience that helped her combine shrewd political insight with creativity. But LBJ regularly put Bess's unflappable nature to the test. "I remember one evening about six o'clock," Carpenter recalled, "when he decided to have a luncheon the next day, for two Prime Ministers and three Foreign Ministers, who happened to be in the country. The comments made by the chef and the head butler when they learned the news are unprintable. A stag guest list of 180 was drawn up and Bess and her assistants worked until midnight telephoning the guests, who generally responded, 'Did you say tomorrow?' Most of the guests were so startled that they forgot to ask who was being honored. This was fortunate, because Bess was not certain until the next morning which of the guests of honor would definitely be able to attend. But the luncheon went as smoothly as if it had been planned for weeks."[19]

State Dinners

Held to honor visiting royalty and heads of government, state dinners were the most elaborate events on the social secretary's calendar. In their five years at the White House, the Johnsons hosted seventeen state dinners, along with many formal state luncheons and official dinners for prime ministers, chancellors, and other heads of government.

But President Johnson put a stop to making state dinners white-tie events. He had never forgotten his embarrassment as vice president attending the National Gallery of Art's unveiling of the *Mona Lisa* on loan from the Louvre Museum. He and the waiters were the only ones wearing white tie and tails. "He was miserable," Bess recalled. "He kept trying to make himself inconspicuous, and he never forgave Lady Bird, who had laid out his clothes." After Johnson became president, he decreed: "No more white tie."[20]

What does one wear to a state dinner?

BESS ABELL: People usually wear their best dress, and it gives them an excuse to go shopping. But there have also been times that people wore things that were too short and maybe less appropriate than they might have been. In the days of the miniskirt, I must stay that we were surprised when Carol Channing came in a dress that was many, many inches above the knee. It was the first miniskirt to grace the White House.

What does one talk about when you're in a receiving line?

BESS ABELL: The Johnsons' receiving line was more than just "how do you do." It was really an opportunity to have a meaningful word then, because the receiving line was basically the only time that they met ninety percent of the people that were invited to the dinner. So there was an opportunity to introduce the visitor from abroad and tell him about the guests.

When the receiving line has ended and the dinner is about to begin, what's the job of the social secretary?

BESS ABELL: The social secretary is always the Chief Worrier. Every big event needs a Chief Worrier. She's probably worrying about the entertainment. Or perhaps they're having some other guests that are coming in after dinner, and she's worrying about them. But [once the meal begins] the biggest items to worry about are behind you—except maybe about tomorrow morning's headlines, she's probably worrying about those.

How does the State Department determine when a state visit is warranted?

BESS ABELL: A state visit is when a head of state comes, a president or a king or queen, as opposed to a prime minister, which would be an official visit. In the days when I was involved, the British prime minister came each year. The chancellor of Germany came each year. The prime minister of Japan came every year. I'm sure there is a lot of knocking on doors saying, "It's my turn now."

The arrival at the North Portico was always one of the Chief Worrier's problems: trying to get the visitor from Blair House and the president on the North Portico at the same moment, without either waiting for the other one. The president would be frequently held up in his office. So there would be much conversation back and forth between myself and the chief of protocol in Blair House, exchanging information. The president was so speedy that they would call me when he left the Oval Office. It took him twelve minutes from the time he left his office, to go to the second floor of the White House to change clothes and be out on the North Portico. So we could always say, "Twelve minutes and he'll be there."

What was the most spectacular dinner that you were associated with?

BESS ABELL: That was the dinner for Israeli Prime Minister Levi Eshkol, which was the first dinner that had been given in the Rose Garden [on June 1, 1964]. It was on an absolutely joyous June evening, with lanterns in the trees, and a beautiful dinner, and wonderful guests. The National Symphony Orchestra played on the South Lawn for [ballet dancers] Maria Tallchief and Jacques D'Amboise, who danced on a stage that had been set up on the South Lawn. And the moon came up as if we had a stage designer plan it. It was really a perfect evening.[21]

Does a state dinner ever get routine?

BESS ABELL: Thank goodness a lot of the things do fall into a routine! You always have to have place cards, and they are always the same, with the gold seal on them. We always had flowers. We always had menus on the table. We always sent out the invitations. So all those things do develop into a pattern, but there are always the last-minute crises, the advanced crises.

One of the grimmest was for the president of Chad [François Tombalbaye] in October 1968. It was also Tyler's very first foreign visitor during his short four months as chief of protocol. Tyler was sworn in on a Tuesday and flew to New York on a Wednesday to meet the president of Chad and bring him back to Washington to introduce him to our president. The day's activities had gone relatively smoothly for Tyler. As the president of Chad did not bring his wife—or wives—with him, I stayed in the White House. Tyler went over to Blair House to pick up the president of Chad and bring him to the White House. This was always something of a problem because we tried to coordinate the president's arrival on the front steps of the North Portico with the arrival of the visiting guest of honor, who would come by limousine from across the street at Blair House.

Generally it works smoothly, but there was always guesswork involved. The president would arrive in the house and I would immediately call Blair House and tell the chief of protocol that he was there, and he would be dressed in a matter of moments. The president really could change from business suit into black tie and occasionally take a shower to boot in about three minutes. He was really the speediest dresser I've ever known. But sometimes the prime minister might be delayed, zipping up his wife's dress or who knows what!

We finally got Tyler, the president of Chad, and President Johnson all down on the front steps at the same time. As Tyler walked in the door he leaned over to me and said, "Honey, the wife of the ambassador isn't coming," which ordinarily wouldn't have bothered me too much. But as she was the only woman in the foreign party, I had seated her on the president's right. She was the only member of the foreign party who was seated at his table. So it meant some substantial juggling of at least four tables in the dining room, and all of those people that I would have to juggle already knew where they were supposed to sit. So I contacted Sandy Fox, whose office, once the seating is done, puts the cards on the table and hands out the escort envelopes to the guests as they come in. I called him up to the second floor with me. I explained the problem to him, and then we started doing an alternate seating plan and marking down, "Well, I'll have to tell Secretary Rusk that instead of at table eight, he's at table two. And we'll have to get to the foreign minister of Chad and tell him he's not at table two, he's at table one."

Simultaneously, I called Mrs. [Mary Edith] Wilroy, a very capable jack-of-all-trades who was the housekeeper at Blair House, and said, "What gives?" She said, "Well, I think that the ambassador just did not want her to come, but I am going to try and get her there, and I think I can. I've told her that she's expected." I said, "Well, tell her that the President and Mrs. Johnson will be hurt if she doesn't come, and if that doesn't work, tell her they'll be offended if she doesn't come." I had spoken with the ambassador of Chad just very briefly. Also, I should mention that the ambassador and his wife had been in this country only about three days, and she was really a scared little butterfly of a lady. I don't think that she'd ever spent much time in a city or very much time in formal clothes or formal situations.

Mrs. Wilroy called me about five minutes later, just before the president was going to take his guest of honor down the steps after they'd had an informal gathering upstairs with the vice president and secretary of state, and said, "She is on her way." She walked in the north door of the White House, just as the president was bringing the president of Chad down the grand staircase, and the ambassador of Chad was with them. He looked like a very surprised gentleman when he saw his wife come in the door. But she looked very pleasant and she handled herself very well and has since told me when I've seen her very occasionally at an embassy party that she was so grateful that we pushed her and encouraged her into coming.

Any other near crises like that that you can recall?

BESS ABELL: There have been loads of them. But probably one of the worst moments that I ever went through regarding entertainment came at a busy time. We were having a lot of state dinners sort of superimposed on top of all the other entertaining that was being done in the White House. The prime minister of Great Britain was coming as the president's guest, with maybe seven or eight days' notice. I think maybe his trip had been planned earlier as an informal working visit, and the president added the dinner to the schedule a week ahead. For a state dinner we always have some form of entertainment after the dinner. Who do you call on with seven days' notice in that busy world of entertainment?

The only person that I could call on was someone who I really considered a personal friend and somebody that the Johnsons considered a friend and vice versa. So I called Bob Merrill, who's a great baritone at the Metropolitan Opera who had entertained at the White House before, and both he and his wife were at home. I said, "What are you doing on—whatever?" He said, "Well, I'm not doing anything. I'm giving a concert the night before down in South Carolina and I'm giving a concert the next day in New York." I said, "Well, that's just great. You can stop by Washington in between times and sing for the prime minister of Great Britain, Harold Wilson." "Oh, that's great. I'd love to. I'll be there." I said, "You and Marian talk about the program and then call me later with the songs that you are going to sing, and I will put together the rest of the program." It was just a very easy thing to put together because his very nice, lovely wife is his accompanist. Since Bob had been at the White House beforehand, I didn't have to go into any complicated explanations.

Bob called me two or three days later and gave me the list of songs that he was going to sing. I took the list of songs down to Liz Carpenter, and she typed up the press release. The next thing I heard was a call from Walt Rostow [National Security Advisor] with sort of a hint of disbelief and a hint of hysterics in his voice. "You can't be serious. You really can't be serious. You're not going to sing for the prime minister who has just announced withdrawal of forces east of Suez 'On the Road to Mandalay'! And you can't sing for the prime minister, who has just devalued the British pound, 'I Got Plenty of Nothin'." I just got on my high horse and tried to explain to Mr. Rostow that music and art were not politics, but we quickly found out with the afternoon papers that where a foreign visitor was concerned, where the prime minister of Great Britain was concerned, art and music were politics!

The State Department types, and the National Security types, said, "You just have to change the program." I felt that it was better to stick with the program and then add a song to make light of it, called, "It Ain't

Necessarily So." But anyway, I talked to Bob and I said, "You better come up with an alternate program, but don't discuss it with anybody if you can avoid it," because, of course, his phone was ringing off the wall from reporters, both the *Variety* types and foreign correspondent types. Since it was the age of the protest, they thought that possibly Bob had planned this program in order to embarrass the prime minister, which was the furthest thing from his thought. He had just picked songs from his light concert program.

So we planned to change the program and sing other songs, and I had another program printed. That morning the prime minister arrived, and he had gotten word, I guess, through our State Department that the program was going to be changed. "Mr. Prime Minister, you'll be happy to know that we're not going to sing those songs for you!" And he told the president: "Now, I can survive the program as originally planned, but I can't survive your changing the program." So I tried to reach Bob Merrill to be sure that he brought the other music with him, and he had already left. But foresighted Bob and Marian Merrill had brought all the music with them, and we went back to the other program and added the song "It Ain't Necessarily So." I think it really turned out all right. But I will always regret, as Bob does, that the prime minister took such a ribbing back home in London from the cartoonists and the humorists.[22]

LYNDON ABELL: Like a lot of people who are socially aware and socially adept, my mother could feel comfortable in really large settings or a variety of surroundings. She was really intelligent and tough enough to get things done. One of her nicknames in the White House was the "Iron Butterfly," and I think she earned it.

CAROL CARLYLE: The Secret Service have nicknames for the president and the first lady. Well, their term for Bess was the "Iron Butterfly." She was this very pretty, fluffy, gracious woman, but when she wanted something her way and she felt it was the right way there was no way they could change her mind. So they called her the "Iron Butterfly."[23]

6

The Lady Bird Special

The Johnsons moved into the White House less than a year before the next presidential election. The oncoming election remained foremost in everyone's mind, and even the social secretary soon became involved in helping the first lady campaign in a most creative way. The Lady Bird Special, a whistle-stop train campaign, left Washington, DC, on October 6, 1964, and arrived in New Orleans, Louisiana, on October 9. In that era, it was common for journalists, historians, and other observers to overlook the contributions of women in the political world—Theodore H. White omitted the Lady Bird Special entirely from his best-selling book *The Making of the President 1964*—but oral histories of the participants recount the excitement, experiences, and consequences of an entirely women-run political operation.

Once the shock and the travail of moving into the White House was over, do you know if Mrs. Johnson ever consciously sat down and thought about what kind of first lady she was going to be?

BESS ABELL: She said, "My role as first lady will emerge in deeds, not words." Yes, she did sit down and think about it seriously, but I think that that was after the election in 1964. She looked on her life at that point—December 1963—as being very short-term. For example, the furnishings up in the west hall, which was the family sitting room, were really almost threadbare. The upholstery in that end of the house takes very rough wear because the west sun streams in there, and it does not last very long. But Mrs. Johnson just would not do anything to the furniture until after the campaign. She said, "There may be another first lady living in this house." She wanted to do everything she could to help her husband, and as that year progressed that was a great deal of campaigning.

Mrs. Johnson was somewhat shy, at least in the early years of her marriage, particularly about making public speeches. Was there any of it left in the presidential years?

BESS ABELL: You get easier about things by doing. I've heard her tell many times the story about Miss Lucy George, the wife of Senator Walter George of Georgia. She asked Miss Lucy, "Do you campaign with Senator George?" And she said, "Oh, yes, I go around with him all the time. I don't make any speeches. I just sit up on the platform to show them I don't have a club foot." This was really, I think, what Mrs. Johnson did in the earlier days of campaigning. She met, shook hands, greeted, licked envelopes, typed lists, and oftentimes, I'm sure, was a helpful secretary to her husband. But I really do not know when she started making speeches or how much of it she did before the campaign in 1960, but that was her first foray into it. She had taken a course, the Capital Speakers Course, from Hester Beall Provensen, who in subsequent years used to help coach her before every big speech. Mrs. Provensen would come over and spend an hour with her at the White House and go over the speeches with her. But in seeing films of Mrs. Johnson, I always thought that she was pretty good in 1960. But then in seeing the comparison you realize how much she gained by doing, how much she learned from it, and how greatly she improved.[1]

Lyndon Johnson committed his administration to passing President Kennedy's stalled Civil Rights Bill. After the longest filibuster in Senate history was finally broken, Congress passed that landmark act in June 1964. Johnson signed it, although he realized it would alienate much of the White South from his party and his campaign for election.

TYLER ABELL: Here she was, the social secretary of the White House. And you would think that a social secretary would have plenty of social things to do, which she did. But she felt strongly that Mrs. Johnson should campaign, and Mrs. Johnson had always campaigned with her husband.

When I was an advance man in the 1960 campaign when Johnson won the vice presidency, occasionally Mrs. Johnson would be there at her husband's side. There were plenty of times when she was not there. But Bess thought, as did Liz—Bess and Liz [Carpenter] were quite a team—they both thought that a whistle-stop with Mrs. Johnson would be a winner.

What had happened politically is that Johnson had taken the Kennedy Civil Rights Bill, which was not going anywhere, and had pushed it through the Senate. It had not yet passed voting rights. That would come in 1965. But the feeling in the South was that Johnson had lost the South because of passing the Civil Rights Bill. And when he pushed it through over

[Senator] Richard Russell's strenuous objections, Russell told him, "You're going to lose the South. The Democrats will lose the South for at least a generation," or maybe he just said, "For this generation."[2]

Nineteen sixty-four was the big campaigning year. Surely you must have been involved in those activities, like the train trip in the South?

BESS ABELL: Oh, the train trip in the South. What an undertaking that was! Mr. Johnson had taken a train trip through the South as a candidate for vice president in 1960, and a lot of the very wise heads in the Democratic Party really did not want the Johnsons to go into the South in 1964. They felt that he was going to lose that part of the country anyway, so why make the effort! I think Mrs. Johnson felt very strongly about this, and I think the president did too. It was the part of the country that they were from and that they were associated with, and they did not want to write it off, and all the Democrats that were down there working for the party and for them. They just didn't want to say, "We've just X'ed through this part of the country because there's nothing in it for us."

Did they do some quiet checking as to what the possible reception might be?

BESS ABELL: Oh, sure, and it wasn't always good. This was really our first experience with pickets. But the train trips involved an unbelievable number of people. It started out with an advance trip, which Liz Carpenter and Joe Moran, who was the head of the advance men, and the Secret Service and probably the communications people took in a plane, which was going to a lot of the big cities. And then we sent out about ten or so advance women who would just move into a town and stay for two or three weeks.

Who were these women?

BESS ABELL: One was Judith Moyers, Bill Moyers's wife. She ended up in New Orleans. I think that Lindy Boggs, Mrs. Hale Boggs—the congressman's wife from Louisiana—went down. Kara Burney, a friend of Mrs. Johnson's from Texas, went down. I don't have that list in my mind to pull out, but these women went and stayed in the towns. And then there was a team of advance men who went out to each of these little towns. One of the assignments that fell my way was working on cars for the train, including a food car. I also worked with the hostesses and on giveaway items and balloons. It was really quite a major undertaking. What I kept looking for was a car for the end of the train that did not have any partitions in it and also had a big platform on the back. We were told that there wasn't any such thing available because those cars went out with bustles. I mentioned it to the president one night and he said, "It's just vital."

It was absolutely madness on his train trip through the South in 1960. His train car had the open platform, a tiny living area, a dining area and kitchen, and two small bedrooms. So, the people who got on at Stop A to ride to their hometown, Stop B, were all in that car, the same car where Mr. Johnson ate, slept, and worked with his secretaries—it was just wild. He said, "You've got to have that kind of car." We called and visited around all the railroad yards, and it just wasn't available.

Then the president called me one Sunday and said, "You call Buford Ellington"—who became governor of Tennessee but at that time was working with one of the railroads, I think Louisville & Nashville Railroad—"you call Buford and he'll find you that car." So I called Buford, and he said, "I never heard of a car like that in this day and age, but we'll see if we can find it." He called me later that night, or maybe early Monday morning, and said, "They've found one over in Pittsburgh, or Philadelphia, on the junk heap, and they are going to put it on the back of a train and get it down to Washington for you this afternoon."

So we went down to see the train car, and it was really in shambles. But it was exactly what we wanted—just an empty car with a great big platform on the back. We had a nice architect come down and design us a striped awning for the back of it, and we also took one of the calligraphers from the White House down, and he drew up the side of the train and how we wanted it painted red, white, and blue. I got the upholsterer who worked on putting fine silks on all the White House furnishings to go and buy the cheapest red and blue cotton he could find and recover all the seats. We painted it blue on the inside and tacked up pictures of the Johnsons campaigning, and it was just great. It was also very hot! The car was really off the junk heap and did not have any modern air-conditioning facilities and had to be air-conditioned with ice. One of the additional jobs of the advance men at each of these stops was to get the iceman to load the ice on the back of the train. So as soon as we pulled into a station somebody out there in the crowd was assigned to load the ice aboard to keep us going until the next stop.[3]

Although the train trip took place in October 1964, Linda Jane Holden, author and garden historian, estimated that planning went on for six months leading up to it. Drawing on Bess's memories, Holden later wrote an account of the trip: "The Lady Bird Special: The Power of a Whistle-stop Campaign."[4]

And Bess was doing all this planning, down to menus. Did she have a large staff to help her?

LINDA JANE HOLDEN: No, just a couple people, but they all worked together, the calligraphers, Bill Gimmel—whose office at the time was right down the hall from Bess's office. And they all really worked together. It was just a very friendly, dynamic atmosphere where everybody was willing to pitch in and do things, which isn't always the case. And so Bill couldn't do enough for Bess in all these drawings and then other times too.

Bess was just so informal and creative. The interior was painted. She did everything without spending any money, also. She covered the seats with this cotton, red and blue, to make it very patriotic and then took family pictures—they weren't framed. She just took masking tape and then taped them to the wall to make them look framed. To make it become the White House on rails. Even though the president wasn't with them the whole time, it was his wife and daughters on this train, so it became the actual White House. And Bess created that. Then all of the people she had to organize, the press people, and the care and feeding and overnight quarters for all these people, that was Bess. Anything that had the whiff of social to do with it, taking care of people, was Bess's duty as social secretary. There's been lots of social secretaries, and certainly everyone brings their own way and their own personality to it but, to me, Bess ranks as the epitome of what a social secretary—beyond just being a social secretary, but a person who loves other people and makes them feel welcome and warm. She's the most hospitable person. I've learned a lot from her in that way.

In the article you have a picture of Mrs. Johnson surrounded by the other women. How did they get recruited?

LINDA JANE HOLDEN: That was Bess. That came through their friends up here that wanted to join in, people that they knew that were part of their team. Bess devised these costumes for them that they wore. That was all her. They were the ones that handed out the goodies, the treats, greeted people at the door, and helped with the crowd flow, getting the people on, getting the people off, and making sure everyone had a picture, that's all Bess.

Lynda Johnson told me, "It was so much fun. They just loved it very much. They were all such good-hearted people. I know I'm really in Bess's camp." But she always had those little gatherings and parties in her office in the White House. People always could drop by for her little cocktails or whatever was going on. She just generated a fun, lighthearted atmosphere that you enjoyed. You just wanted to be a part of it. So that's why all these people signed on and wanted to be a part of it because of that. You work hard, but you just wouldn't want to miss it because Bess made it fun.[5]

Initial Resistance

Liz Carpenter, who handled Mrs. Johnson's press relations, confirmed the president's keen interest in the whistle-stop trip.

LIZ CARPENTER: The president wanted her to go on the whistle-stop because he knew her value. He was sold on a whistle-stop, having been on one in 1960, as a way of campaigning. In fact, it was Harry Truman who said to him, "You know, there are a lot of people in this country who don't know where the airport is, but they know where the depot is. Go out and find them." Sure enough, there are more that know where the depot is. So, before we went to Atlantic City, the president asked me to come up with an idea for how to best campaign in the South.

I met with a number of southern governors in Atlantic City. We began with one idea that governors would maybe have a reception for the first lady in each statehouse, but the Republican legislatures were coming to be very alive in the South. Some of the governors were worried that they wouldn't be able to use their state capitols for this. As a matter of fact, we weren't too sure it would work either. The South was going through all the birth pains of civil rights. At that point it was a heck of a lot better to have meetings outdoors with everyone standing.[6]

Was Mr. Johnson involved in all the planning for this?
BESS ABELL: Yes. Not down-to-the-minute details, but he was very much involved and I'm sure was on the telephone with people saying, "How's it going to work?"

Did any of the male politicians worry about the women running this show?
BESS ABELL: Oh, yes. Some of President Kennedy's staff had stayed on at LBJ's request. Most people, I think, stayed on. And they were all involved in the campaign. [Presidential aide] Kenny O'Donnell is the person that I remember taking a very dim view of these ladies doing this train trip through the South and [Presidential Campaign Director] Larry O'Brien less so. O'Donnell just did not think that it was a good use of resources. It was going to be expensive. You were going to lose all those states anyway, so just write them off. They did not want Mrs. Johnson to do anything. They were really just opposed to it. I think all of that is just what kind of

women you are used to and what kind of respect you have for them. They really did not think that Mrs. Johnson could make a contribution. They did not know any women like her.[7]

Was there any bit of chauvinism, do you think, in that, or just the political calculation?

BESS ABELL: I have to think it was chauvinism, because they were used to Mrs. Kennedy, who was a great lady, but she did not want to be involved. She really was not all that interested in it. Mrs. Johnson was from the South, and she just did not want to write off those eight states. I don't know how much good it did, but it made great worldwide copy. She was on the news every night, on the front pages, and it gave her an opportunity to call on the governors of those states, all the wives of the governors, and the senators. There were some of the congressional people that came aboard and some who didn't. I think that all of the officeholders did speak with her on the phone. Some of them would speak with her and say, "Oh, Lady Bird, it's so nice to talk to you. I love your Lyndon, but I just can't support him this time around."[8]

TYLER ABELL: Neither Mrs. Johnson, Bess, or Liz wanted to write off the South. They were all southern ladies. Kenny O'Donnell and some other Kennedy-type leftovers who were still in the White House said it was a complete waste of money. You weren't going to accomplish anything for the great expense to run that train as it did from Alexandria to New Orleans.[9]

LIZ CARPENTER: Mrs. Johnson decided to go on the whistle-stop. It was a fantastic job of engineering. I went out and advanced it down the train tracks ahead of her and then came back and laid the whole thing out in front of the president. And again, this is why you love Lyndon Johnson. I tried and tried to meet with Kenny O'Donnell about this campaign. Kenny O'Donnell had no respect for any women in politics whatsoever. The whole attitude of the Kennedy men who worked in this operation was to keep women barefooted and have them on their feet, preferably pregnant, on Election Day—but nothing beyond that. O'Donnell wouldn't even meet with Bess and me to talk about this until I laid the whole plan in front of the president.

The president yanked him up there on the second floor of the White House, and we got out maps, and the president was obviously so enthusiastic about what Mrs. Johnson could do on a train trip that we sat there and planned it. I enjoyed watching O'Donnell being brought around by the President of the United States on the value of women, and he had to suffer three of them—Mrs. Johnson, Bess, and me, for that period.

The president knew that Mrs. Johnson would be loved in the South. He knew that he did not want to default the South. They were hearing from so many of their friends that were saying, "You've forgotten about us. We aren't important. Our votes don't count." So her real role was to get on a train and go in eight states, four days, forty-seven speeches, and say, "This president and his wife respect you and you are loved." And to also say, because you had to at each stop, "We stand on the civil rights program. This is the New South," and try to lift them to something better.

Well, two days before we were going to announce it—and we had the whole thing worked out on paper—Mrs. Johnson (and this is the lesson she had learned from her husband) called me up to the second floor and she said, "Before we put this out in the paper, let's make the courtesy calls." She got on the phone and for about eleven hours we stayed on the phone. She phoned every governor of a southern state and every two senators. And the conversations were something like this: "Governor, I'm thinking about coming down and campaigning in your state, and I'd love your advice."

Of course, we didn't want their advice because we already had the whole thing worked out. She'd listen for a long while, and they loved to give advice. Then she'd say, "Well, we were thinking about coming through on such-and-such a date and wouldn't you like to get on and ride with us some of the time?" So many times the answer was, "Yes." There were some hilarious "No's." I'll never forget one senator, Willis Robertson of Virginia, when Mrs. Johnson got hold of him, he said he was going to be antelope hunting. But the fact that she knew to call ahead before they read it in the papers is sheer Johnsonian performance. She had learned it at his elbow, and it paid off tremendously because I think we got four of the governors and a number of senators that we wouldn't have if we had just announced she was going.[10]

Complex Logistics

Bess transformed an old wreck of a train car, named the *Queen Mary*, into the colorful Lady Bird Special. Beyond redecorating, she choreographed the journey, organizing volunteers, recruiting entertainers, dispersing the many bouquets of flowers bestowed upon them, and planning different southern dishes for each state.

Was it difficult to arrange for people to get on at one town and ride to the next stop?

BESS ABELL: All those things were difficult, but most of the time it worked. It really worked as a pretty smooth-running machine. It was hard to remember which town you were in at times. The president rode with Mrs. Johnson from Washington to Alexandria. Lynda took, I think, the first two days of the trip, and Luci took the last two days of the trip. There were myriad details that had to be worked out for getting the people to Stop A so they could ride to Stop B and be introduced, but it really worked very well. The last car was our living room car; then the next car was Mrs. Johnson's car. In the dining area of that car worked her two secretaries, Ashton Gonella and Mary Rather, who made that trip with us. And then the third car was a car with four offices in it; I had an office; Liz Carpenter had an office; and there were two others; and then a large living room space. That is where the people for Town B would get on at Stop A. They would get on that car and there was always somebody like John Ben Shepperd, Buford Ellington, and Bill and Hazel Brawley there to greet them.

Bill Brawley, from South Carolina, used to be in the post office department, but I don't know whether he was then or not. But he and his wife had responsibility for the southern states for the Democratic National Committee, and that's why he was with us. So there were always two of them there and generally four. They would gather everybody aboard, do greetings and introductions, and give coffee and rolls. Then during the ride from Town A to Town B those people would go up into Mrs. Johnson's car and meet her, have their picture taken with her, and give her anything that they had for her, like a bouquet of flowers, a homemade cake, a bushel of apples, or a mincemeat pie. They would then move into the last car, the living room car, and at Stop B they would be introduced by Hale Boggs and get off.

We also had to get rid of all that stuff that was presented to Mrs. Johnson, or we would have had to add a number of cars to the train, and it was already plenty long enough. When you got to Town C, Mary Rather or Ashton Gonella would have written a note signed by Mrs. Johnson to the old folks' home or the orphanage or the hospital, saying, "I was given these lovely flowers on my train trip through the South and I hope that you will enjoy them." And then those were given to the advance men at Stop C to take to their destination.

We couldn't do that with food, however, because the Secret Service was such a bear about it. The staff could eat it on the train if we wanted to, but

Mrs. Johnson or Lynda or Luci were not allowed to have that food. But the rest of us, if we decided to take a chance, the Secret Service really did not quarrel, although they did not approve. They made us throw away the food.

There was one fly in that smooth-running machine, though. We got ahead of ourselves and gave away a bouquet of roses before it had been presented! I think it was handed to a motorcycle cop, but we got it back just as the train was pulling out.

Mrs. Johnson was on stage for the whole trip, and it was really an exhausting trip for her. But there could not have been an easier way to make all those stops than traveling with your office and everything with you. One of the great burdens, I think, when you go on a trip like that is getting back home and writing all those thank-you letters for all those bouquets and all those mincemeat pies. So these were all done on the train and mailed at the next stop.[11]

Was it all on one railroad line?

LIZ CARPENTER: No, we had about four different lines. Working that whole system out with the railroad companies was really something. But here's the thing. You got these fantastic telegrams from little two-bit towns along the way. I'll never forget one from a place in North Carolina, like Ahoskie, saying, "Nobody important has been through here since Buffalo Bill. Please have your train stop here." Well, stop we certainly did, even though it required some of the advance men pulling the weeds in the middle of the tracks, because some of these tracks hadn't been used for a long time. But it is a great way to campaign. You're right in the heart of town in so many of these towns. And if we had run this time [in 1968], I was hoping we would do one through Ohio.

Along this track, for instance, in North Carolina there are thirteen stops you can make in one day. It's almost the same in each town. International Harvester is on one side of the street, J. C. Penney's on the other. When you are in the towns of fifty thousand or less, people come from hundreds of miles around. When you get to the cities, they've moved the depot out to the suburb, and you have to get off the train and go downtown and lay a wreath. That's just the politics of it.

At one place, I remember so well, a woman came up to Mrs. Johnson and said, "I got up this morning at three o'clock and milked thirteen cows so I could be here." Well, you know, it is a great way to see the face of your country, and we're not all a sophisticated urban society.

We had a marvelous time. We really adored it. And all that music! We had a tape recording that played over and over again on the back of the train "Happy Days Are Here Again" and "Hello, Lyndon" alternately. We'd turn it on when we'd start slowing down going into a town and then turn it on as we headed out of town.

What determined where you stopped?

LIZ CARPENTER: Well, timing, space of the trains—we looked at some of the schedules the president had used in 1960 and Harry Truman had used before—the gathering places for the counties, where you would be at different hours of the day. We wanted to go into the towns that nobody else could get into. Anybody can get into Atlanta and out with their hide on even if you're for a civil rights bill. We took Savannah. It's tougher. We took Charleston. It's very much tougher. But she was going to the places that probably nobody else could get in and out of. And in some places, you know, they weren't all applauding.

[You stopped] where you needed votes; where the tracks went; where you could get to by nightfall; all the things that shape train schedules. Being on the back of the platform about seven a.m.—the farmers get up early—for a first show on the back of the platform. Through dusk-dark, and you could get ten to fifteen stops in a day that way with thousands of people at each stop.

We blanketed the press in these areas for days before and afterwards, and [LBJ] was the most insistent in saying to me, "How many advance men do you have out?" And I'd say, "Well, we have twenty guys out throughout towns along the way." He'd say, "That's just not enough, and I don't want just men. It's the women who'll get out there, and get the garden club groups down." And he says, "They have more stickability." So we ended up sending men and women into every single town.

They were generally people from here who were originally from that area, but people who had either worked on the Hill for congressmen or senators he knew. We used an awful lot of staff people who had worked for Senator [Richard] Russell of Georgia, or for some of the senators—[Sam] Ervin from North Carolina for there. They know the territory. They know the bases to touch. They know how to get the crowds.[12]

LUCI BAINES JOHNSON: What I remember is when we would stop, Bess would get herself off the train out there and she would be conducting a school play, literally. She would know that these people needed to come after these people, and these people come before, because if you get these people to come first, then they could be the lead for those people who had something to follow up on. I'm sure there were surprises. I'm sure that there were things that happened that were not anticipated, that were difficult. But I am also equally sure that Bess was in control. I think her main goal was to try to make two things happen at each stop: for Mother to have a chance to share what she felt and what she had to say; and for Mother to hear what the locals had to say.[13]

Did you have enough food for everybody?

BESS ABELL: Yes. We had sweet rolls and coffee in the living room car in the morning, and then we switched to soft drinks and nibbles around noon. We served cocktails and soft drinks around four-thirty or five. We had different hors d'oeuvres every day, all things from the South, like little bitty fried chicken legs. Betty Talmadge, Senator Talmadge's wife, gave us some of her hams from her ham business. So we had ham biscuits when we were rolling through Georgia. And we had shrimp when we were heading along the Gulf Coast, all kinds of good things. The dining car was full all the time.

Who were some of the entertainers who participated in the Lady Bird Special?

BESS ABELL: The entertainers that we had, not on the train with us, but they flew ahead to the major stops. They were the Brothers Four, the Bitter End Singers, and Bob Newhart. They really never met Mrs. Johnson because they would leave just as we arrived and head for the airport and climb on the plane and head for the next stop. I think when we got to New Orleans we managed to get one picture of Mrs. Johnson with everybody.

What you had to do was to call up and ask the Brothers Four, "Do you have two days of your life that you can give us?" Both the Bitter End Singers and the Brothers Four had done a program for us at the White House. They had been a part of the big Salute to Congress, a show that the president had on the lawn in 1964, and at that time they said: "Gee, if there is anything we can do, we want to."[14]

Did the president talk with Mrs. Johnson at great length before she left on how to handle such crowds and what she ought to be doing, or was this pretty much her initiative?

LIZ CARPENTER: They talked a whole lot about it because I felt that he was somebody that missed terribly being along. He joined us at Raleigh, North Carolina. I said, "We're going to need beefing up by the time we get to Raleigh," and he said, "I'll be there." He knew we needed a stimulant then to keep the train going. The president was there to say good-bye to us in Alexandria, and he was at the end of the tracks in New Orleans. I always felt that he was sorry he wasn't along every bit of the way. But he was never prouder of her—to be a woman who carried a train through a really difficult part of the country and did it with great crowds and with great applause.

But the thing that made this unique is we sent out about sixty women. They would go into a town three or four days before and have press conferences and boom the fact that the Lady Bird Special is coming to town. One of them was named Mrs. Robert E. Lee [Phyzzie Lee], and I wish to gosh every one of their names had been Mrs. Robert E. Lee. It was a great asset. But all of these good-looking, able women were very much considered at the head of the ranks by the president. He never underestimated their value, and he was the one that insisted on advance women.[15]

One of the many advance agents for the trip, Neal P. Gillen, recalled Bess's strategy for building a crowd at each stop.

NEAL P. GILLEN: It was Bess's idea to send in advance women to work with the garden clubs. Hallie Young, Howard Young's wife, arrived in Norfolk a few days after I did. Howard Young worked with Voice of America. Hallie was a very capable organizer. She met with the garden clubs and various women's organizations and got them committed to the event. In Virginia at that time, women were the power behind the thrones. They played a very important role, and it was Bess's insight to actively involve women in the campaign. It was a strategic and wise decision on her part. It really worked. As Liz Carpenter explained to me, "If the wife is involved in the project, the husband and the whole family have to come." So, insofar as building a crowd, it was relatively easy.[16]

Did everyone overnight on the train?

LIZ CARPENTER: Yes, slept on the train. We had press cars on the train. The press had their typewriters and their bathroom and their berth all on the same train, which also had advantages.

It is a fantastic way to campaign. It's the best of all ways. When we were getting ready to leave here, I guessed we would have fifty reporters, and we had two hundred and twenty-five. Their papers were paying their way. We started turning down requests. It must have been an experience for some of the foreign press because we didn't have room, and we weren't running in Europe. But at least fifteen foreign reporters came along. Mrs. Johnson saw them privately just to try to clue them in on what American politics was like.

There were a lot of reporters along who, interestingly enough, don't like to fly and are scared to admit it. They all wanted to cover a political trip, and so the train trip was going to be their brush with politics.[17]

LINDA JANE HOLDEN: They had bunks. And there were two dining cars. Mrs. Johnson had a car and then there was one for the press. That's where Liz Carpenter would hold her afternoon press conferences to form her message for the day—get that out to the people. Bess made that point. I just remember her saying, "As we choo-choo-chooed down the track, more and more people started coming." There was one stop where people held up signs saying go away. Bess said there were moments where they were frightened for their safety. But the Secret Service helped with that.[18]

Encountering Hostility

"Don't give me the easy towns, Liz," the first lady requested when they planned the itinerary. "Anyone can get into Atlanta—it's the new, modern South. Let me take the tough ones." Consequently, they stopped in areas where resistance to the Civil Rights Act ran strong. "But we have to go," Lady Bird insisted. "We must let them know we love the South. We have not turned our backs on them. I don't think there's much chance of carrying it for Lyndon, judging by the letters I get from my Alabama cousins, but at least we won't lose by default."[19]

Did you have contingency plans for possible trouble? You were, after all, moving through the Deep South, which was not exactly congenial in some places.

BESS ABELL: We did have one threat to Mrs. Johnson when we went into northern Florida, and the Secret Service were terribly edgy and nervous at that point. We were crossing a long, low railroad bridge, and they had gotten a threat that it was going to be blown up. I think there was a helicopter overhead at that point, and there was a boat on at least one side of it, maybe two sides. I don't know whether they sent another train over it before entering or not, but anyway we crossed it. It was a long bridge, several miles over the water, but we got over it safely.

You actually got a better response than at least the general public had anticipated. There were a lot of local southern politicians who came when people had expected they wouldn't.

BESS ABELL: Mrs. Johnson handled it very well. She handled the ugliness very well, and I think she came out the winner. Like when [Texas

Congressman] Bruce Alger's group hit her over the head with a sign at the Adolphus Hotel in Dallas on the eve of the 1960 election, which everybody said carried Texas for the Kennedy-Johnson ticket. People in the South don't like to see a lady slighted like that, especially one of theirs. I think Mrs. Johnson's southern accent got thicker as we moved through the South too; certainly Luci's did. Luci got such a southern accent that I would not have believed, but it just came out. It was something that Mrs. Johnson had been moving away from with the speech coaching, but she got back there into the South where she had spent those summers as a child, and it all came back thick and fast.[20]

LIZ CARPENTER: We were out to woo, and we were out to woo with real courthouse politics on that train. We would put on forty or fifty local people. There were some who didn't show, but in a way, it was a little bit like the domino theory. The first two or three stops were so successful that the southern politicians began to be getting more and more aboard, and there were more people boarding than we had even counted on. You know how it is. They look to whether the judge or the sheriff showed, and they did show.[21]

Did you attribute the opposition to the civil rights issue?
BESS ABELL: Yes, I mean, Johnson said, "It's the right thing to do. But we're going to lose these states for a generation," and did.

Mrs. Johnson ran into some hecklers along the way, didn't she? There was visible opposition.
BESS ABELL: Visible and noisy hecklers, but she was wonderful. She was terrific. On those four days, all those stops, we traveled a little further south with each passing hour. In Savannah or Charleston, there were hecklers out there that just were not going to shut up. Mrs. Johnson was just very stern and schoolmarmish when she said, "In this country we hear all views. I've heard yours, and now I want you to be polite and hear mine." That worked a couple of places. It was not successful in Charleston. It was where [Representative] Mendell Rivers was. But I thought his speech was ghastly anyway.

But there were signs along the route that would say "Black Bird, Go Home." I remember that being on a big banner or sheet that was held at the back of the crowd at a train stop. There were two young men, one at either end of this banner, "Black Bird, Go Home." As she talked in this nice, lovely southern accent, talked about all her Alabama kinfolk, the sign kept getting lower and lower and lower. Finally, it was on the ground, and I think those two fellows went away.[22]

Were her feelings hurt by that sort of encounter, just on a personal level?

BESS ABELL: I'm sure they were. I'm sure they were. But she respected people, and she is just the kind of person that she would say, "Well, they're just misguided, but they're good people." She was a sunny person.[23]

Lindy Boggs, wife of Congressman Hale Boggs, and later a representative herself, was cochair of the Lady Bird Special and did advance work for the trip. She recalled some of the opposition they faced.

How about South Carolina?

LINDY BOGGS: South Carolina. Oh, dear. I do remember that we had a little bit of difficulty in South Carolina at first. But again, there was a fairly well-organized women's group in Columbia, the state capital. They turned out in great force. So it had the good effect—this all-women's team—of making the women proud that the candidate had chosen women to advance, had honored us with this real responsibility, and had chosen women as the ones who really could affect a success. They were very helpful in this regard. They were enthusiastic about our assignment and felt they couldn't let us down and couldn't let his opinion of women down. So it did have that effect.

Do you have any recollection of the way Mrs. Johnson handled these incidents of heckling?

LINDY BOGGS: I have many recollections of the way she handled the instances. We had many security problems along the route, as you can imagine. We had a little engine that went ahead of the train. I had so much experience by then, you see. I had done one train; I knew how to do another one. I had also learned that what I needed to do in the advance work was to leave a person who went with me in each state. Before then, I had just assigned a state to one person in the team who would phone back as we went along the route. The second time around, I left a coordinator in each state. Then she was the representative of Mrs. Johnson, and all factions could talk to her.

I had a committee of young people because we went through some college towns. One of the enthusiastic young people said, "You know that engine that goes in front of the train? It has that whole open car behind it. Don't you think it would be marvelous if we put everybody in their little LBJ costumes, and as we went into a college town, we could all be on there and get off?" Nobody, of course, realized that it was a security measure to have the engine in front of us.

We had many security problems. By that time, of course, we had the Secret Service and the various agencies of the government in all of the different states who were responsible. When we went over water—we had a bomb threat, so we went over a causeway from Florida into Alabama. Mrs. Johnson was always alerted to the problems and always very calm about it, very certain that they would be taken care of.

There was a group that started out in Columbia, South Carolina. It was a right-wing group, and the leader was an older gentleman with a crutch. He would give signals to these young people with his crutch, when to begin to chant, and so on. Lady Bird took it very well. The men along the route got horribly upset! They were defending their lady. I think perhaps if they had left it to the ladies that it would have been better.

I remember getting into Charleston, and they were quite raucous there. I was so pleased that whoever had been the chairman of the stop at the previous large city was otherwise engaged, because he had become so upset. Hale was going to be chairman, and I knew he wouldn't get upset, that he was accustomed to hecklers. And he got totally infuriated! Lady Bird always handled it properly and well. She finally, very gingerly, called everybody in and suggested that the best way to handle this was either to ignore it or to let her say, "Now you've had your say. Now allow me to have mine. Then when I'm finished, you may have yours again." It worked perfectly.[24]

Civil rights activist Virginia Foster Durr recalled in 1967 a similar incident when the Lady Bird Special stopped in Alabama, as well as the nervousness of Southern Democratic politicians about being seen anywhere near the train.

VIRGINIA FOSTER DURR: In 1964, when she came down on the Lady Bird Special, my husband and I drove down to Mobile to see the train come in. As she got off the train, the streets were pretty well crowded with people, and a great many Negroes, but the politicians were totally absent. There was, you know, quite a bit of enthusiasm for her, but when she got to the place where she was going to speak and I looked on the platform, there was only one Alabama politician that I recognized, which was Senator [John J.] Sparkman.

When she got up to speak, I'm sure that these little boys had been paid to heckle her and to interrupt her because every other breath they would interrupt her and say something nasty or just yell, "Down with Johnson, down with Johnson." Bird stopped in the middle of her talk and looked out at them, and she said in this very sweet way, "Now look, I believe as firmly as you do in the right of free speech, and I think you have a perfect right to express your opinion to me. But I think you should give me a chance to express my opinion, and then you can say what you want to." Well, just because she was so ladylike about it and so sweet and gentle, they did hush up a little while so she could finish her speech. When it was over and she got quite a lot of applause then, too, and the crowd was quite enthusiastic. Luci was with her, and she got a big hand from all of the young people.

I remember Senator Sparkman, I saw him afterward, and I said, "John, you really deserve a gold cross for having courage enough to stand on that platform by Lady Bird when all the other politicians had disappeared." He said, "Well, I hope it's going to be a gold cross. I'm afraid it's going to be an iron cross." But he did stand by her.

Then the Special pulled out, and she had surrounded herself with a lot of southern women that came from Alabama, like [Presidential Special Assistant] Doug Cater's wife [Libby Cater] and a number of other southern women who worked in Washington and had connections here. That was a very brave thing for her to do, because in 1964 the South was so strongly against the civil rights bill and they were so angry about it and the [Barry M.] Goldwater sentiment was so strong. To come back into the South with a lot of women and face those hostile crowds and travel all through the deepest part of the South and subject herself to this kind of heckling and hooting and howling was an extremely brave thing. I think that she showed at that point another quality that we Southerners admire so much, which was courage, real moral courage. So I have a great deal of affection and admiration for her, and I think that she's been a remarkably good wife to Lyndon.[25]

How did Bess describe some of the negative aspects of that tour?

LINDA JANE HOLDEN: That it was painful. I was just in Charleston and I thought about this when I was walking the streets of Charleston. They pulled their shades down and put "We're for Goldwater" signs in their windows. The Charlestonians were really rude to Mrs. Johnson, and so that hurts. Then the next day, one of the local papers chastised them and said such rude behavior won't be tolerated here again. But, yes, they weren't accepted everywhere. That's just hard.

The Lady Bird Special had a locomotive going ahead of it.

LINDA JANE HOLDEN: They did, running ahead. There was something they thought looked really suspicious because of that locomotive going ahead. They subjected themselves to stopping anywhere because they would just slow down when they were going through the different towns. Liz Carpenter had done a good job with sending out the advance people to prep. So if there was a good crowd there they would just, on a whim, slow down and stop and then do their thing there. It was kind of, "This is what we're planning for today, but we might do this, this, and this too." They wanted to be responsive to the people. That was the whole point, to get the South on board, literally.[26]

James R. Jones, who later served as President Johnson's chief of staff, recalled how he got his start on the Lady Bird Special.

JAMES R. JONES: They were putting together this special train trip, starting in Washington, winding up in New Orleans. Tommy Boggs [Washington attorney and lobbyist Thomas Hale Boggs Jr.]—obviously, his family was very much involved with that—Tommy asked if I wanted to advance one of the stops. I said, "Sure." We had just graduated from law school, and I didn't have anything to do right away except I had some Army duty that I had to take care of. Because the experienced advance people had all been taken over by the president's campaign, we built a brand-new team. So we had an advance man school.

Even though I had only advanced, I think, one trip, maybe two previously, I taught the school about what you do as an advance person. We had, I think, forty-seven stops, and we had a little over twenty advance people. Almost all of them had never advanced before. So instead of just one stop, I ended up being in charge of all the advance operations and the movement of the train, keeping everything on schedule, and, of course, I stayed on it the whole time. What I am told is that at the end of the train trip, Lady Bird Johnson was impressed and mentioned it to her husband: "There's a young man you ought to get on your staff." Now I'm sure that Bess Abell, and Liz Carpenter, and the first lady's team had a lot to do with that too, but I never found out for sure. But that's how I got to the White House.[27]

New Orleans Finale

After four days and 1,628 miles, the Lady Bird Special reached the end of its line in New Orleans. Scholars of the election have judged that the first lady's whistle-stop had enabled the Southern Democratic Party "to mobilize its entire apparatus in whatever locale she passed through." Although Barry Goldwater carried five of the southern states—South Carolina, Georgia, Alabama, Mississippi, and Louisiana—Lyndon Johnson carried the rest.[28]

When Mr. Johnson met you in New Orleans, did you get thanks from him for all your labors?

BESS ABELL: I never saw him really, except on the platform. I think that he was really pleased with how it worked out.[29] The president wanted to call and read you what the *New York Times* and the *Washington Post* and the *Washington Star* were saying about the trip. He was very supportive of the trip.[30]

It seems to have been a remarkable success, which must have been a great relief to have it finally over with.

BESS ABELL: Yes, but we lost all the states [except Virginia, North Carolina, and Florida]. But we missed it! We really missed it. We wanted to take another train trip. We loved it. We ended up with a flying Lady Bird Special, which went to three places in Texas and into Oklahoma and Arkansas. On that one we took a few hostesses. At each stop the hostesses would get off the plane and hand out candy that said, "Hello, Lyndon" and balloons and pennants. We talked about going out through Pennsylvania and Ohio, but we never did it and ended up with the airplane. It was a very expensive undertaking, as you can imagine.

I think that everybody who was along on that trip, from the guys from the White House garage who were along to handle baggage and junk that came aboard, to the European press, the photographers, the staff that was along, we all loved it.

As we moved from one area to another, they [the train crews] coordinated it, but I think that we worked mainly with the Southern Railroad. No, we worked with Atlantic Coast Line, too, very much. But one train company was responsible for the food and dining operation. I think maybe that turned out to be Atlantic Coast Line. And they loved it, adored it. And afterwards, everybody wanted to have a party for all the people who were onboard.[31]

LIZ CARPENTER: But it was a fabulous trip, and the real value of it, if you want to look at it from pure politics, is that for four days you stayed on the big news shows, [NBC's] Huntley-Brinkley. You had five minutes every nighttime you can't buy or afford to buy in a campaign. And we were on it every night because it was unique that a woman was doing it; in some ways, I guess, because there was controversy along the tracks.

It was female run. We did a whole lot of extras that you don't normally do on trains, with happy hours for the press and with serving the specialties of the house on the dining car of whatever state we were in. Hale Boggs and other southern men were along. But we were calling the signals.

To me, the biggest thing that [Mrs. Johnson] did politically was the whistle stop. It went so well that when we got to the ranch, the president, who was so proud of her he was about to burst, asked us to go on a flying whistle-stop through Arkansas, Oklahoma, and I believe it was Northern Texas.

She doesn't like to go beyond the strength of her endurance, because she likes to do everything she does well and the best she can and not be fragmented. We were at the end of our rope physically by four days.

But the president talked to her many times along the way, and there's no tonic for her like his words of confidence and faith. It's just like a magic wand had been waved over her.[32]

LINDY BOGGS: Going into New Orleans at the end of the 1964 Lady Bird Special train, [LBJ] was very exuberant, because going into New Orleans at the end he joined us. He had heard rumors that there was infighting in the factions and that there wasn't going to be a sufficient crowd. Instead, there was just a marvelous, wonderful parade out of season. Of course, it's always the season for a parade in New Orleans, but we had a real Mardi Gras parade, with floats and everything representing all the southern states, and an enormous crowd. We had the southern states, and we ended up with a statue of [Simon] Bolivar to show his connection with Latin America, and all of this. He was so amazed that his advance information had been different than what the situation truly was that, going into New Orleans in the 1964 campaign trail on the train, he reached over and took my hand and said, "Don't worry. My attitude is different this time."[33]

In this kind of thing, with the enormous amount of work and physical strain of conventions and the train trip, does Mrs. Johnson ever get tired, cross, lose her temper?

BESS ABELL: She's so in control of herself and her emotions. Does she get tired? Yes, absolutely, bone-tired! But she somehow had that self-discipline to push a little bit harder and get out there and do.

She never had a tendency to get cross with people who just happen to be close to her? I suppose what I'm doing is sort of unconsciously comparing her to her husband.

BESS ABELL: You can't do it in that regard. She would soften the blows that a lot of people would get from the president; a tongue lashing that would come from him would sometimes be followed by sweet words from her. Did she ever lose her temper? I honestly can't remember. Liz told me that the angriest she ever heard Mrs. Johnson was when she was in her bedroom at the White House and she had walked into the room, or was in the room, and the maid was drawing the shades in the room to darken it— but it was still twilight. And Mrs. Johnson said in a very strong, forceful voice, "Don't ever pull the shades until the last drop of sunlight is gone. I want to enjoy every bit of it." She said that was the maddest she'd ever seen her. She really does enjoy the daylight hours. When she'd take a nap, whether it was in a hotel room in New York or in her room in the White House, she'd never pull the shades.[34]

TYLER ABELL: There's a spike that Bess thought up. A golden spike that she invented for Mrs. Johnson to give out to people to celebrate the accomplishment of the train. They're all engraved with Mrs. Johnson's initials and the Lady Bird Special. It's not a golden spike. It's an iron spike, painted gold. It was Bess's idea along with using the railroad car the way she did.

Bess's spike is engraved: "To Bess, with happy memories of our whistle-stop tour, October 1964, Lady Bird." I think this is what inspired Lindy Boggs to give Bess a "Streetcar Named Desire" for her charm bracelet.

The president got on the train for the last lap, and they pulled into New Orleans. They didn't carry very many states, but they did carry a few. I think they carried Virginia and Florida. They didn't carry South Carolina, Alabama, Mississippi, or Louisiana. But the record will show what they carried and what they didn't. But they did make a difference. Johnson's vote in the 1964 election is still the largest percentage that anybody has ever gotten, even though he didn't carry as many states as Nixon in 1972. Nixon carried everything but Massachusetts.[35]

NEAL P. GILLEN: The follow-up after the whistle-stop was amazing. The advance men and women submitted a list of people to be thanked, and people got letters from Lindy Boggs, Carrie Davis [wife of Congressman Cliff Davis], and Mrs. Johnson within a week or so after the event. It had a significant effect. I got follow-up from people in telephone calls and letters. The pictures took a little more time, but all of that was there. The president watched it very carefully. He joined the trip twice, first in North Carolina, and then he met her in New Orleans at the end of the trip.

There were many editorial cartoons. One shows a couple of good old boys, rednecks, and a drawing of the train, saying, "What's old Lyndon up to?" I think it was the political success story, the best strategic move of the campaign to plan that trip. The proof is there because Johnson carried Virginia and North Carolina. He lost in South Carolina, Georgia, Alabama, Louisiana, and Mississippi, but that was expected because of civil rights. And the Democrats lost a few southern congressional seats. It was a turning point. President Johnson knew that the South was going to turn. But that trip was key to Johnson's victory.[36]

7

White House Weddings

Having known the Johnson daughters since they were children, Bess Abell offered advice and assistance at the White House and organized their weddings. As much as she admired Lady Bird Johnson, she understood what the first lady's priorities meant to her children.

BESS ABELL: She's a marvelous mother; she has given those girls a great deal. But if there was ever a choice between husband and child, the choice was always the husband. If it was a choice between campaigning with her husband and leaving her children with Zephyr Wright [longtime Johnson family cook], she would go with her husband. I'm not sure that there is anybody else in the world as selfless as she is. Other people always come first, but in that scale, Lyndon Johnson is always at the top of it, and the girls come next.

Did the girls learn to accept this?
BESS ABELL: I don't know that any child can learn to accept being number two anymore than any husband could learn to accept being number two. Lynda was always very much involved in her father's life. During the days when we were out on Thirtieth Place, she would come home from school in the afternoon and almost the first thing she would do—well, the newspapers were always put up on her bed. In the normal household they would be put in the trash, [but] they were put up on Lynda's bed so she could read them when she came home from school. She was a student of history, as well as current events, and she would almost always get on the telephone to somebody in her daddy's office and say, "What about such-and-such a bill? Did the vote come up on that today?" And she really stayed in touch on the things that were happening on the Hill and the things that involved her father's life. Luci was more interested in the page boys than in what the page boys were carrying.

Did you find yourself in the position of the big sister to Lynda and Luci?
BESS ABELL: No, not really. I enjoyed both girls, but I can't say that I ever had a special closeness with either one of them. I think I made the

most points with Luci when she discovered that my handwriting was like her mother's, and she said, "Can you write the note to Miss [Katherine] Lee, [principal] at National Cathedral, for me?" It was legitimate; her mother was away then.[1]

LYNDA JOHNSON ROBB: I'd say Bess was very faithful, vivacious, attractive, and unflappable. I just thought her elopement was just the biggest romance I had ever heard of. Oh, this was so exciting. I can't say I thought of her as a big sister, but she was certainly somebody I went to for advice.[2]

LUCI BAINES JOHNSON: Bess was comfortable. She was able to build a confidence with my mother on lots and lots of levels because there was a sense of, "We've shared a similar walk. We understand each other. I can rely on her." I don't remember when Bess came to The Elms. She was just there. I do remember how grateful we all were that it was long before November 22nd.[3]

Was there any effort made in 1964 or 1965 to find something for Lynda and Luci to do?
BESS ABELL: I really don't know if there ever was a concentrated effort on that. Luci, because of her own problem being left-eye dominant when you're supposed to be right-eye dominant, was a very poor student at National Cathedral and made very, very poor grades. Dr. Robert Kraskin found that Luci had this problem, and she started taking eye exercises that solved her problem. It was just amazing how her grades went up from C's and D's to A's and B's in a matter of months. She then had an interest in working with children who had that sight problem and the learning difficulty that comes with it. Lynda, on the other hand, when she graduated was interested in finding a paying job. You know, it's very hard to hit the pavement and hunt for a job when you're the daughter of the president.

Lynda eventually wrote for McCall's *magazine.*
BESS ABELL: She took it very seriously, and I think wrote some quite good pieces.

Were you close enough to see what it was like for the Johnsons to be raising a pair of teenage daughters in the White House?
BESS ABELL: Mrs. Johnson and the president, I think, never wanted to shelter their children from public life. There are many people in the

political arena who want to keep their children away from it, not let it touch them. But the president and Mrs. Johnson felt that there were so many benefits that would come to them that they wanted to involve them in everything from campaigning to official trips abroad with their parents and state dinners at the White House. Mrs. Johnson would from time to time ask one of the girls to stand in for her to receive a group at a tea or coffee. She always wanted them to come to the state dinners when they were in town. She would also tell them when she invited them that if we ended up with too many people, they would have to eat in the Navy Mess with the staff, and they were both good sports about it. They would put on their best dress and go and greet and meet and have a marvelous time with the guests during cocktails. The guests would go in to dinner, and the girls would join the military social aides and me and go over and have dinner in the Navy Mess and then make a beeline back and greet some of the guests who were coming in at ten o'clock for the entertainment.

Perhaps the girls saw more of their parents in the White House years, living over the office.

BESS ABELL: That's true. Mrs. Johnson, of course, saw much more of the president too because he would be working in the house, and then he would go to the office and come back for lunch. I guess it was probably the only time in his life that he ever had lunch at home.

Did the girls' dating activities cause any special difficulties?

BESS ABELL: It caused a lot of difficulty for them. Both of them, when they finally nailed down their husbands, did it really within the confines of the White House rather than outside the White House. It was much easier for the daughter of the president to see a movie in the theater there or to play bridge up in the solarium than it was to go out to a restaurant. It's the only way to get away from the Secret Service agents, and it's one of the effective ways of carrying on your romance privately and not on the social pages of the Washington papers.[4]

LYNDA JOHNSON ROBB: I had this nice young man from the Navy Academy that I was in love with, and he was on a naval cruise. He was supposed to be coming into Naples. And, of course, I couldn't meet him. I had to be chaperoned all the time. The fact that I had Secret Service didn't matter. It was the looks of things. Bess had to be my dueña and watch over me on this trip.[5]

Lynda got an awful lot of publicity from dating the actor George Hamilton for a while.

BESS ABELL: I liked George very, very much, and I think he really came along at a marvelous time in Lynda's life. I think through George she learned that there was more to being a woman and a person than just being a good student. It was really because of George that she began to take an interest in clothes and makeup.

There was some indication at the time that Mr. Johnson was not overly fond of George Hamilton.

BESS ABELL: I read all those things, but I never heard the president say anything but nice things about George. I truthfully have no knowledge of how he felt about the possibility of Lynda marrying George. He has always said that he thought his girls had good judgment, and they were going to have to live with the man they married, not him. He thought it was up to them to pick out who that man in their life was going to be, and not up to him and Mrs. Johnson. But I've only heard the president say nice things about George, and in my dealings with George I always found him to be a real gentleman and not in any way taking advantage of his association with Lynda, although I'm aware that during that period his price per picture went up astoundingly.[6]

The Wedding Planner

You were a wedding planner. What was that like?

BESS ABELL: Oh, it was great fun, and it was especially great fun for me, who never had a chance to plan her own wedding, because Tyler and I eloped, so there was never any chance to do that. So we had two big weddings to plan. Every once in a while, when one girl and I might be talking about something that might happen, she'd say, "What did you and Tyler do? Oh, now I remember, you didn't do anything."[7]

JAMES R. KETCHUM: The weddings were the logical extension of what she was doing for the President and Mrs. J. Bess would come up with all kinds of things to meet their aid and comfort. And she'd be there with it.[8]

LINDA JANE HOLDEN: She was a mastermind. She had a big map that showed everyone's positions—especially for Luci's wedding because so much happened there at the White House with the reception. She had to move them off-site and then back on-site. Lynda's was all at the White House, but Luci's was outside. Her big map that showed where everyone was to be, where things were, the flows, and things like that. She had to deal with all the bridesmaids and on that flurry of all that pink, and keeping the irons going. Liz Carpenter did the press relations, but everything else was all planned by Bess. She knocked herself out to please the Johnsons, to make sure it was what they wanted and what their daughters wanted. To me, it seemed like Bess was a part of their family. They had that kind of relationship, that rapport that lasted so long.[9]

Luci's Wedding

After she converted to Catholicism, Luci Johnson chose to be married in the Shrine of the Immaculate Conception. But as usher J. B. West noted, "The White House was decorated to the hilt for her reception. Bess decorated, choreographed, stage-directed, rehearsed. Liz Carpenter dangled tidbits of information to the press about every possible detail involving the wedding, with the exception of the wedding gown." He recalled that on the morning of August 5, 1966, "I asked Bess to walk around the house with me, inspecting every room, going over the reception scenario, being sure there were to be no changes." But of course, no matter how much planning, she would confront unexpected developments.[10]

BESS ABELL: There were a couple of things that didn't go quite right with Luci's wedding. The thing that we had messed up on was Luci's wedding dress. Lynda could go to a designer and say, "Show me some sketches." She could look at a photograph, a drawing, and decide "This dress is the right dress for me and let's go ahead with that." Luci didn't think that way. She wanted to see the dress, zip up the dress, and wear the dress. She wanted to be sure it was the right dress, and she also did not want Pat Nugent, her fiancé, to see the dress before he saw her in it.

Foremost thing in my thoughts on Luci's dress was trying to keep it a secret. Not the wedding, but the dress. I went up to New York and visited a lot of bridal houses to look at dresses for my "younger sister" who was in South America and was only going to return something like two weeks before her wedding—that was my ploy. We picked up a number of dresses to take home and show to her mother and mine, and then took them back after Luci had tried them on.

We found a bridal designer named Priscilla of Boston, a lovely woman who makes beautiful bridal dresses, and Priscilla [Comins] was making a beautiful dress for Luci. Then the president called me at home. It seems that David Dubinsky had come to him. Mr. Dubinsky was head of the International Ladies' Garment Workers' Union, and he said, almost with tears in his eyes, "I can't believe that you're letting your daughter get married in a non-union dress. It's just awful, and I don't know what to tell my members, that the President of the United States is letting his daughter get married in a non-union dress."[11]

Most of the good bridal houses at that time, and probably still are, are non-union. They tell me that they pay higher wages, but that they are not union houses. So the president really was very upset about that. He said, "You just have to have that dress made with a union label on it. I don't care what happens, but it has to have a union label on it. It's just too embarrassing and too wrong, and you shouldn't have done it that way in the first place." And he was right. We shouldn't have, but we did.[12]

I said, "I'll talk to Priscilla in the morning and I'm sure that we can work something out that will make you and Mr. Dubinsky happy." I loved Mr. Dubinsky. So the next morning I called Priscilla and explained the situation. She said, "It's not a problem, Bess, I promise you. There's a bridal house in the same building as my office, and I've already talked to her. We're going to make another dress and it will have a union label in it. We'll send you both dresses at the same time. What you do with them is up to you." So I clipped that union label out of one dress and sewed it in the other! Brides are supposed to wear something old, something new, something borrowed, and something blue.[13]

LUCI BAINES JOHNSON: Never, ever, ever in my wildest dreams, at nineteen years of age, would I have thought to make sure that the people who created my wedding dress were in a union shop. It didn't occur to me. I got to choose the dress. Well, women's garment workers had been long-time staunch supporters. We just couldn't do that. So I have two identical wedding dresses. One that was made with Priscilla of Boston at her place and another that was a copy of it in a union shop. Bess got thrown that. "Now, next." Never chastised me. Never.[14]

BESS ABELL: It's hard to imagine, even looking back on it, what a big deal it was, but everybody was after the design of that dress. They all wanted to know what it was, and whoever found it out would have a great big scoop. The newspaper people were going into bridal houses under all kinds of guises, trying to get pictures or details about Luci's wedding dress.[15]

Didn't Women's Wear Daily *publish a sketch of Luci or Lynda's dress?*
BESS ABELL: They published them both. They were more accurate on Lynda's than they were on Luci's—they really didn't get Luci's.

Was there any retaliation against Women's Wear Daily?
BESS ABELL: I think that the retaliation really worked to *Women's Wear Daily*'s benefit. I think their circulation went up by something like a hundred thousand after all the fuss about the wedding. Liz Carpenter told them after they broke a release date, which they said they weren't bound by because they did not come to her press conference—they got it from somebody else who was there. She refused them credentials to the wedding, so there was sort of a battle on the front pages between Liz and *Women's Wear Daily*. I think they both feel they won.[16]

Liz Carpenter barred the publication from covering the wedding or the reception after it broke the embargo and published sketches of the bride's and bridesmaids' dresses.

LIZ CARPENTER: It was one of the problems, and one of the most public problems. They were trying to release and do a lot of sleuthing around on what Luci's wedding gown would look like. Luci wanted the right to wear her wedding gown for the first time with her groom never seeing it. So we had a flap on that.

There were other crises—the wedding cake, for example. I had announced that we were going to have fresh lilies of the valley on top of it, and I got a frantic call from a public servant—not a crank—who let me know that there was a public health bulletin out which said that lilies of the valley drip a juice that gives people hallucinations. They can wander around as though they're in a coma. Well, I could see five hundred wedding guests wandering around as though they were in a coma, and I tried to convince Bess of this. She thought I was crazy, but we got the public health bulletin, and so we sprayed the lilies of the valley. These are minor crises, but they're funny, and it's multiplied in the humor when they occur in the White House, of course.[17]

In her memoir, *Ruffles and Flourishes*, Liz Carpenter lamented that the problem of surviving a White House wedding was "intensified because we still had business as usual on other East Wing activities, while trying to plan the wedding and satisfy the insatiable appetite of the press for wedding details."[18]

BESS ABELL: Then we made another mistake in Luci's wedding, which upset the president terribly. The wedding was out in the National Shrine on a very, very hot day in August, in the middle of a very, very hot week in August. It was going to be a long ceremony. The wedding ceremony itself, the mass, etc., ran about an hour and fifteen minutes, and the Shrine was hot. Two days before we had a call from American Airlines—it was during the middle of the airline strike—saying, "We have all this air conditioning equipment which we ordinarily use in our planes, and our planes aren't flying anywhere. We've been reading about how hot it is in the church and we could bring these machines out and we'd be happy to do it with no publicity, no nothing, and air condition the church for you. We can set them up late in the afternoon, run them all night long, run them up until just before the guests are ready to come in and then turn them off, and you'll have enough cool air in there to keep all those people very, very comfortable." I was ecstatic about the idea! I discussed it with Clark Clifford, our unofficial legal wedding adviser, and he said he thought it was just fine, so we proceeded ahead with it, telling them, "Yes, we would love to have it."

The air conditioning trucks were on their way out to the Shrine. Jim Reynolds, who was assistant secretary of labor and who had been very much involved in the airline negotiation and had taken time off from his problems with the airlines to help me get out of the mess with David Dubinsky and tell me what we could do to make Mr. Dubinsky happy and make the bride happy. And right in the middle of his airline negotiations, here we presented him another problem. He just hit the ceiling, as did [Secretary of Labor] Bill Wirtz. I think Bill called the president and said, "You just can't do this. These airlines are on strike, and it's just going to blow the whole thing sky high."

That's when the president called and said, "If there was a mistake to be made on this wedding and you haven't made it, it's because you haven't thought of it." He was furious with me, and with Liz, and his wife, and everybody. We called off the air conditioning. I've always given Bill Wirtz what-for about it because Lynda passed out from the heat and everybody else nearly died. I had known how hot I was going to be so when I got back to the White House after the ceremony I had another dress there to change into. I just perspired all the way through mine. There were a lot of other people there who wished they could have changed. But it worked out all right. Luci got married, despite the lack of air conditioning.[19]

BRIAN LAMB: Bess had a terrific relationship with the president. He respected her. You could just tell. He didn't respect everybody. He made it very difficult on people. But when Bess would walk up to the President of the United States, he listened to her as he would his wife, thank goodness. He barked at her from time to time, but she knew how to deal with it. But he barked at everybody. He barked at me. I mean, that was one of my favorite things.[20]

The other side of that coin, when things went well, did LBJ compliment you?

BESS ABELL: Oh yes. I loved working for him. I loved it because you always knew where you stood. You did not have to hear about it from the fifth assistant secretary that you had screwed up or that you had done something wonderful. He picked up the phone and called you himself. He said, "Oh, you're the smartest person in my administration. I should have you in my cabinet." He would just puff you up and make you feel great. And then he could bring you down to earth.[21]

How did Luci take all of these controversies?

BESS ABELL: Luci was very, very much in love, and she really didn't let any of that bother her. The only thing that I remember that really upset Luci, and I always will be sort of annoyed at the bridesmaid who caused the problem. I had worked out where the girls and boys in the wedding party were going to stand and who they were going to walk out with, not by who they were madly in love with or who they had an enormous crush on but by height and who would look the best.

After the rehearsal, the day before the wedding down at the Shrine, one of Luci's bridesmaids just really fussed at Luci, and I think broke down into tears because she couldn't understand that Luci would make her walk out with Joe instead of Bill, whom Luci knew that she had fallen madly in love with during all the wedding parties. I thought, "Of all the things to come and worry a bride with the night before she gets married, when she's got enough other things on her mind!" So Luci was very tearful too. In any case we changed the walking-out order to make the girl happy, and then it made some other little girl very unhappy—one of those very silly things. But I really don't think these things bothered Luci. She was an excited, thrilled little girl who was getting ready to be a grown-up wife.[22]

LUCI BAINES JOHNSON: When I married for the first time, my understanding was I got to choose the groom, I got to choose the bridesmaids, I got to choose the dresses, and that was all I chose. Absolutely everything else was what my mother and Bess would do, down to every flower in the cathedral. Well, the day or two before, I developed some horrible reaction to chrysanthemums. They're real hardy, hardy, hardy flowers. I was marrying at the National Shrine of the Immaculate Conception on August the 6th in the middle of summer. So having hardy flowers was real important, but having hardy flowers that all of a sudden you cannot use because the bride's going to be going, "Achoo, Achoo, Achoo, Achoo, Achoo, Achoo." I don't know how Bess changed all that at the last minute to still make things look beautiful because I had unhinged all the detailed planning, unintentionally, but nevertheless did. Never an admonition. It was just beautifully, beautifully, beautifully done, every detail. And I did not get to choose any of it.[23]

At the Shrine, Lady Bird Johnson was relieved to find that "Our missal had been marked 'stand,' 'sit,' 'kneel'—one of the thousand and one logistic triumphs for Bess, who knew that we, sitting in the front row, would have difficulty following the ritual."[24]

LUCI BAINES JOHNSON: The choice of the wedding cake was done by our White House pastry chef. But Bess knew that if something had a fruitcake connotation, that it would do two things. That was part of a Southern tradition, and it would stay moist longer. And so it tastes better later. And when you were building a cake up like that, you needed to make sure that that was part of it. She had little heart-shaped boxes with a piece of wedding cake in them to give to every person who attended the wedding to take home as a souvenir.

I heard that Bess also suggested a place for your honeymoon, and she even went there ahead of time.

LUCI BAINES JOHNSON: Rebekah Harkness had been instrumental in the White House acquiring a quality stage to perform on that could be moved in and out that was state of the art. In doing that, Bess had come to know her, and she knew that Mrs. Harkness had a home in the Bahamas that was secluded and private and could maybe be a fabulous honeymoon place. She wanted to go to make sure that it was not a part of a portion of Nassau that was racially restricting because there were places back then that were. She had to be able to make sure that she could provide my father that certainty, that they wouldn't have that surprise. Bess was all about doing her homework. There were lots of jobs that she was given where she didn't have at her fingertips all she needed to know. But she knew what she needed to know to get what she needed to know. She had no problem admitting her ignorance. She had a problem not having figured it out and how to resolve that. So that no place I went, nothing I did that would come back to embarrass my father.

The press was interested in everything, and especially in everything that you didn't want them to know. If you didn't want them to know it, then it became the forbidden fruit. Forbidden fruit's been interesting to human nature since the beginning of time. For years and years, even if you knew where your honeymoon was, you didn't tell anybody. That belonged alone to the bride and the groom. Well, there were four people in that marital bed. There was my husband, there was me, there was Bess's image, and then there was a Secret Service right at the door. I mean, Bess chose all these kinds of things. And we said, "Yes, Ma'am. Thank you very much." With her, she came to you with a recipe of events of what was going to happen—I think the discussion may have taken place with my mother—but by the time it got down to me, it was more of a "she said it, I did it" kind of thing. She was my mother's emissary. If Bess told me, it meant that Mother approved it. But she had found a route for us to leave the White House reception and get out and get transportation to get on a plane to go to New York City to stay at the home of Mary Lasker, my father's good friend. Spend the night there and then get on a commercial plane the next day to go to Nassau.[25]

Lynda's Wedding

"A few minutes before 4, I took my place at the head of the stairs," Lady Bird Johnson recorded of her daughter Lynda's wedding to Chuck Robb on December 9, 1967. "Bess, still calm in all the tumult, was the major-domo, and at her signal I took White House Aide Brian Lamb's arm and walked down the stairs past the throngs of wedding guests in the entrance foyer and down the hall, to the masses in the East Room."[26] That marked the first wedding ceremony in the White House since Theodore Roosevelt's spirited daughter Alice married Nicholas Longworth there in 1903.

You must have known then-Captain Robb before Lynda.

BESS ABELL: Yes, I did, because as social secretary, I interviewed the guys who were prospective social aides. So in effect I hired him and brought him to the White House where they really did meet. Chuck was around the White House for I guess almost a year before he and Lynda really had a date.

Lynda and Chuck Robb became engaged after a birthday party that White House curator Jim Ketchum threw at his home on Capitol Hill for

Childhood photo of Bess Clements. (Courtesy of the University of Kentucky Libraries.)

Earle Clements joined the Army in 1917, rising to the rank of captain. (Courtesy of the Abell family.)

Sara Blue Clements. (Courtesy of the Abell family.)

Fourteen-year-old Bess Clements dancing with Lieutenant Governor Wetherby at her father's inaugural ball, December 1947. (Whit Wooton, ©USA TODAY NETWORK.)

Sorority sisters Bess
Clements and Sue
Wetherby, daughter of
Kentucky governor
Lawrence Wetherby,
October 4, 1951.
(Charley Pence,
© USA TODAY
NETWORK.)

Bess Clements as
Kentucky's princess in the
1952 Cherry Blossom
Festival, with her escort,
Lieutenant P. Zuckerman,
at a party given by the
Kentucky Society of
Washington in Vice
President Alben W.
Barkley's office. (*The
Courier-Journal*, © USA
TODAY NETWORK.)

Bess Clements, 1954 graduate of the University of Kentucky. (Courtesy of the University of Kentucky Libraries.)

Senator Earle C. Clements (*left*), Senator Lyndon B. Johnson (*center*), and Senator Richard Russell (*right*). (Courtesy of the University of Kentucky Libraries.)

Senator Lyndon B. Johnson and Lady Bird Johnson host a reception in honor of the wedding of Tyler and Bess Abell, shown with her parents. (Courtesy of the Abell family.)

Tyler and Bess Abell greeting House Speaker Sam Rayburn. (Courtesy of the LBJ Presidential Library.)

Marriage and military life both began in January 1955 for Bess Clements Abell and Private Tyler Abell, who was stationed at Fort Devens, Massachusetts. (*The Courier-Journal*, ©USA TODAY NETWORK.)

Tyler and Bess Abell with their sons, Lyndon, three, and Dan, five, in 1964. (*The Courier-Journal*, ©USA TODAY NETWORK.)

White House social
secretary Bess Abell at
work in her White House
Office in 1965. (*The
Courier-Journal*, ©USA
TODAY NETWORK.)

Making a last-minute adjustment of a table setting in the White House state dining
room, Bess Abell oversees dinner preparations in honor of King Hussein of Jordan in
1964. (*The Courier-Journal*, ©USA TODAY NETWORK.)

Bess Abell assigns tasks to the White House military social aides before an event. Liz Carpenter called them "Abell's Army." (Courtesy of the Abell family.)

The Lady Bird
Special en route
to New Orleans,
October 1964.
From left to
right, Luci
Johnson
(holding sign),
Jan Shepard, Liz
Carpenter, Lady
Bird Johnson,
Joe Moran, and
Bess Abell.
(Courtesy of the
LBJ Presidential
Library.)

Liz Carpenter, John Roche,
Bess Abell, James Symington,
and Ashton Gonella serenade
President Lyndon B. Johnson
(*front and center*) aboard Air
Force One, returning from
Korea in 1966. (Yoichi
Okamoto, courtesy of the LBJ
Presidential Library.)

Bess Abell with her parents at the 1967 Kentucky Derby. (James N. Keen, ©USA TODAY NETWORK.)

Bess and Tyler Abell at the 1966 Kentucky Derby. They first met at the 1950 Derby and had their first date at the 1954 Derby. (Charles Fentress Jr., ©USA TODAY NETWORK.)

Bess Abell, Lady Bird Johnson, Tyler Abell, Lyndon Abell, Dan Abell, and President Lyndon B. Johnson in the Yellow Oval Room at the White House after Tyler's appointment as Chief of Protocol in 1968. (Yoichi Okamoto, courtesy of the LBJ Presidential Library.)

President Johnson greets Tyler and Bess Abell, with her father and mother, at the White House wedding of Lynda Bird Johnson and Chuck Robb. (Kevin Smith, courtesy of the LBJ Presidential Library.)

Lady Bird Johnson with her chief aides, Liz Carpenter, Bess Abell, and Ashton Gonella. (Yoichi Okamoto, courtesy of the LBJ Presidential Library.)

Joan Mondale made the vice president's house a showcase for the arts. She stands here at right with Lady Bird Johnson and Tyler and Bess Abell. (Courtesy of the Abell family.)

As executive assistant to Joan Mondale, Bess Abell helped the Mondales settle into the vice president's house at the Naval Observatory. (Robert Steinau, ©USA TODAY NETWORK.)

Bess and Tyler Abell seated with Margaret Lynn Brewer, a world civilization teacher in Scott County, Kentucky, after presenting her with the 2016 Earle C. Clements Innovation in Education Award. (Matt Goins, courtesy of the University of Kentucky Libraries.)

On the front terrace of the Kentucky Governor's Mansion are grandchildren Solomon Abell and Sarah Abell, seated, and behind them Bess Abell, Sue Wetherby, son Dan Abell, daughter-in-law Ann Hunter, and Tyler Abell during a "Kentucky roots" family trip. (Courtesy of the Abell family.)

Bess Abell poses in the Red Room of the White House during a visit by President Francois Tombalbaye of Chad on October 2, 1968. (Robert Knudsen, courtesy of the LBJ Presidential Library.)

Warrie Lynn Smith, a close friend of Lynda's. On the morning of the party, Smith called to ask if they could add two guests to the dinner. "Lynda flew in very late and very upset last night," she explained. "She apparently has parted company with George [Hamilton], and she'd like to come over. And there's one aide who always makes her happy and smile. His name is Chuck Robb and he would like to come along."[27]

JAMES R. KETCHUM: She and Robb had dated a few times before then, but never really to a point that they had after they left our house about 11:30 at night. They had a long discussion and, at some point in that discussion, he asked her to marry him. She then went back home, where Mrs. Johnson was in bed with the president, and Lynda wants to talk to her mother. So she goes in on her hands and knees and she pulls at her mother until her mother wakes up and says, "What?" Lynda motions to her, so she came back out into the hall with her and they sat down, and Lynda told her mother that Chuck Robb has asked her to be his wife. This then started what ended up being a December wedding.[28]

What was it like getting married in the White House?
LYNDA JOHNSON ROBB: Oh, it was the best of times and the worst of times. Getting married was wonderful, period. It was so exciting, and you had all the pomp and ceremony. It was also difficult because there were so many people we *had* to invite, that my parents felt that we needed to invite. People who were not necessarily my close personal friends or even my father's and mother's close personal friends, but people that were in positions that we needed to invite. So I look back and I think, "Why did we invite this person?" And that was because they were some leader in the Senate or somebody in the House that was a real good friend, helping Daddy on a piece of legislation.

Then, of course, this was the time when the Vietnam War was really beginning to get hot. Luci got married in 1966, and I laughingly say that people liked us better then and she got better wedding gifts. By the time I got married, we didn't have as many friends. We certainly didn't have as many that felt like they needed to send as nice a gift on occasions.[29]

There was a certain solemnity about my wedding. Because we knew that all these gifts were going to be packed up because we weren't moving into a house. He was going to be going away. Because of the war, I think, ours was a little bit more constrained and serious. It wasn't quite as light-hearted. When Luci got married, it was before the Vietnam War got to be an issue. Now, having it at the White House, I never thought that would protect us in any sort of way from any demonstration. Probably, I was just self-centered enough that it just wasn't an issue. Bess took care of all of the little details. I picked out my dress and I picked out my bridesmaids. But I always knew that we'd be doing it in the East Room.[30]

There were so many people that came to the wedding that Chuck and I never really got to see. There was one friend of his that drove from Ohio. People came from all over. A lot of my friends, high school friends, grade school friends that I didn't ever really have a chance to talk to because after the ceremony we went back upstairs because they had to fix up the East Room where we were married. They had to take down the altar and push the people into another area, and it took a long time. Then we went down and stood in line.

White House receiving lines are different than most wedding receiving lines, aren't they?

LYNDA JOHNSON ROBB: Standing in line with Daddy sometimes could be a long ordeal because he would stop and talk to everybody, and we would try to get a picture with each person. I stood in line for hours and hours, and I had a very heavy wedding dress. It was a wonderful dress, a beautiful dress, but it was satin, and it had beading on it. My shoulders were just aching because it was very, very heavy. That was one of my least favorite things about it.[31]

Well, everybody felt they had to go through the receiving line. And Daddy had a picture taken with them. We had a picture taken with almost everybody. Then we spent days and days and days after we got back signing the pictures to people who came. Of course, it wasn't just having a picture taken with the bride, because receiving-line pictures are never any good. They're just awful. I am facing one direction. You are facing another direction. Someone's over there. You have half of Mother and a little bit of Daddy. And there is Chuck's dress uniform. So the pictures are not anything worth having, except that, one, it proves you were there; and two, since Daddy was on one side of me, you got a picture of the president, which for a lot of people was a big deal. Daddy had photographers take pictures all the time. But he knew that for a lot of people that would be a wonderful souvenir for them to have, a picture with the president.

Daddy would stop and talk to everyone, and say, "Can you remember when Lynda was just this tall?" A lot of them had grown up with me. So that was wonderful. But it was a lot of people. And we didn't have any terrible disasters. Bess and Liz worked so well together. They both had a lot of laughter in them. They were not very, very solemn, official, protocol—they veered on the side of opening things up, not closing them down. Somehow, we found ways to keep everybody happy. We didn't have any disasters that happened—I can't think of any.

We did have one terrible hitch, but it wasn't Bess's fault. We were getting married in the afternoon and going off on our honeymoon. In order to be able to get out of town in time, we had chartered a little plane. It was going to fly us to our honeymoon destination. A night or two before the wedding, Daddy said, "Oh. You're going to have to cancel that. Because you don't know this, but the company that owns the charter company is going to be bought by one of the big military industrial complexes," the ones that Mr. Eisenhower so worried about. So here we are, on our wedding night, and having nowhere to go. I don't know if Bess had worked that out. Whatever she decided to do, and whatever advice she may or may not have given my husband, I don't recall. We did fine, but it was not what we planned.[32]

Afterwards you thought, "Oh, gosh, I didn't enjoy this" in the same sort of way you would like to. Because they said, "You have to leave now because nobody else can leave until you leave." I really wanted to go back downstairs to the party and enjoy it. It was wonderful pomp and circumstance, but some of the ordinary things I missed out on. But it was a beautiful wedding, and we never could have done it without the help of lots and lots of people, particularly Bess, [longtime staff member and family friend] Willie Day Taylor, and Liz Taylor.[33]

What's the difference obviously between a White House wedding and a non-White House wedding?

BESS ABELL: They were two entirely different weddings.[34] Lynda's wedding in the White House was much easier because although it was a little more complicated moving people around, you had a lot of people help you move those people around. Also, I had borrowed from Admiral [William] Rayburn out at the CIA four walkie-talkies like the Secret Service now have so that we had little earplugs. I had one, Carol Carlyle had one, and Barbara Keehn had one, and then maybe the lead social aide so that we knew what was happening where.

The guests came through the East Entrance, like practically all guests come in now, and then came through the east corridor, and then up the staircase and into the East Room. We did not have enough room for chairs for anybody except Chuck's mom and dad and Lynda's mom and dad. I think everybody else stood. So there were people in the East Room where the ceremony took place, and then there were people out in the hall behind stanchions. There were also various press people who were stationed along the way so that afterwards they could have a get-together and give a pool report for all the reporters that were not there. One reporter who was responsible for giving her part of the pool report just said, "Well, I'm really sorry, but I was so enamored of looking at George Hamilton [who attended the wedding] that I didn't see anything else. I'm really sorry, but I can tell you everything about George, who he talked to, what he was wearing, and everything."[35]

We had this altar in the East Room that we had made out of putting together some pieces of the stage that was used in the East Room. They were panels that looked very much like the paneling in the East Room itself, and so there was a little riser and then these panels and then a lot of greenery and so forth. There was a little hole that was drilled in the panels and the greenery for a reporter to be behind that, so that she could observe the bride and groom, see whether or not they had fainted or stuck out their tongue at one another, or whatever, and that person who fit there was Bonnie Angelo, a great, great reporter who was at that time with the *Time* bureau in Washington. Later she was, I think, head of the bureau in New York, and then head of the bureau in London, and so forth. But she was the only reporter who was small enough to fit in that space, so that was Bonnie's assignment. She got that assignment because of size, not because of great intellect. But she could have gotten it because of that, too.[36]

LYNDA JOHNSON ROBB: We had people standing just cheek-to-cheek. We came down the stairs and turned left to go into the East Room. You had just a small amount of space between these people on both sides, wanting to see the dress and everything. It was a short service. Everybody had to stand, except a few older relatives who did have chairs in the East Room. You had all these people in the East Room and then you had to, somehow, get them out of the East Room and find a place to put them, so you could set the East Room up as a place to have the cake.[37]

CAROL CARLYLE: The wedding was quite a chore. We had to set up the East Room and expanded areas for the ceremony. Then we had to take people to the other side of the White House while we tore that down and set that up for a sit-down. Normally, when we had an event, we had walkie-talkies so we could be in different places executing this event because there was no way we could walk around and get from one side of the room to the other in thirty seconds because there were so many guests. I was on the stage when Lyndon Johnson and Lynda Bird were coming down the stairs into the ceremony. I would have to cue Bess to cue the orchestra to cue the next person with our equipment. This was very modern at the time for us to have and do. But I can remember being well-equipped to execute the event. And I don't think there was a mishap at all from my vantage point. It turned out to be spectacular, and the pictures show it.[38]

BRIAN LAMB: Bess was the one in charge of running the wedding, and we were obviously all involved. It was fun. There was at least a twenty-five-page directory on every step of the way on what the wedding would do. We had meetings together with all the aides on what we were to do. She ran it like a military operation. She always knew what she was doing. And by the way, the thing that was interesting about Bess is everybody liked her. All the aides liked her.[39]

8

In Time of War and Protest

Bess Abell was more than a social secretary, commented presidential aide Jack Valenti: "She was an emollient, softening every crisis with an elegant imperturbability which mystified and calmed me. The rafters could be shuddering and the entire White House falling down about our heads and Bess would stand there, undismayed, smiling easily, never a tinge of despair or panic. She never raised her voice. The words would come slowly, every edge of hysteria carefully smoothed away, with only sounds of softness patting one's ears."[1] These attributes helped greatly as the war in Vietnam escalated, interrupting White House events and providing a trying backdrop to day-to-day living.

BESS ABELL: Well, first of all, you have to imagine, Lynda and Luci's rooms faced Pennsylvania Avenue. There were demonstrators out there through the evening. They would go into their rooms to go to bed at night, and there were chanters out there, "Hey, hey, LBJ, how many kids did you kill today?" And on it would go.[2]

The White House Festival of the Arts

In 1964 LBJ named Princeton University history professor Eric Goldman as special consultant and liaison with the academic world. Johnson expected Goldman to persuade the nation's top scholars, thinkers, writers, and teachers "to generate fresh, new and imaginative ideas for the benefit of the government."[3] Working with Bess, Goldman helped plan the 1965 White House Festival of the Arts. She had in mind an event dedicated to performance artists, while he wanted to include writers and intellectuals. She warned him that they could be "troublesome," but he made his choices and issued invitations. One went to poet Robert Lowell, who promptly accepted but soon afterward changed his mind. He withdrew publicly, citing his objections to the president's foreign policies and asserting, "Every serious artist knows that he cannot enjoy public celebrations without making public commitments." His declaration caused an uproar. "We didn't miss Robert Lowell at all," Liz Carpenter commented, "but the press, with their insatiable appetite for controversy, spent most of their talents on who wasn't there, rather than who was."[4]

Lowell's withdrawal pressured other invited speakers to take a stand. Critic Dwight Macdonald attended, but circulated a petition denouncing Johnson's foreign policies. Novelist John Hersey insisted on reading passages from his nonfiction account of the bombing of Hiroshima. Lady Bird Johnson saw this as an affront to both Presidents Truman and Johnson. She pointedly told Goldman, "The president and I do not want this man to come here and read this." He decided not to take her admonition as an order and warned that Hersey would pull out of the festival and create more negative publicity. Liz Carpenter suggested that since Hersey had been invited as a novelist, he should be asked to read from one of his novels, but Goldman would not compromise. He hoped that reviews of the festival would credit the White House for offering a salute to the American arts that "made no compromise with quality or conventionality," but instead had to admit that the event had been "an unmitigated disaster." Shut off from access to the president, Goldman resigned the following year and proceeded to write a defense of his role in the affair.[5]

White House curator Jim Ketchum watched these events unfold.

JAMES R. KETCHUM: It was a who's who in every single area of performing arts. You had ballet out on the stage on the South Lawn where you had the symphony. You never would have tried this even if you'd had a year to plan for it, but the fact that they only had about eight to ten weeks! Goldman on behalf of Johnson would pick up the phone, and the director of the Whitney [Museum of American Art] would say, "Certainly we can do this." They brought in the Smithsonian to help construct. They brought in the National Gallery of Art to do a lot of the registrarial work, the Library of Congress for prints and photographs. It was all the king's horses and all the king's men. They really did put Humpty Dumpty back together again, except for the Dwight Macdonald flap and what Robert Lowell had been saying to the press.

Yet these people who did show up, with the exception of Macdonald, no matter what their objections to the war they put their best foot forward and were extremely polite. But Johnson just could not stand to think that he was being personally taken on by somebody who was passing a petition around. I think most of the opponents of the war were quite horrified to think that was happening as well. That is not quite the way the White House saw its role as far as being the host with the most. When you think of the checklists of the Endowments [for the Arts and Humanities] and other enterprises such as that, it showed an administration that was absolutely daring in its attempt to bring front and center for the American public to appreciate and understand and to honor these individuals and what they had contributed. We'd come a long way from Fred Waring and the Pennsylvanians during the Eisenhower administration to Marianne Moore reading her poetry in the Red Room.[6]

BESS ABELL: The time that protest invaded the White House—I tried to avoid that because I kept track of these full-page ads that ran in the *New York Times* every Sunday, sometimes during the week. They would have people, artists, writers, signing petitions to the president. I kept track of those because I did not want to invite those people to a state dinner. I did not want them to be sending ugly regrets. We did not need that. We wanted a pause. But an intellectual had been added to the White House staff, a man from Princeton named Eric Goldman. Eric had this idea of a White House Festival of the Arts, which we had already been thinking about in my office. I was doing X part of it and he was going to do Y part of it, which was inviting writers to come and read their works.

I was really concerned about that because I thought that he ought to compare his list of writers to my list of *New York Times* advertisements. But he didn't. When I said, "Now, Eric, we want to have the writers come in the day before and test the mics, to be sure that the sound levels are right, and then have the podium at the height that they want and make sure there are no surprises." He said, "Oh, you just want people to come in there so you can censor them!" I said, "Eric, I promise you, they will be glad to have been here and not just arrive that morning and be presented with lights in their eyes." So we finally went ahead with that, and they did come. Several of them came over and thanked me and thanked Eric for having them come see the room and test things out.

Eric had invited Robert Lowell. Lowell had written an open letter saying how terrible the Johnsons were, and how terrible this whole administration was, and he was not going to come to the White House.[7]

You tangled a bit with Eric Goldman on that, didn't you?

BESS ABELL: Eric was always a problem. He was a prima donna. My feeling was always that the White House did not have room but for one prima donna, and that was the man who earned the right to be. I really did not have much use for other people who needed their hands held, and Eric was one of those people. I never did have a great deal of respect for him.

In his chapter on the Arts Festival, I think I was the main villain, and I think maybe Mrs. Johnson was the next main villain even before the president. But I understand that in the rest of the book he had some terribly nice things to say about her. I'm afraid that Eric's ego got in the way of his historical perspective in talking about the Arts Festival.

Eric takes that as his own idea, the brainstorm that had been bursting within his breast trying to find an outlet, lo, these many months since he had arrived at the White House. I don't detract from him for it because I think that he did have good thoughts. But he takes credit for that when I really think I deserve a lot of the credit for it. I had originally talked to the president and Mrs. Johnson about it before Eric ever got involved in it. He brought me into it when I went over to his office one afternoon and said: "Eric, we've just got to do something cultural!" He acts like I don't even know who John Hersey is. So the whole thing really leaves me sort of cold. Eric was a real bad egg in the whole thing. He says that he didn't know why the president delayed so long in planning the Arts Festival. He knows very well why the president delayed so long, because the president told us all why he delayed so long, and we knew it at the time!

It was because of the war in Vietnam, and it was because the president had received some criticism for entertaining at all in the White House. A number of people thought we should have gone back to the days of World War II when there was absolutely no entertaining in the White House. I did not agree with that, and I do not think it was purely because I would not have had anything to do if we had traveled that route.

What was the president's reaction as the Festival of the Arts began to be more and more troublesome?

BESS ABELL: His reaction was—I think Eric was accurate on this—to have less and less to do with it and wondering why the hell he had gotten involved in it in the first place. But the point is that the problems did not have to come. The problems were basically created by Eric. When the president finally went ahead with it, I guess I thought that I was in charge of it and Eric thought that he was in charge of it. I'm always somebody who tries to work with somebody else. Eric had some marvelous, very, very good, useful ideas—a lot of them a whale of a lot better than mine. He certainly knew the poets and the writers better than I did.

134 WASHINGTON'S IRON BUTTERFLY

But I would never have called Robert Lowell and asked him to participate in this. If he was a conscientious objector in World War II, he would certainly have a problem with the president about [Vietnam], and therefore, I would not have selected him. When Eric told me he had called him, I just really nearly had a heart attack. I said, "You can't have!" He said, "No, no, you have it all wrong. Robert Lowell realizes what we are trying to do, and he realizes that even though he does not agree with the president's foreign policy, that he is grateful for what he is doing in the arts, and therefore he wants to be a part of it." Of course, the next we heard, Robert Lowell had written an open letter to the president and delivered it to the *New York Times* about a day before it reached the president.

Goldman describes a couple of occasions in which you and/or Mrs. Johnson talked to him about the guest list and the selections that "the guests will read," in the case of Arthur Miller, John Hersey, and Mark Van Doren. Were you talking on President Johnson's instructions?

BESS ABELL: No. I wanted to do something that would be a plus for the Johnsons and a plus for the arts. I did not see any need in giving a forum to people who were going to embarrass the president. I think, however, as it turned out, I did wish that the president had come to the Arts Festival and had given that day to it and had talked with these people informally; that he had walked around with John Hersey and talked with him informally. I do think that the president really made a mistake in shutting himself off from these people. I think that even if they did not sell him on their point of view, that he could have given them an understanding of his problems that would have stayed with them longer. But when a man is president and he only has twenty-four hours in every day and he's got to sleep a few of them and he has all these things coming at him from all different directions, and he says, "I don't have time to do that. Can't these people know that I just made a speech on television the day before yesterday and said all these things?" But you just have to keep saying them. It's just like advertising Coca-Cola. When you get so you just cannot stand to hear it anymore, I guess that is pretty good advertising.

Did you or Mrs. Johnson or anyone else try to talk the president into spending more time there?

BESS ABELL: I don't know whether Mrs. Johnson did or not, but I did unsuccessfully. And I think that maybe Jack Valenti tried to encourage him to spend more time there, but it was really a lost cause. I was glad that he came to the dinner that night. And, of course, the credibility gap has always been with the White House or any other political office or any other business office. You tell white lies, and our white lie in that was that the president never had planned to be involved in anything else. I do not think the president, when he signs up to say, "Yes, you can have an arts festival at the White House," he doesn't simultaneously sign up to say, "and I will be there for twelve hours," from poetry readings through a jazz concert at the end.

Eric's whole approach to this was really different than mine. He looked on it not as a college seminar because that is low-rating the Arts Festival and low-rating what Eric thought of it. But that was more what he thought of it, a very free-flowing sort of thing. I, on the other hand, looked at it as a tightly programmed piece of entertainment. It was too complicated not to have a tight schedule. The only people that he had contacted were the writers. I had gotten in touch with the drama groups, with the symphony group, with Duke Ellington, and with the Joffrey Ballet. I had reached all the narrators who were to introduce the programs, except for Mark Van Doren, whom Eric had spoken with.

But Eric could not understand why we needed this rehearsal, and I tried to tell him that you cannot have a ballet troupe get up on a stage and not have rehearsed it on that stage and with that lighting and that music, and then he understood that. And I said, "The same thing is true with the writers. They need to come here and see that stage and try out the microphone and see if the lights are shining in their eyes. This is the first thing on the schedule, and we want to do it right." And he said, no, he would have no part of it, and I said, "Well, with your permission I would like to call these people and not make it a requirement but to explain to them why we want to do it." And each one that I called to ask if they could come down on Sunday before the festival to see the stage, test the microphone, check the stands, test the lights, was grateful and said so at the time of the call and on Sunday when they were there. Basically, they said, "I'm terribly nervous about this, and this will give me a much easier feeling."

When Mark Van Doren read his introduction on Sunday, I was really just sick at my stomach and sick at heart because his whole tone was more Robert Lowell. You could tell that he was in a way distressed about it. So I spoke to Eric after that and I said, "I really hate to see the Arts Festival open this way. If it does, that's going to be the whole story of the day, and there are too many other wonderful things that are happening here, and it's probably going to be the whole story anyway. The whole Robert Lowell thing will be the lead of everybody's column, both in New York and in London. But I hate to see it start out on that vein." I think Eric later wrote that

I was shaking my finger in his face and saying, "If you don't do something about that, I'll tell the Big Man on you," or something like that. Anyway, whatever he has me saying is so out of character with me that even if I was furious with him, I would not have done it.

Eric said yes, he thought that was a good point, and he was going to go back to the hotel where the Van Dorens were staying over, at the Hay-Adams Hotel, and discuss it with him. And he did and Mr. Van Doren did change the tone of his introduction.[8]

Eric Goldman puzzled others on the White House staff, who held conflicting views about him, including curator Jim Ketchum and special assistant to the president Douglass Cater, who had his own roots in the intellectual community.

JAMES R. KETCHUM: Goldman was gone about six months after the Festival of the Arts. He had a terrible time getting along with Bess and Liz. I don't know why. Boy, he was a super guy. I think that Johnson gave people a little bit of freedom, but not so much that he could not reach out in about three seconds and grab them back. But there is no way to describe what a decent, interesting person Goldman was.[9]

DOUGLASS CATER: When I arrived in May of 1964 Eric was already there. I had read that he was to sort of serve as the transmission belt for ideas from the intellectual community. I remember I contacted him about prospective ideas he might have received that would be useful for a speech that the president was going to give out at Irvine, California. This was at the dedication of a new campus out there. But I had comparatively little dealings with him over the years. I found he was a rather prickly kind of fellow, and frequently it was more difficult to deal with him than to leave him alone.[10]

Lady Bird Johnson recorded that postmortem meeting in her diary. "We discussed the one-by-one hammer blows of the front-page stories—New York Times, New York Herald Tribune, even the Washington Post. All of them seemed to delight in faulting their country and their president. They accented only on Robert Lowell's not coming, John Hersey's coming and lecturing, Dwight Macdonald's passing around a petition for his fellow guests to sign, disapproving of the president's foreign policy. There is some uncertainty as to whether he got four or seven signatures out of three hundred guests. I'll take a 293 to 7 majority any time!"[11]

Antiwar Protestors

It was a period of great turmoil in the country, much of it relating to the war, but also cultural upheaval and the assassinations. How much of the White House is a cocoon and how much of that outside reality penetrates?

BESS ABELL: Oh, you're very aware of it. You're very aware of it, because you read the newspaper and people talk to you, and if you were me, you have a mother-in-law who is marching against the war. One time, Luvie [Pearson] called me and said, "Can you make arrangements for me to pick up Danny and Lyndon after school? I want to take them to an outing." I said, "Sure, Granny. Where are you all going this afternoon?" She said, "Well, actually, Dr. Spock is in town and we are going down to picket the White House." And I said, "Granny, no, you can't do that with Danny and Lyndon. I don't want my son named Lyndon Abell to be down there saying, 'Oh, my Mommy works there.'" I said, "Please, take them to the zoo or something, or go see Dr. Spock yourself, but don't take my kids down there."

We were very aware of what was going on, and it tampered with any guest list that I had anything to do with. My office, Barbara Keehn and I usually added what we called "sparklies" to the list, which would be the movie stars, entertainers, football players, or Olympic swimmers or skaters, something that we would sprinkle into the guest list. So we paid attention to that and when arranging entertainment for state dinners.[12]

Did you ever have an entertainer refuse because they wanted to be paid or would not come because of politics?

BESS ABELL: No, because we didn't ask them. Most of them usually came from New York. I think we sent them shuttle tickets, and a driver would pick them up at the airport. We would put them up at the Hay-Adams Hotel. They would come to dinner and had a program with their name on it. They were treated well. One of the many wonderful things about being at the White House were those White House telephone operators who could find people. This will really date me, but one time I was trying to reach Bing Crosby. I reached Mr. Crosby, and we were chatting, and I said, "Mr. Crosby, where did the White House operators find you?" He said, "I'm on a sailboat off Tahiti." So they were wonderful.[13]

Bess "borrowed" Carol Carlyle, a secretary for Tyler at the post office, for her own staff.

CAROL CARLYLE: When you worked for Bess, you didn't discuss politics on a daily basis. We had a mission. We had a job. We were running the

White House events. So, sometimes, you didn't focus on what was going on around you outside because we were so busy. It was the Vietnam War, whatever human rights that Johnson was pushing. You were aware of it and you were involved, but your mission was making the White House events function. So sometimes that wasn't as strong a presence in your thinking.[14]

BESS ABELL: Mrs. Johnson had a series of luncheons, and she actually started this on foreign trips when Johnson was vice president. The first foreign trip that she went on, the State Department planned her itinerary, and they did not know what to do with the wife except send her to an orphanage or hospital. Mrs. Johnson just knew, knew in her bones that there were more interesting and more useful things that she could be doing on these trips with her husband, so she asked if she could have an opportunity to meet interesting women.

In Tehran, instead of having a luncheon where she would be seeing the same women who would be at the dinner that night with their husbands, she met the dean of women at the university; she met the woman who ran a travel agency; she met a woman who ran a boutique; she met a woman who made jewelry; she met the first woman lawyer in Iran who had written her own marriage contract. I remember being there with one woman, I think this was maybe the university president or dean of women, and this woman was being asked by an American Embassy wife, "What does your husband do?" She pulled herself up, and she said, "I'm here because of what I do, not because of what my husband does." And these women were all so pleased and delighted to be recognized for something that they did.

She continued that at home and abroad. We never had a good name for these luncheons. They were called, very unattractively, I thought, but we never could beat something with nothing. They were called "Women Doers' Luncheons."[15]

Eartha Kitt

On January 18, 1968, Lady Bird Johnson held a Women Doers' Luncheon on juvenile delinquency, and President Johnson stopped by to make a few remarks. When the president started to leave, the singer and actress Eartha Kitt rose from the audience to confront him about what he was going to do about "delinquent parents," those who had to work all day and could not look after their children. After he left, Kitt denounced the Vietnam War: "We send the best of this country off to be shot and maimed. They rebel in the streets. They take pot and they will get high. They don't want to go to school, because they are going to be snatched off from their mothers to be shot in Vietnam." The first lady rebutted: "Because there is a war on—and I pray that there will be a just and honest peace—that doesn't give us a free ticket not to try to work for better things—against crime in the streets, and for better education and better health for our people."[16]

As the public protest over the Vietnam War increased, did that kind of problem show up in other parties and in assembling guest lists for other occasions?

BESS ABELL: Absolutely. And, of course, we did not always save ourselves from it. But I used to clip out of the Sunday *New York Times* those full-page advertisements signed by a long list of people, a lot of them in the entertainment world, that were saying, "Dear Mr. President: You have killed so many North and South Vietnamese. How can you sleep at night?" It would have been very foolish on my part to invite someone to come and sing at the White House, or do a poetry reading at the White House, who had the month before or the week before signed one of those ads. In the first place, I think that the person who got the invitation would have been the most surprised individual of all.

It's one reason that we ended up having so much ballet toward the end. Every once in a while, somebody would say, "Gee, the president really likes ballet!" And I'd say, "Oh, yes, he likes ballet and music too." But the truth of the matter is that ballet dancers don't generally have political opinions, and the rest of the world of the arts—certainly the folk singers and the actors—it wasn't chic to be in that world unless you were marching on the White House against the war in Vietnam. I felt this with a number of my friends. I know that Peter, Paul, and Mary, the folk singers, spent an evening with Tyler and me, really late into the night after a concert of theirs. I think we wound up about four-thirty in the morning, talking about Vietnam. And they said at that time that they had not gone over to the other side, but how difficult it was for them because all of their friends, and even their manager, was really down on them about it.

By performing in the White House, were they subject to social pressures among their peers?

BESS ABELL: No, because they did perform in the White House and they did some things for us in the campaign. But that was in 1964, and that was before it had really gotten chic to march on the White House and march on the Pentagon.[17]

Of course, you also had Eartha Kitt.

BESS ABELL: We did have Eartha Kitt, but not to entertain, and she was not on *my* guest list, either.

LIZ CARPENTER: Eartha Kitt was chosen because she had testified in behalf of the president's bill [on juvenile delinquency] before a House committee. She had talked about what could be done on crime. If Kitt had come to the White House and told about the ballet classes that she teaches as a volunteer in Watts, it would have been a whole different ball game. But she came and for reasons that I do not know but only could guess that she was a declining actress looking for a stage. She decided to throw in the Vietnam War and get fiery about it, and so she really undermined her own race because for the first time, a First Lady was trying to tackle the subject of crime, and she diverted everyone's attention to Kitt and Vietnam while someone was trying to address her problems.

I checked her out with two or three people at Justice and so forth and asked if her name had ever showed up on any kind of ad protesting the president on Vietnam. It had not. It still has not. In fact, as far as the Vietnam War, the day that she appeared at the White House luncheon, she had asked a congressman to make an appointment for her at the Pentagon to see about going to Vietnam to entertain the troops. She did not believe enough entertainers were helping our boys. She canceled the invitation, and the most surprised man in Washington was the Army colonel who she had an appointment with at four o'clock that day to work out a two-week trip touring in Vietnam, when he heard on the radio of her blast at the first lady.[18]

BESS ABELL: At the luncheon, Kitt was late, late, late. The ladies already had sherry and orange juice in the Blue Room, and we were getting ready to take her plate off the table. The ladies had gone into the Family Dining Room, and just about that time, Kitt came up the stairs to the main floor. She came across the foyer, this large marble foyer, and she was doing large dancers' leaps. It was quite stunning and beautiful, but I thought she was going to crash into me in the doorway. So I moved sideways, and she went into the Blue Room, and I said, "Oh, Miss Kitt, the luncheon is actually started but I will take you to your table." She went in and sat down.

The butler who served that table said she never ate a thing, but he kept filling up her wine glass and she kept emptying it. So I guess she was high as a kite. The president came in and was making some remarks to the women who were there, saying how terrific it was, and women could make anything happen. As soon as the president left, Eartha Kitt stood up and started talking to Mrs. Johnson about how terrible it was that we were sending these boys halfway around the world to die, and she had just had this baby pulled out of her gut and she didn't want him going over and dying in Southeast Asia.

Betty Hughes, whose husband was the governor of New Jersey, and the Hugheses had a batch of children and some of them were serving in the Pacific. I will say, it's the one time I remember Mrs. Johnson being taken off guard, but Betty Hughes picked up the ball and ran with it, about what a wonderful country we are and we are here to talk about "What Citizens Can Do to Insure Safe Streets" and make good things happen for our country.[19]

I actually have a photograph somewhere of Liz and me, taken that day, because we were, the two of us, sitting at that big table in the State Dining Room being served lunch while this was going on in the other room. I think it's in a scrapbook that Liz gave me, called "Low Moments at the White House with Bess Abell."[20]

Do you think that this was sort of an impromptu decision on her part, or do you think that it was all along calculated?

LIZ CARPENTER: I think that she was always looking for headlines. I think they could have taken any kind of turn. To the best of my information, and I did considerable checking, it happened in an impromptu way. She has a lot of problems. One of them was she was dieting, and she didn't eat a bite at the lunch. She had had some drinks. The second thing is she is a declining actress looking for publicity, and she was determined she was going to get it. Her agent had called me and asked me if she could make a speech. I said, "No, we have speakers." But it ended up that she got the headlines.

However, here again, Mrs. Johnson was determined to convert what that bad blast had been into constructive action. We got ten thousand letters on the Eartha Kitt thing. The phones rang off the hook, and I had the staff in my office to take every single phone call, who called, and what they said. They were 95 percent in behalf of Mrs. Johnson and indignant that anyone would talk to a first lady that way as a guest in their home. But about five national organizations put out press releases as a result of hearing about it. Maybe they wouldn't have heard about it if there hadn't been that angry voice, so that we got our story out. And to every one of the ten thousand letters, we sent a letter saying, "It is too bad that angry voice tried to turn our attention, but if you were serious about doing something about crime in your city, here are eighteen things you can do," and we listed each one of the eighteen things, such as, "You can have a survey and check on the amount of street lighting in a neighborhood because where streets are lighted, less crime occurs." And so good things came out of it, but it was an awful moment, of course.[21]

EARTHA KITT: I didn't want to go, because I thought oh, those politicians, those luncheons what are they going [to] mean? But the White House kept calling me and saying, "Yes, Mrs. Johnson definitely wants you to come." So okay, I go. . . . The title of the invitation was "Why is there so much juvenile delinquency in the streets of America?"

I heard a lot of people get up and say things like, "Well, it's very nice, Mrs. Johnson, that you're planting seeds along Route 66, and if you put trees in the center of Harlem on Seventh Avenue, I think that would—" What was on the invitation? All of them were fawning up to the boss, so to speak. . . . Finally, I raised my hand to a point where she would recognize me, and I said, "I think we've forgotten about what the subject of this luncheon is all about." I recited what the subject was. I said one of the reasons why our boys are running away from the United States—because they come to me wherever I am in the world and they tell me what they feel. Our position in Vietnam, they don't like it: "We've been there long enough to realize that we cannot win this war. It's a silly war, it's an unwinnable war, and we don't want to go. It's not that we don't love America, but we don't want to be involved in this war." So I told her what the boys had told me. I said that's why they smoke pot because they just want to go to sleep until everything is over." . . . One woman was sitting to my right. She leaned over and whispered to me, "Thank you, Eartha, for saying what you said. We all feel the same way, but unfortunately 75 percent of the women in this room's husbands work for President Johnson." So they couldn't say anything about what they really felt. I found out what was actually felt when I was in a car . . . and I heard on the radio, "Eartha Kitt made Mrs. Johnson cry." I didn't see her cry.[22]

What was Mrs. Johnson's reaction after the luncheon was over?
LIZ CARPENTER: Deep despair because no one enjoys having such an ugly exchange. And it came as such a shock, and I think she was very blue about it. I think she really, you know, you reexamine your own thoughts and think how in the heck did this woman get on the list? And that was one of the questions we had to answer. You think, "Gosh, I should have been smarter than to invite her." We didn't know much about her. The only thing

we knew was that she was one of the few persons in the performing arts who had ever made a statement on crime.

I think we all felt that we could kick ourselves for doing it, and probably I suffered more than anyone, because I had gotten the name. And you did not know how it was going to come out for twenty-four hours. But we got busy fast to make it come out right. You can't bury your head in the sand on those things. You've got to face it. And Mrs. Johnson was never one to turn her face from a problem just because it's ugly.[23]

JAMES R. KETCHUM: The next day it was Mrs. Johnson who was very, very upset, who did not know whether she had handled things properly or not. That's all she wanted to do. She wanted to be assured. Liz and Bess and I were the three people that were there. Liz and Bess assured her that she was just perfect. But it bothered her.[24]

An Unexpected Summit

In June 1967, during the Vietnam War and immediately following the Six-Day War in the Middle East, President Johnson held an unexpected summit meeting with Soviet premier Alexei Kosygin in Glassboro, New Jersey. State visits include an exchange of gifts, but the impromptu meeting left no time to shop.

Is there a backlog of gifts for when you've got to do something in a hurry? How does Mrs. Johnson reach in her knapsack and pull out something appropriate?

LIZ CARPENTER: Well, by having Bess, who has a whole office full of kind of standard things [and] in this case, a gold Hamilton wristwatch. Bess keeps a few on hand, and we happened to have the Early American mirror, which was used by bridal couples in New England in the early days and was a nice antique to give, that had been planned for a subsequent visit. We had to pull up something in a hurry, so those were handy and available. No, there wasn't any time to go out and shop in this case. There are some standard books that Mrs. Johnson likes to give.

So she anticipates that kind of thing?

LIZ CARPENTER: Yes, and I think through experience Bess has learned to never be caught empty-handed. The president told Bess to spend imagination more than money. I think that our gifts were much more thoughtful and personal. We didn't just give Steuben glass out on an assembly line. You often tried to find out a hobby of a person and then choose a gift that went with this hobby. The president really enjoys gadgets, and so he liked to give Accutron clocks and that kind of thing. But often you could do a gift for practically nothing.

For instance, when Bess found out that the prime minister of Japan had been a postman, she found an antique post office box through her husband, who worked at the post office department, and fixed it up. And the prime minister was absolutely enchanted. When we found out that Éamon de Valera, the president of Ireland, had been born in this country, we found his birth certificate and had it framed nicely. There's something that's tasteful, meaningful, costs twenty-five dollars in contrast to five hundred dollars.[25]

The 1968 Disturbances

On March 31, 1968, President Johnson announced on national television that he would not run for reelection. Five days later, the assassination of Dr. Martin Luther King Jr. led to major riots across the country and in Washington, DC. Fires and looting erupted just blocks from the White House.

Lady Bird Johnson was in Corpus Christi, Texas, on April 8, 1968, when she reported in her diary: "Bess called me from the White House. Obviously she was very much upset. She did not think we should go on with the state dinner on Wednesday night. The curfew was still in force. She described the incessant barrage of TV coverage . . . of looting and fires . . . of seeing policemen stand by while people knocked the windows out of stores, grabbed TV sets and loaded them into cars. . . . It was as though I were talking to an inhabitant of another planet."[26]

Patricia Perkins Andringa was then serving as a White House intern.

Did you ever see Bess very discouraged about something?

PATRICIA PERKINS ANDRINGA: I did see her distressed when Washington was on fire. There were riots and a lot of tension. I remember her calling me and asking if I was okay, and did I need to come stay with them. It was amazing that she was still thinking of her intern. I never once felt as though she was out of control or she was flustered. She was very high energy, yet there was a great calmness in the way she operated. Nothing appeared to be an emergency. Just the way she pushed me out there to greet guests; I don't know whether there was something going on behind the scene or not, but it just flowed. Bess was a very classy lady, and she cared deeply about what she was doing. She seemed to love people and handled them well. I never heard her say a negative thing about anybody, ever. She just always had a positive, optimistic approach.[27]

Senators Eugene McCarthy and Robert Kennedy vied in the primaries for the Democratic presidential nomination until Kennedy's assassination. At the Democratic National Convention in Chicago, Vice President Hubert Humphrey became the party's nominee, but his triumph was overshadowed by violence in the streets. Bess and Tyler attended that tumultuous convention.

So the turmoil on the streets, in the park, and the hotel didn't directly affect you?
    TYLER ABELL: It didn't directly affect us, although it certainly easily could have. That was such a disaster. It was just something that everybody who was there realized that the Democrats had serious problems because these hippies were trying to make things as difficult as possible to carry on a convention. It was an antiwar movement, but it didn't accomplish anything except that it cost an awful lot of money. They threw stink bombs in the Hilton Hotel, which made the place smell like vomit. So they didn't make any friends. That's the wrong way to run a protest. And the things that they did were just awful. They smeared excrement on the policemen and then complained that the policemen were beating them up. I remember a friend of mine, Bob Martin, said he was walking along the street and this bottle of a beer was thrown out of a hotel window from he didn't know how high up. But it just smashed on the sidewalk right next to him. If that had hit him, it could have killed him.
    Bess and I were staying in a suite that a friend of mine had in the Blackstone. We were happily a few blocks from all the disastrous activity, but it was a very welcome few blocks. A friend of mine, Jack Nelson, who had also been an advance man for Johnson, was on the staff of the convention and he had worked out the security, which was a disaster. Jack forever tried to hide the fact that he'd ever had anything to do with the security of the 1968 Democratic Convention because everybody was issued these very elaborate magnetic cards and you had to use your card in order to get in or get out of the convention. Very, very soon, it became obvious that the cards were not working and there was no way of fixing the problem. So the security went back to the old system of trying to identify each person by some sort of driver's license or other identification card. There was a lot of attention paid to it because reporters could not get into the convention legally because their card wasn't working. Then they had to show up with

some sort of other identification. So, naturally, they were very put out and ran very uncomplimentary stories about how poorly organized the convention was.

Did you or Bess have any role to play in the convention, or were you just there as observers?

TYLER ABELL: At that time I was in the private practice of law, and I was very soon to become chief of protocol again. At that moment I was operating as a lawyer, and I did a certain amount of lobbying work and representation. But Bess was there, basically, as my wife. Certainly, as social secretary to the White House, she did not need to be there and possibly the president would have been mad at her if he had known she was there. So we never made a thing about her being there.

Why would that have angered LBJ?

TYLER ABELL: Well, maybe it would and maybe it wouldn't have. If you worked for him, you should work for him. And he wanted you to work for him, not for somebody else. So Bess ran the risk that he would decide that she was doing something out there besides working for him and would have been annoyed about it. But it did not work out that way, so it was not a problem.[28]

The unpopularity of the war worked against Humphrey throughout the campaign, but he soldiered on. In November, he lost to Richard Nixon by less than one percent of the popular vote. The end of the Johnson administration closed that chapter in Bess's life.

9

Part of the Family

BESS ABELL: I loved working for the Johnsons because if you did something that the president liked, you didn't have to wait to hear about it from the third assistant secretary somewhere, you heard about it from the "Man."[1]

President Johnson's confidence in Bess's abilities was reflected in a telephone conversation he had with her on April 17, 1964, as they were planning for the first meeting of his Commission on Heart Disease, Cancer, and Stroke.

BESS ABELL: Mrs. Johnson said you wanted to do your remarks outside, and my suggestion would be that you do them in the Rose Garden. We could bring the people directly into the Rose Garden. You could come out and give your remarks, and then everyone could go upstairs for drinks, and dancing, and seeing the White House. . . .

LBJ: You can't get them all in the Rose Garden, can you?

BESS ABELL: Well, we can get some of them on the Overflow. That's the best place you can do it. You can say the garden was so pretty today, and the day was so pretty that you wanted them to see this part of the White House.

LBJ: All right. I think that's just perfect. I'm glad you're a can-do girl.[2]

That confidence encouraged the Johnsons to give Bess wide latitude in a variety of activities and to call on her for any number of projects. She became the first lady's confidant, adviser, and traveling companion. They treated her—as they did the rest of their staff—as part of the family.

TYLER ABELL: It's impossible for anybody who has not experienced it to see what happens when you join the White House. It was almost minutes after Johnson became president that a technician from the White House Signal Corps showed up at our residence to install a special phone, which was a direct line to the White House. Our regular phone never stopped ringing. Just everybody who thought they knew me or Bess, in any capacity whatsoever, called. You can't imagine how important they think you are, however lowly ranked you are, if you are part of the presidential party. It's called the Imperial Presidency, and it got that name I think very realistically, because it's overpowering. But Bess managed to survive all that with just unimaginable savoir faire.[3]

Special Projects

What special projects did the first lady work on?

BESS ABELL: Mrs. Johnson was associated with beautification, which is such a sissy word. You never said it! There were two things that she did that she said, "I hate those words, but we can't come up with anything better." [She meant the Beautification Project and the Women Doers' Luncheons.] She started in her hometown, which was Washington, DC. There are triangles all through the city, and entrances to the city that are beautifully landscaped. For many years after she left Washington, she used to get a batch of letters from taxi drivers, thanking her for making their jobs so nice in the springtime, when they would drive in from National Airport and all the daffodils were in bloom. Then, when she was back in Austin, well, she had another hometown to take charge of. She worked on the hike-and-bike trail that goes around Town Lake. The mayor and city fathers of Austin wanted to name it Lady Bird Lake. She said, "No, no, no. If you want to do that after I'm dead, that's okay, but not now." The day after she died, they changed the name from Town Lake to Lady Bird Lake.

What was Mrs. Johnson's reaction when she as first lady was compared to other first ladies?

BESS ABELL: It's very hard for any first lady to be compared to another. I guess maybe you'd feel like the second wife. Nobody really likes to be compared to anybody else. I never really heard her remark on it. I'm sure that it probably didn't please her, no matter how she was compared. I remember something that she said before they left Washington when she was accepting an award and very, very much in the twilight of departing the White House. She said, "Just because I planted flowers doesn't mean another first lady has to water them." You know, "Don't compare me." She also pointed out to many of us that the first lady is not elected, she is selected by one person.

Did Mrs. Johnson by any chance sort of deliberately try to avoid anything that could be considered as imitating Mrs. Kennedy?

BESS ABELL: She didn't deliberately avoid it, no. She continued Mrs. Kennedy's program of adding furnishings and paintings to the White House collection. She was deeply interested in it, but she did not want to make that her cause. That's going to be a continuing project, and I hope that every first lady will be equally interested in it. You may have one marvelous table, but that doesn't mean that sometime in the future one that's better isn't going to come along.

Preservation was very informal under Mrs. Kennedy, and President Johnson by Executive Order set up the Committee for the Preservation of the White House that had some private-sector members appointed by the president and then some members because of their positions, like the head of the Smithsonian and the head of the Park Service, the director of the National Gallery.

After the election, did Mrs. Johnson begin to give more thought to what she would do?

BESS ABELL: She wanted to have a project so that her time wasn't just spent posing for publicity pictures and shaking hands and giving tea parties. She wanted to have a project, something that she could identify with, something that she could constructively do, something that would be involved in some way in the president's program. And I honestly don't know how many different things that she considered.

And eventually she ended up with the Beautification Project.

BESS ABELL: Yes, there were many meetings up in the Queen's Sitting Room with people like Mary Lasker, health activist and philanthropist, and Stewart Udall, Secretary of the Interior, just planning and thinking toward what she could do, what form it should take. She didn't want to approach beautification of the whole country, it was too big a job to tackle, so she took Washington, which had been her home for more than twenty-five years, and established the First Lady's Committee for a More Beautiful National Capital. And there was of course a great deal of fallout from that all over the country, with other groups being formed in other cities, governors' wives taking it on as their project, and mayors' wives.

The White House did a great deal to encourage it. Whenever Mrs. Johnson had an opportunity, for example, to meet with a group of governors' wives, there would very likely be talk about beautification. A lot of it was natural fallout, a letter from a mayor saying, "I want to do this. Can you help me," or, "I want to do it, and this is what I'm doing."

She later on also got actively involved in antipoverty affairs.

BESS ABELL: That started, of course, in 1964 before the election. She wanted to visit and do things that would call attention to contributions that her husband and the Democratic Party had made to the country. Her first trip into a poverty area was to my home state of Kentucky in May of 1964, when she landed in Lexington and then drove up into the mountains and visited a farmer. We had to walk about a mile back up the creek road. Then we went to a little one-room schoolhouse, which was getting some school lunch money. One of the things that impressed me so much that day was the teacher saying how much just that one glass of milk a day meant to the diets of those children. They had grown two inches more, on the average, than children who didn't have it. I think Mrs. Johnson went to a one-room schoolhouse too, so she felt at home there.

All of these things made a great impact on her. She would meet people on these trips, like the lady who was the head of the school system there in Lick Branch, Kentucky, in Breathitt County. Later on, for example, when she would have one of the Women Doers' Luncheons, she would reach back in her memory on those trips and bring those people to Washington. One lady I think did come to Washington for two of the luncheons, quite some time apart.

On trips like that, how would you select places? I mean, why Lick Branch, Kentucky?

BESS ABELL: This was done with the assistance of some of the people in the departments who would know—the Agriculture Department that was giving money to farmers for crops could help you on selecting the farmer.

She leaned on advice from the departments to pinpoint these things. You might have a choice of eight things in eight different states. But that was the input that helped you select where you were going. I will tell you it wasn't selected because of ease of transportation. It's "one of those places you can't get there from here."

Did you do any speech writing for Mrs. Johnson?

BESS ABELL: The only things that I wrote at all were the little remarks that Mrs. Johnson would make before introducing the entertainment after state dinners. Other than that I had no hand in it at all. They were always very, very short because she didn't want to have to be worrying and thinking about a speech all the way through a state dinner. That was left to the heads of state, and so it was usually something very short, not more than a couple of paragraphs at the outside.[4]

MARY LYNN KOTZ: J. B. West, the chief usher, had a compact little office, and it was right opposite the South Entrance, where all the visitors arrived. So we were all invited by Bess to come and help her with a great greeting for all of the visitors. I will never forget that we were standing there when Madame Chiang Kai-shek came. And Lady Bird said, "How do you do, Madame Chiang? I'd like to introduce you to my right hand, Bess Abell." That was just marvelous. How better to introduce Bess Abell than as Mrs. Johnson's right hand? Because I always teased her that she was the real Lady Bird because she organized her life, and she was so appreciated by everybody in the White House.[5]

Touring the White House

While President Johnson met with members of Congress in the East Room, Mrs. Johnson regularly led their spouses on tours of the Family Quarters. One evening, as the group began ascending to the second floor, Bess ran up to curator James R. Ketchum and J. B. West to alert them that the president had invited Texas governor John Connally and his wife, Nellie, to spend the night. Their luggage had been placed in the Lincoln Bedroom, and the bed had been turned down. With the tour on its way, they did not have time to summon a maid. "Quick, we've got to make the bed," Bess whispered.[6]

JAMES R. KETCHUM: J. B. West, Bess Abell, Mary Kaltman, the housekeeper, and I raced into the Lincoln Bedroom to put things away because we knew that [the tour] was going to be coming along, the spouses of the people meeting in the East Room. The bed had to be made up, a coverlet pulled down and shams returned and so forth, and clothing had to be put in the closet, and suddenly, there are four of us around the bed—and the door opens up and Mrs. Johnson looks and has all these people staring over her shoulder. We said, "Oh, come right in." It looked like a Marx Brothers movie, but she quickly explained to everybody what was going on. She'd forgotten the Connallys were there, but she didn't miss a beat on it. She never did.[7]

What were you interacting with Bess about?
JAMES R. KETCHUM: Well, the curatorial program is responsible both for the permanent collection—and we're talking about things that went

back well into the nineteenth century and things that had been acquired since the spring of 1961. There were many things that had not even been cataloged yet by the winter of '63. Remember, we started out with two people in the office. We had to build from there.

Bess, in many instances, either knew or was aware of a donor. She would make sure that they could be at a reception or sometimes even a state dinner. That was a bridge to the world that we were trying to conquer. She could put the frosting on the cake. I don't think there was a day that went by that we didn't spend some time in each other's office. She was always coming over to the White House proper from the East Wing. She would be walking right by my door, so it wasn't a problem. And many times when she'd be with Mrs. Johnson, Mrs. Johnson would give her things to discuss with us, and she would stop on her way back to the office. Sometimes it was something Mrs. Johnson wanted to discuss with several of us, so I might be included in that. J. B. West would be as well. And so it was all just kind of part of the extended family. You did become family, there's no doubt about it. It was just great to go to work every day and know that if you needed a support system, it was there.[8]

Serving American Wines

Breaking with tradition, Lyndon Johnson decreed that only American wines should be served at White House functions, including state dinners—a significant recognition of the advances in American wines. Once again, Bess played a role behind the scenes. She later recalled, "One of the nice fringe benefits of the job, was that we got to do the wine tasting."[9]

TYLER ABELL: Tom Bendorf was a great pal of Bess's.[10] He had been an administrative assistant to Clair Engle and had helped him get elevated from the House to the Senate. Tom represented the winegrowers of California, which he'd gotten close to through Senator Engle. So when Bess went to the White House, Tom called and said, "You've got to start serving American wine. The winegrowers of America are great. They make really good wine, and there's no reason in the world why you should continue this business of Jackie Kennedy's serving French wine. We're not here to help the French. We're here to help the Americans." Bess said, "Well, it'll be a big break for us to push the French wines out. And I've got to be sure that the American wines are at least as good, and maybe better." So Tom Bendorf said, "Well, we'll show you that they're better."

He rented a room in the Madison Hotel. I don't think it had any furniture. It was just a big empty room. And on one wall he had cases of French wine, and on the opposite side he had cases of American wine. He had an expert wine taster there who would take a bottle out of one case on one side of the room and say, "Now, this is this type of wine." He would describe a little bit about what it was and where it came from. He'd open it up and pour a little bit into each of two or three glasses. After we'd tasted the wine, he would say, "Now, this is the equivalent from France." Then he pulled out the bottle and said, "This is what I think would be the direct comparison, and you can tell me if you think it's the same or better or not as good." We stayed there for at least an hour tasting different wines, and Bess said, "Well, this is absolutely very helpful, and I'd love to participate. I think it would be very important for America to show that our wines are what we serve. When I went to Turkey, the Turks didn't serve me French food, they served me Turkish food. And I think that's the way we should do it here. But I have to be sure that if I order wine for a particular dinner, that you can supply enough of it." And they said, "Absolutely, that will be done. First thing, soon as you decide what kind of wine you want, we will tell you the kind you should have, and we'll ship you enough. You just tell us how much you want, and we'll ship it to you. And if we can't supply enough of it, we'll have to think of a wine, a slightly different wine that will serve your purpose."

So that's the way it worked the whole time that Bess was social secretary. And there was never a time when they served French wine.[11]

In 1969, the president of the Wine Institute stated, "No president has done more to further the interests of the American wine industry than President Johnson," crediting him with stimulating the popularity of American wines.[12]

Personnel Matters

What was Bess like as a boss?

CAROL CARLYLE: Her demeanor was always very smooth, very calm, never raised her voice if something wasn't right. She would show you or correct you, but you never felt that you were being talked down to. It was almost like having a peer as a boss.[13]

An intern recalled her experience in Bess's office.

PATRICIA PERKINS ANDRINGA: On my first day there, Bess sent me home, saying, "Put on a dress for the evening. You're going to attend the state dinner." While I don't remember for whom the state dinner was for, I will never forget being seated next to Secretary of State Dean Rusk. That's an amazing show of confidence that I would not make a fool of myself or say something inappropriate to the Secretary. Bess gave me the opportunity to talk to such a distinguished, intelligent, soft spoken, important person. Another time that stood out was when the president was entertaining the top educators and businessmen of the country for dinner. For some reason, everyone was running late or whatever. Maybe Bess did it on purpose, I don't know. But as people were starting to arrive, she said, "You need to go greet them." Remember, I was a rising, college senior. "Just welcome them to the White House and show them where to go." So I did as I was told, and one of the guests was Kingman Brewster, who happened to be the president of Yale at the time.[14]

As staff manager of the White House Social Office, Bess had to cope with various personnel matters, including her own salary.

TYLER ABELL: Before Bess first went to the White House, she was making $6,000 a year. So when they put her on the White House payroll, they put her on it at $6,000 a year. It took her a couple of years before she finally got up the courage to say that she wanted a raise. But she found out that everybody else in the White House was making a lot more money than she was. And so she finally got up her courage, and she called Marvin Watson, President Johnson's appointments secretary, and said, "I want a raise. I want to make $20,000 a year." And they gave it to her. In those days an assistant secretary of state made $20,000 a year.

BESS ABELL: There was a lot of monkeying around. I needed another person working in my office. I called Tyler and I said, "Can I borrow Carol [Carlyle]?" who was the secretary in his office. "Just over the Christmas season when we're just drowning in things." He said, "Sure, when do you think I could have her back?" I said, "I don't know, we'll wait and see." She stayed until Johnson left the White House. But she stayed on the Post Office payroll all that time. I'll bet you dollars to donuts that's still going on. You borrow people from other agencies, and you just don't send them back.[15]

All personnel matters went through Marvin Watson, the president's appointments secretary who exercised virtually unlimited authority and became one of the obstacles Bess had to overcome. In 1966, Bess appealed to Watson to get a raise for Fred Jefferson, one of the employees of the Social Office. He worked as a messenger and driver and occasionally filled in as an additional butler. Bess regarded him as indispensable and felt he deserved a promotion and raise. But Watson denied her request.[16]

TYLER ABELL: Fred Jefferson was always marvelously helpful, always trying to do special errands for Bess. He was just a really hardworking guy because he did an awful lot of work, real work, in the office, and was the messenger and the driver. One day, Bess decided that he was absolutely entitled to a raise. She asked Marvin Watson if she could get him a raise, and Marvin said, "No. No. We can't possibly do it. There's no money in the budget for it. That's all set by the Civil Service."

So Bess called up her friend, who was then head of the Civil Service. She said, "I've got this man who's working for me, and he absolutely should have a raise, and I hope you can figure out how to give him a raise." The head of the Civil Service said, "Well, I'll send Ned Coffey over there and he'll inspect everything, and see what's going on, and see all the work that's been done, and so forth and so forth, and he'll figure it out." Ned Coffey came over and watched all the things that Fred Jefferson did. Ned Coffey said, "Well, Bess, Fred Jefferson is doing the work of two people. So we will give him a raise by giving you another person." Bess said, "I don't care how you do it, that's fine by me." Then she called Marvin Watson and said, "Marvin, I'm taking care of this matter with Fred Jefferson by hiring another person. I'm just so grateful to you for letting me work this out with the Civil Service." Marvin said, "Oh, that's great. I'd like very much to meet the new person." Bess said, "Well, then the next time there's an opportunity, I will introduce you." Not too much later, Fred was tending bar in the White House for a big party and Bess said, "Well, I want you to meet the new employee, Fred Jefferson." Marvin said, "I've been had."[17]

BESS ABELL: Two things I very much wanted to do, I wanted to have a White butler at the White House, and I wanted to have a Black social aide, the military officers who were social aides who helped with ceremonies and so forth. To get the White butler, you had to talk to Charles and John Ficklin, the brothers who were the maître d's, saying, "Can't you all get some White guy who can work with you all? I think that we need an integrated staff."

And then with the military, I said, "Can't you all find any single Black officers who can come and work with this wonderful group of people?" They finally did send me somebody, and I said, "He's great and I like him. He'll work out fine, but he's so White, we can't get credit for him."

The White butler was very British, and the first state dinner that he was serving J. B. West was aghast to find this white butler on his hands and knees in the East Room cleaning up a spilled drink. J. B. didn't tell me this story; the butler told me this story. He said, "Mr. West came over and said, 'No, no, no. No, no, no. I'll clean that up.'" And the butler said [with British accent], "But Mr. West, I'm on the staff."

In 1968, James R. Jones replaced Marvin Watson as appointments secretary, the equivalent of President Johnson's chief of staff. He described relations between the president's West Wing and the first lady's East Wing.

JAMES R. JONES: There was always a tension between the two, although it was not warfare. It was just, starting with Marvin [Watson], he had been given the orders to cut back on spending, cut down on staff. And the East Wing had Liz Carpenter and Bess. Both had good ideas that they wanted to implement, so they needed money. There was always that budget tension as to whether or not they got enough or not. But it was very, very cordial. That was the nice thing about being in the Johnson family, so to speak. While you still had the aggressiveness in terms of trying to get ahead, you did not have the meanness. You did not have the intrafamily fighting like so many other administrations have.

It was just trying to implement the many things we had to do. I knew that Bess was very close to the Johnsons and that she was well regarded, that she had had lots of experience in Washington politics through her family. And she was an intimidating-looking person. She was erect, very good-looking, but all business. So that was kind of the first meeting I had with her. Then you find out later after working with her that she had a real warm side to her.

She had a hard act to follow because Kennedy's social secretary had captured the press, had really good relationships with the media, and they put on good programs that advanced President Kennedy's plans for what he wanted to accomplish. Like everybody in the Johnson sphere, she had a difficult act to follow. But I never heard her complain. She put her programs together and oftentimes, they entailed money or budget. She would say why and what it was going to do. And oftentimes, she did that with the president. I didn't have that many interconnections between Bess and the president, but my sense was that what she did was not something that he had expertise in. The president totally trusted her. When she recommended ideas, it was not that he questioned whether it was right or wrong. It was informative as opposed to trying to be convincing.

It was very interesting because the president could get exasperated sometimes with Mrs. Johnson, either that she was pushing him too much on something he didn't particularly want to do or things like that. But you had to satisfy Mrs. Johnson and her team. You were not to step on them or mistreat them or anything like that.[18]

Lady Bird's Joy of Life

BESS ABELL: The Wildflower Center—first called the National Wildflower Research Center and then became—over Mrs. Johnson's initial protest because she did not want it named after her—but after it had been in business for I guess about eighteen years it was renamed the Lady Bird Johnson Wildflower Center. But she always had a joy in life and a joy in discovery and in doing something new.

I was with her in the Virgin Islands. She had gone down to give the graduation address at the University of the Virgin Islands. After the ceremonial activities at the university we went over to the island of St. John for two days of R&R—Rest and Relaxation. I had brought along my mask and flippers and snorkel to go out and see the wonderful things in the clear water of the Caribbean. She wanted to go too. So we got a mask and flippers and snorkel for her. I had been with other people when that was the first time, they had put a mask on their face and breathing through a tube through the water and it takes time getting used to it, and a little bit of discomfort. But for Mrs. Johnson as she put that mask on and put her face in the water and realized that she was like her very own glass bottom boat, and she could see what was on the floor of the Caribbean. She could see all these beautiful fish and the coral, and she just never wanted to take her head out of the water.

We had this ranger-naturalist with us, a man named Noble Samuels, who knew all the flora and fauna, whether it was above the earth or below the water. At one point she was swimming along with Noble, and she took her head out of the water and she said, "Noble what is that silvery fish with the long mouth?" Instead of answering her directly he pointed to another quite wonderful, colorful fish and told her about that fish, what it did, and what its name was, and what it ate. It was sometime later when we got back in the boat Mrs. Johnson said to Noble, "That long silver fish with the long mouth, that was the barracuda, wasn't it?" He said, "Well, yes, Mrs. Johnson, but it wasn't going to bother you."

So it was a great day of discovery of things in the water and what they did and what they ate. She was back in the water the next day and enjoyed snorkeling since then. I think she was about fifty-five then. And to show that she is always doing new things, it was about two years later, I think, when she was fifty-seven that she learned to water ski.

When Mr. Johnson was vice president, the ambassador of Iran used to send over to the vice president's house about every six or seven weeks a big box of pistachio nuts from Iran and also a wonderful generous tin of that fabulous Iranian caviar from the Caspian Sea. The Johnsons just delighted in that, enjoyed the pistachio nuts, and reveled in this fabulous caviar from Iran. After they had been in the White House for several months, Mrs. Johnson called me and she said, "I keep signing these letters to the ambassador of Iran thanking him for the pistachio nuts and thanking him for the caviar. Where are the pistachio nuts and where is the caviar?" I said, "Well I have no idea. I thought that it would be going to you." But upon a little investigation I found that the Secret Service just destroyed any foodstuffs that were sent to the president or his family. So I relayed this to Mrs. Johnson and said that the Secret Service said that they were sorry, but any foodstuff that came to the president or his family had to be destroyed. There was a long pause, then, in the conversation with Mrs. Johnson. She said, "Well, you call the Secret Service and tell them to send me the pistachio nuts and the caviar and I will take care of destroying it personally."

One time I was in Texas with Mrs. Johnson—this was before the days of plastic, of credit cards and ATM bank cards where you could just plug a card in and, assuming you weren't overdrawn at the bank, you could get some cash—well, this is before those days. I had stayed down in Texas longer than I had anticipated and I'd run out of cash, so I had asked Mrs. Johnson if she would cash a check for me. She said, "Yes, indeed." We drove to the bank and I wrote her a check, and she was going to take it into the bank and cash it. She looked at it and she said, "My goodness, you and Tyler have a joint checking account?" I said, "Well, yes, ma'am." She said, "My goodness, I wouldn't have a joint checking account with the Angel Gabriel." I kept the bank account with Tyler, but I used the $750 Mrs. Johnson paid me to open my own bank account.[19]

Bess at Home and at Work

PATRICIA PERKINS ANDRINGA: Since [Bess] became like a big sister, we talked a lot. What I often saw was somebody who had two young boys and was very concerned about the amount of time she was working at the White House, the effect this was having on the boys, and the fact that she couldn't get to some of the things they were doing. I don't think she ever said she was worried about her relationship with Tyler, that was a given, but she was concerned about her kids. She was so conscientious. So I don't know how much time she had for a light side. However, the fact that she didn't get uptight, that she seemed to have her stress under control, leads me to believe that there was a lightness there which enabled her to do as much as she did.[20]

What's it like to be the husband of the social secretary in the White House? Isn't that an awfully time-consuming job for your wife and the mother of your children?

TYLER ABELL: Yes, it was time-consuming for her, but compared with life right now I frankly wouldn't say it's a hell of a lot different. Bess's time seems to be consumed anyway. I guess a lot of people would have objected to it. I liked it very much; the kids liked it. Bess did a wonderful job at being social secretary and did a very good job as a housewife and mother. I know that sounds corny, but it's true.

What were the circumstances of your being named protocol chief?

TYLER ABELL: I was practicing law. I had been down in Florida on some kind of business, and I'm sure that I was also combining it with politics, considering what time of year it was. I got off the plane at National Airport and called Bess and said, "I've just got a short time before I go to West Virginia. Why don't we eat lunch?" So I picked her up at the White House. She said, "My God, the damnedest thing has happened. The president just called me and said he'd been trying to reach you and couldn't reach you, and that he wants you to be chief of protocol. What do you think?" I said, "I don't know. What do you think?" So we discussed it all through lunch. She explained exactly what he had said, which was that he had been very nice about it. He did not say, "You have to take it" or anything like that. He said, "If Tyler can work out a leave of absence from his law firm and would like to do this, I'd like very much for him to do it. But if he cannot do it, if it is inconvenient for any reason, I'll understand. Have him give me a call back before four o'clock."

Normally when talking to a chief of protocol I'd feel obligated to ask him how he got along with the White House social secretary.

TYLER ABELL: Bess and I got along very well. That was not true, though, of other chiefs of protocol. She really got along well with Jimmy Symington and pretty well with Angie Duke [Angier Biddle Duke]. I remember

Angie one day got into a problem with her. It was one of the very early state dinners, and Bess had arranged a beautiful theatrical presentation for after dinner. The president came out of the dining room and started marching on down to the East Room where the stage had been set up, and Angie Duke ran ahead and said, "Quick, start the performance." Bess, who had been scurrying off doing something else, didn't realize that any of this was happening, and they started the performance before a whole lot of other things were done that were supposed to have been done first. Bess was really sore about that one. Angie sent her a big bouquet of flowers the next morning, apologized, and made up for it. But I had no problem with the White House social secretary![21]

LUCI BAINES JOHNSON: Bess would come to my mother before every visiting head of state arrived to say: This is the way they believe. This is the way they think. These are things that are important. This is what they're allergic to. These are the people that will be difficult for them to feel comfortable with. These are the people that would make them feel valued. So when Tyler became chief of protocol, Bess then had two jobs. She was my mother's social secretary, and she was Tyler's professional right arm and expected to provide him a lot of that, too. Now I think they had always provided each other that their whole life long. But that was just what she did.[22]

Last Days in the White House

What was the mood like after Johnson announced that he was not running?
CAROL CARLYLE: We were shocked. We were speechless. We all sat down and cried. And the next day we just had to go on. We did whatever was planned. I mean, we were still busy. The hardest day was our last day there where, I think, at midnight, we managed to carry the last things out of our office and cried walking down the street that the world had come to an end. But it was hard. I'm sure that in all administrations the personnel go through this.

Did Bess have a way of sort of keeping the boat afloat?
CAROL CARLYLE: Just by her demeanor. She was very even, very level-headed, very calm, and brought that feeling to all of us. We had some good times, too. One of our projects was working with a company to manufacture the china. Each president can have china if they want china. Well, there wasn't enough china to entertain 300 guests. You would have to mix

the patterns up. So we determined that it was time for some Johnson china. It was going to have flowers on all the dessert plates. The dinner platters were all the same, but each dessert plate had a different flower from every state. Well, the dishes came in and the dessert plates looked like you put this decal on them and they came from Woolworth's. Bess said, "We can't accept this. This is wrong. We can't accept this."[23]

JAMES R. KETCHUM: We had a situation that occurred when a good portion of the Johnson china had to be rejected, the dessert service. For Mrs. Johnson, flowers were everything, for the detail and the design. The dessert service was made up of state flowers. Each state had its official flowers. Tiffany's design studio was responsible for the designs. A young French designer named Andre Piette. He did a fantastic job on everything from soup course to main course, but he did a horrible job on dessert course. These designs were not worthy of F. W. Woolworth.

When they were seen, and when Walter Hoving, chairman of Tiffany & Company, came down to counsel with Mrs. Johnson, and Bess, and myself, he agreed. He then had to face up to what we told him, that anything that is ordered by the White House, even though it is rejected by the White House, has to be destroyed by the White House. They used to just dump it in the Potomac River, but that became fodder for all kinds of collectors when the river was dredged.

So Bess had a suggestion that we make a humongous poster, and that we put a name on it like Marvin Watson. Also other people over in the West Wing who had been holders of the keys during the last three or four years of the administration and made life very difficult from '65 on. We had a tray of glasses with about four different kinds of champagne, and we went down to one of the bunker rooms in the sub-sub-basement. We put the poster up at one end, and we took the dessert service, one plate at a time, and we hurled them, one right after the other. We tried to hit the target as many times as we could. In this instance, no one needed to get on any psychiatrist's couch and vent their spleen because it was all taken care of courtesy of the rejected White House china.[24]

J. B. West recalled that since legally the flawed plates could not be returned for other use, Bess solved the dilemma by inviting a few of the staff to a party in the White House basement. They found the dessert plates stacked in the middle of the room, with a poster on the wall featuring everyone's least favorite presidential assistants. "Heave away!" she shouted, and they smashed all 220 pieces of china.[25]

The Children's Garden

How did Lady Bird Johnson's children's garden become a reality?

BESS ABELL: One thing that the Johnsons left was the children's garden at the White House. What happened was Liz Carpenter ended up with some money left in her travel budget, and she said, "We have to spend this, because if we don't, Mrs. Nixon will spend it." This was after Christmas of 1968. Mrs. Johnson said, "We've already made our gift to the White House." We thought we needed to do something that fits her, something on the White House grounds.

I called Edward Alexander, who had done a lot of beautification projects with Mrs. Johnson and with his boss, Edward Durell Stone Jr., founder of EDSA, a premier landscaping design firm. I said, "Can you get a shuttle to Washington and we'll pick you up this afternoon so you can look over the grounds and see if you can think of anything that would make sense?" So he did. He walked around the grounds, and he found this wonderful spot where Mrs. Kennedy's trampoline had been. It was perfect to plant a little apple tree and dig a pond. This work was done in freezing weather in January, when they were putting the finishing touches on the inaugural stands out on Pennsylvania Avenue.

The Johnsons at that point had two grandchildren, Lucinda and Lyn. They had to put their little hand and footprints in stone plaques. I think Lucinda and Lyn are quite cross because their prints are only in cement. The [George H. W.] Bushes came in years later, and they had their grandchildren's prints done in bronze. Do you think that we could get Lucinda and Lyn's paw prints done in bronze?[26]

LYNDA JOHNSON ROBB: They found a spot where the trees made sure that you couldn't be seen from the gates. It had a little pond with some little fish and was kind of a grotto. You had a nice, comfortable bench to sit on, so you could go out and sit and rock your baby, or at least sit in the sun with the perambulator. At that time, Lucinda was just a few months old. It was a place that I could take her outside to get some sunshine, and people couldn't see us. Mother and Daddy paid to have all of that fixed up with some sweet little words. And then we put our handprints and footprints in cement. But you can imagine trying to do that in January with a child that is three months old and a little boy who is only eighteen months old.[27]

LINDA JANE HOLDEN: My book was on the White House gardens.[28] What I really was interested in talking to Bess about was the children's garden at the White House, which is a garden that Mrs. Johnson created on the eve of their departure from the White House in 1969. Bess knew the whole back story of that garden. Bess is very much like Bunny Mellon: Neither one of these women ever wanted to take credit for all that they did. I sort of began to feel like it was my mission to give credit where credit is due, because Bess was just so clever and imaginative, full of spunk and life and zest.

As she talked about the children's garden, she always put everything in the context of Mrs. Johnson. She didn't call her Lady Bird. She called her Mrs. Johnson. She tried to give Mrs. Johnson credit, but I just read between the lines and realized what had really happened. It was a farewell gift, an alleged farewell gift. Whereas Liz [Carpenter] had already identified a farewell gift, a vase or something that was being left to the White House as the Johnson's farewell gift. But Bess went to Mrs. Johnson and they had this discussion, this conversation, and it was the context that, "Mrs. Johnson, you're really a gardener, what about a garden?"

Bess came up with this idea to put this garden down where the children's garden is today, which was an area that was on the south grounds, on the lower part of the grounds, near the tennis court. It had been used by Jackie Kennedy for her trampoline. She had them plant a green wall of hollies and azaleas that would give her privacy. It ended up being just an empty area, so it was ideal for a private garden. Mrs. Johnson had become a grandmother while living in the White House. So the idea was that she would bequest a grandmother's garden to future first ladies—because she liked to walk her grandchildren around the south grounds in their buggies. But there was really nowhere for privacy. Even the Rose Garden and the Jacqueline Kennedy Garden, they're very public gardens. But this one was sequestered away, and it was designed for children. It had a slate terrace. They put a pool in there and an apple tree. Bess had the apple trees because the kids could climb it and they could also pluck apples in the fall. Then she had the surrounding area planted with flowers of the seasons—mostly flowers with big heads that children could pluck with their hands and play with.

The pool was very shallow. On the eve of their departure, which was in January 1969, the garden had been quickly thrown together. They had an inscription in the stone saying that President and Mrs. Johnson had given this garden as their gift to the White House. Then Bess had the grandchildren put their hands in the cement with their names and date. When they had this little dedication ceremony, they all walked down.

Irvin Williams, who was the head gardener at the time, he and Bess both, separately, told me this story. Luci Johnson's son came running in and then fell right into the pond, in January, with his little coat. They rescued the child, wrapped him in Bess's coat, and took him back up to the house to change him.

So you're saying that the idea for that garden originated with Bess?

LINDA JANE HOLDEN: Yes, and her wanting to leave a lasting memorial and tribute to Mrs. Johnson. She loved Mrs. Johnson. Even years later, when I was talking with her about this book, she was very emotional. I was just struck with the way she just loved Mrs. Johnson.[29]

What is the relationship between the first lady and the social secretary? There's got to be a very high level of trust.

BESS ABELL: The Johnsons adopted their staff as family. I don't know how that tradition is with other administrations, but it was part of the Johnsons' personalities.

I don't like comparisons, but I at one point called somebody in my office who had worked in Mrs. Kennedy's social office, and I asked them to bring something up to the second floor of the White House. They wanted to really be sure that they had heard what I said because afterwards they told me that was the first time that they had been on the second floor of the White House. But that was not how the Johnsons operated. They brought us in as guests. We were part of their life, part of their family. It was a great thing to be a part of it. They really did adopt you.

Most of us who worked for President and Mrs. Johnson became a part of their family. They were interested in us. They were interested in our children. They were interested in what we were doing. We were just a part of their life and vice versa.

I think everybody that worked for them in the Senate, the vice presidential, the White House years, really felt a part of their family. And they made us part of the family. They included us in special events. They would invite staff members to sometimes come to state dinners, sometimes for a reception. Toward the end of the Johnson administration, the president and Mrs. Johnson wanted to be sure that everybody who worked for them was invited to something or another, and we began having more and more people come in after dinner for dancing at events. In fact, one evening, at one of the last state dinners, the president was dancing with various people, and he was dancing with one woman named Betty Tilson, who worked in Mrs. Johnson's correspondence office. He came over to me afterwards and said, "Now, what does Betty Tilson do?" I told him that she wrote absolutely the very best letters, drafted the very best letters for Mrs. Johnson. He said, "Oh." Then he went over and asked Betty to come to Texas with him.

And, by golly, Betty and her husband, Don, moved to Austin, Texas. Don got a job down there. I think maybe he worked for the government anyway, and he got a transfer to a job in Austin, Texas. Betty and Don became a member of the Johnson extended family.

They included us in Christmas. They became a part of our joys, a part of our sadness, and we were part of theirs. Another thing is that the family quarters of the White House were open to staff. That area of the White House in past administrations had a line across it, and you didn't go up that elevator to the second floor. But with the Johnsons there were meetings up there, there were luncheons, dinners. It was just a part of the house that we knew as well as the state floor.

The last night in the White House, the Johnsons held a party for the staff?

BESS ABELL: The second to last night they were there they had a party for the members of the president's cabinet and their wives, and the last night they were in the White House they had a party for their staff, where we took pictures and shared memories. It's a very special memory, looking back at that dinner in the family dining room upstairs, and cocktails before, and coffee afterwards in the Yellow Oval Room, with that lovely view out the window across the South Lawn to the Washington Monument and the Jefferson Memorial beyond, the prettiest view in the White House.

Toward the very end of the Johnson administration I was driving out of the White House grounds with Mrs. Johnson. We were going off to some embassy reception, and it was a lovely evening. The sun was setting, and the sky was beautiful. You could see the inaugural platform going up on Pennsylvania Avenue as we were going out the north gate. I said to Mrs. Johnson as we were leaving this beautiful house, "Are you going to miss all this when you're back in Texas?" And she said, "Oh yes, I'm just going to miss it. I'm going to miss it like a front tooth. But, you know, there's just absolutely nothing in the world that would make me willing to pay the price for another ticket of admission."[30]

More than one of your cohorts has said it's a job in which you can never relax. Is that true?

BESS ABELL: Not for me. I had a wonderful time. At the tail end of the administration, when the Nixon troops were going around and checking out office space and so forth, I decided there were so many long faces around there, I would start having a party. I brought in a lot of booze and food to my office, and in the morning we would have Bloody Marys, and then, I don't know, then we'd have some sandwiches, or maybe somebody from the kitchen would bring over some shrimp or something, and we'd have maybe some wine. Sometimes there'd be mimosas in the morning, and then in the late afternoon we'd break out the hard stuff. We would have martinis and whiskey sours and scotch and soda.

One time, Liz [Carpenter] was in the office, and I just thought we needed to lift spirits. A couple of people from the new Nixon team were coming by and surveying the scene and saw this "party" going on in my office. They came by and they were shaking their heads, and they asked, "How long has this been going on?" Liz said, "For five years. Can you believe it? For five long years this has been going on!" And they just shook their heads as they walked away.

January 20, 1969—do you have memories of the last day?

BESS ABELL: Sure. I was at the White House. I had cleared out my office. The president was in the Red Room, and the Nixons had arrived, but President Johnson wasn't ready to go yet. He was still signing appointments. He wasn't going anywhere. I think he named Liz's husband to something, maybe to the naval board. Les had been in the Navy. I wish I'd known what was going on. I would have gotten him to name me to something.

Tyler was escorting the diplomatic corps to the inaugural ceremony and afterward hosted them for lunch at the State Department. I went to Clark and Marnie Clifford's. They were having a luncheon reception at their house on Connecticut Avenue for the Johnsons and the Humphreys, members of the Cabinet, and a few White House staff who were still around. After that, most of us went out to Andrews Air Force Base to wave good-bye to the Johnsons. There was LBJ going up the stairs to Air Force One for his last ride home with his little grandson, Lyn Nugent, in his arms. I was surprised to see Republican Congressman George Herbert Walker Bush there also saying good-bye to LBJ, a fellow Texan, instead of being down at all the whoop-de-doo for the new president. Because of that I've always had a special warm spot in my heart for George Herbert Walker Bush.[31]

10

Joan of Art

Contrary to F. Scott Fitzgerald's assertion that "there are no second acts in American lives," Bess Abell returned to the center of the political world just eight years after the Johnsons left the White House. In 1976 she joined the campaign staff of Joan Mondale when Joan's husband, Senator Walter Mondale, was nominated to run for vice president with Jimmy Carter. When they won, Joan asked Bess to become her chief of staff.

LBJ was an unhappy vice president, although most vice presidents are thought to be unhappy in that job, so there was nothing unique about that.
    BESS ABELL: Well, I worked with Fritz Mondale, and I did not think he was unhappy. I think that was because of the way Jimmy Carter decided to change the vice presidency.[1]

TYLER ABELL: Mrs. Mondale called her right after the nominating convention in 1976 in New York. Mrs. Mondale called our hotel room and asked to speak to Bess. After the call Bess said, "Mrs. Mondale wants to see me. We've arranged to meet in her room at two o'clock." When she went over there, Mrs. Mondale said, "Everybody's told me that you're the most important person for me to hire, so I'm going to hire you right now. I hope you'll go to work for me." Bess said, "Yes, I would like to do that."
    In some respects, this was a repeat. But Mrs. Mondale was quite a bit different from Mrs. Johnson. Of course, they were very close to the same age. Joan was probably four or five years older than Bess. Not much more than that. They had kids that were almost the same age. There was a little more of a friendship atmosphere than an employee–employer. Bess did help Joan become the person that did the arts because Bess thought that every first lady should have some sort of a program that they promoted. For Mrs. Johnson, it was beautification. For Joan, it was art.
    After they won the election, Bess wanted to be chief of protocol. I know that she talked with Fritz Mondale to see whether or not he would ask Jimmy Carter to make Bess chief of protocol. It must've been a very strange

conversation. I never asked Bess to tell me any more about it. But the situation was strange because, of course, Joan wanted Bess to stay as her assistant. Bess was made chief of staff for Mrs. Mondale. She had the job of running the Mondale house. They moved out of their house on Newark Street and into the vice president's house. And they were the first vice presidential couple to spend any significant time in that house. Rockefeller was the first vice president who had access to the house. But he had a much better house in Foxhall Road. And he spent one night in that house, which is another different and interesting story.[2]

WALTER MONDALE: When I got nominated for vice president, we were sitting there wondering what the hell we're going to do now. Who could we get to help Joan? We both came up with Bess's name almost instantly. Joan wanted Bess. I wanted her to have Bess. Would Bess be available? We called her, and she came over to see us. We popped the question, and she was all ready for it. She said, "Let's go," and she was just a great presence with Joan on the trail, overseas, whatever it was, in those meetings that we have about how we're doing, how it's going. She was back in the White House because that's where we were again, and she knew all about that stuff and she was the steady hand. Joan trusted her and she, I think, liked Joan and they made a very good couple and they saw the world together.

The way you presented it just now, it sounds like you were very much aware of Bess. It wasn't plucking a name out of the blue. What preceded your selecting her?
WALTER MONDALE: Joan and I would go to the White House once in a while for social events and usually Bess was around there, and she was so kind and welcoming to everybody. It was really stunning to me, when I got nominated, the first thing we knew was that Joan had to hit the road and she needed help. She can't do that alone, and who should it be, and within a few seconds, both Joan and I came up with Bess's name.

Bess was not a neophyte. She'd been around politics for a long time with her dad and in the White House with the Johnsons. She knew what the hell was going on. She's very sharp, and I remember how thrilled Joan and I were when she said she could do it. Immediately, Joan and Bess went off somewhere and started talking about the campaign and how they would organize it.

During that campaign, what was Bess's role?
WALTER MONDALE: She was Joan's right-hand person. She would travel with her. She would do the planning. She'd coordinate between us

and Joan. She had a good political mind. She'd be on the strategy sessions. She was just what we needed, and Joan had every confidence in her. There was not a slight bit of doubt about that.

Joan was supposed to go on the road and campaign, which she did by the thousands of miles, and Bess was always with her. She was supposed to go to women's groups and try to tie down the women's vote. She wanted to emphasize the arts, and so the idea was that she would, among other things, try to make a special entree to the arts community around the country, which is a pretty big group, and she was great at all of those things. Bess knew what it was. Joan could get tired easily. It was just something in her makeup, and Bess was always strong and could fill in when Joan was exhausted.[3]

MICHAEL S. BERMAN: I remember Bess telling me in New York, right at the end of the convention, that she'd gotten a call from Joan and that this happened almost immediately. She quoted Joan as saying, "Everybody has told me that the most important thing for me to do is to hire you. So I want to hire you."[4]

BESS ABELL: Well, I tell you, I was shot with luck after the Democratic convention in 1976 when Joan called and asked if I would join her on the campaign trail. What a great adventure that was.

When the campaign started, I remember it starting as a whistle-stop from New York to Chicago and ended with great enthusiasm and much excitement in Minneapolis. Long days, short nights, and many speeches and many fans. People were always asking her, "If Fritz is elected vice president, what will you do?" and she said, "I would like to work with the arts. That's always been part of my life." So that is what she wanted to do and what she set out to do.[5]

Joan Mondale was the *very best* traveling companion. In one respect she was too good. It was 1976—Joan was campaigning coast to coast—north, south, east, west. After Labor Day we were off on our first "on our own" campaign trip. Oh, we had been on the campaign train from New York headed to Eugene, Oregon—the town where Joan was born. Someone on the campaign staff met Joan at the plane, gave her an outline of a couple of events that night and an overview of what to expect the next day. After Joan met the local campaign staff, she made an informal talk, thanking them for their hard work, long hours, and commitment to electing Jimmy Carter and Walter Mondale. Joan and I were delivered to the motel with an outline of the next day's schedule.

When I woke up I headed to the lobby, for orange juice, coffee, a couple of pastries, the morning papers, and then back to Joan's room to be sure she was up—and to talk about the day ahead. When she opened the door I was stunned. She was not only up and dressed, but the room was neat as a pin. The bed was made without a wrinkle. I asked: "Has the maid been here already this morning?" "No," Joan answered. "I always make my bed."

I suggested: "Where will the maid think you spent the night? Perhaps with that woman traveling with you? Or with one—or all three—of those good-looking secret service men?" Of course, such thoughts had never crossed Joan's mind, as I went around unmaking the bed and tossing the bathroom towels about. I am happy to report that was the last time Joan made her bed on the campaign trail, and there was no better traveling companion.[6]

WALTER MONDALE: Joan and Bess got along very well, and they both campaigned well together. One of the things that the Carters needed, they had no Washington experience. They'd never been in office in Washington, because I remember when Carter was going to go to the White House to see the president and we were in the Blair House and he asked me what the White House was like. I said, "You mean you've never been to the White House?" He said, "No. Never been there," and now he was going to be elected and take the place over. Amazing.[7]

Where Bess had worked on Lady Bird Johnson's personal payroll during LBJ's vice presidency, Joan Mondale became the first vice president's wife to have had an official staff, recalled Judy Whittlesey, who served on that staff.

JUDY WHITTLESEY: When she worked with Mrs. Johnson, Bess talked about having a little office in their home in Spring Valley. There wasn't a vice president's residence then. The Rockefellers symbolically were at the vice president's residence, but not really. The Mondales were the first vice presidential family to actually move into the vice president's house and live there and for Joan to have a staff that essentially took some staff allocation from the vice president's total budget and complemented resources and personnel.

Joan had an office in the Old Executive Office Building. I've been back there in subsequent administrations, and it's in the same part of the building, but it's grown. Bess and Joan created something that has multiplied with time because it was no longer unusual. It began to be expected that a second lady would have a mission and a staff, and so they broke ground in that.

What was your impression of Bess Abell?

JUDY WHITTLESEY: Hugely creative and with an absolutely wonderful network of people. I didn't know at first because Bess was a new colleague and friend, but I began to realize how broad, and deep, and wide her personal network was, because anything that you wanted to get into, Bess said, "Oh, we'll call so-and-so." It would be a door-opener to someone who could help do what you needed to do. That was also true with journalists because of her time with the Johnsons and just her life. She knew a network of journalists and women correspondents, who were a limited group because there weren't as many women in journalism. It certainly is much greater now, but typically the people who were assigned to lifestyle feature kind of writing were women. Bess had known them and opened doors. They were people who helped tell stories about the things that she and Joan were taking on.[8]

TYLER ABELL: I can't imagine, frankly, that Fritz would have wanted Bess to leave his wife to become chief of protocol. Jimmy Carter might've been better served with Bess as chief of protocol. He probably did not want to offend his vice president or Mrs. Mondale by stealing somebody and making them chief of protocol if he could have had somebody else just as easily, which he did. He did choose a woman, Kit Dobelle. Bess, in her traipsing around with Joan Mondale, had needed some help and had gotten Gretchen Poston to help her. Gretchen Poston was a friend and a political activist. Gretchen wound up having Bess's old job as social secretary.[9]

DEBORAH M. SALE: I came to work for Vice President Mondale as an advance person. I first met Bess at advance school in Minneapolis because she was a member of the senior staff and we were all there to be trained. Vice President Mondale said the most intelligent thing I think I've ever heard anyone say to a political staff that was going to be scattered around America working for him. He told us that he reserved the right to make his own enemies. This is something that a lot of people in political life should hear, I think. Bess never did need to hear that because Bess didn't make enemies. She had an incredibly lovely style in dealing with everyone, and made people feel that they wanted to do what she wanted them to do and therefore didn't have to demand. I don't think she ever really did demand, not at least in terms of what I saw. I mean, she could be steely, I think. She was very clear about what she wanted, very clearheaded, and very strategic too.[10]

Running the Vice President's Residence

"My new job . . . meant big changes for the Mondale family," the vice president wrote. "We moved out of our house on Lowell Street in Northwest Washington to the vice president's residence at One Observatory Circle off Massachusetts Avenue. Ted, Eleanor, and William, now teenagers, found themselves in the media spotlight from time to time and handled it impressively. Joan, who had begun to establish herself as an arts advocate of national stature and had written a book, *Politics in Art,* soon found new venues for her skills. Thanks to President Carter, she became honorary chair of the Federal Council on the Arts and Humanities, where she established herself as a champion of art in public spaces and helped establish a set-aside for arts funding in the construction of new federal buildings. Although she missed our house and neighbors on Lowell Street, she soon transformed the vice president's home into a showcase for prominent American artists . . . and before long she was known around Washington as 'Joan of Art.'"[11]

When you entered the vice presidential residence, did Bess have a role in decorating or making decisions of what came over from your house on Lowell Street?

WALTER MONDALE: Bess was involved in everything. It's not hard to define everything, and she would help Joan figure out what she was going to do. We were the first really active vice president to be in that wonderful house, and Bess had a knack for that stuff because she'd been in the White House for four years. She knew something about it, and so she was ideal for making the arrangements in the house for trying to decide what the rules are going to be and, once again, hitting the road. That's what she did.

What was her interaction with your kids?

WALTER MONDALE: They needed to know the rules too, and they went out on the road a lot. It was kind of a free-spirited family. These kids I'm sure wanted to be part of a campaign. They wanted to go out and speak. They loved their mother, and the kids traveled with her once in a while. We had Ted, Eleanor, and William, and they were all hotshots. They loved to do this stuff, and Joan knew, of course, and Joan and Bess would probably have to consider what they were doing and why they were doing it.[12]

Michael S. Berman, an aide to Walter Mondale in the Senate, became the White House counsel to the vice president.

MICHAEL S. BERMAN: No vice president had ever lived there before. Rockefeller was the first vice president in which the residence was available. He had set it up. He created a special bedroom for himself with a special bed. He did some remodeling so the bed would fit the house, and he never spent a night there because his own house, which was a couple of blocks away, was more comfortable.

They didn't move in right away because nobody had ever lived there in a real sense. So when we took it over, there was a bunch of things to figure out. There was a staff of Navy Stewards, and they were trying to be very helpful, but you had to provide your own food. So it took us awhile to really get them acclimated to moving in from their house in northwest Washington.[13]

Bess organized social events for the Mondales and continued making guests feel at home, although sometimes they also needed a little policing.

BESS ABELL: When I worked with the Mondales, we were having a press Christmas party, and there was this journalist there, whose name shall not be mentioned. She had a fur muff that she was holding in one hand like this. I came up and I said, "Oh, I love that," and put my hands in it like this. She had two little sherry glasses that had the vice presidential seal on them. I said, "You really don't want to do that. You ought to put those back."

Did you know that something was in there?
BESS ABELL: No, it was an accident. I said something about, "I love those fur muffs. They must feel so good." Clunk.[14]

How did Bess and Joan work together? What was the arrangement like?
JUDY WHITTLESEY: When the Mondales moved into the vice president's residence, and Bess set up the office in the Old Executive Office Building, Joan was at the house and Bess was in the office. Joan didn't come into the office that much. Bess would go out and meet with her. It was usually ceremonial or very specific activities, but Bess would meet with her and they would go over plans and activities. Joan wanted to continue being involved in pottery, which was really important to her. She had classes one day a week that were important to her. Her tennis partners from her Cleveland Park neighborhood were important to her. The neighborhood vegetable co-op that she was one of the instigators of was important to her.

Bess figured out a way to be respectful of the things that Joan wanted to do and the pieces of her "civilian life" that she wanted to bring into public service with her, how to integrate that into a schedule for official functions and traveling that would accomplish the things that needed to happen to pursue the mission, which they had determined was supporting the arts in America, with a particular interest in craft. That was an interest of Joan's and a very unsupported aspect of the arts in America at that point. It was popular locally and in communities, but in the arts at large, it was not at that point.

They staked that out as an area where Joan could make a difference. I'm not quite sure what the conversations were like at the beginning that established the division of time. I just know that it worked. Joan was able to maintain the things she liked. I learned that from Bess, so that when we went on to the general election in the 1984 campaign, there was a day set aside as the pottery day, the tennis day. We built on that respect for the things that were important. And Bess clearly worked out something that worked well for what she and Joan thought the office should do, that we all should do, and that satisfied what Joan wanted to do personally.[15]

Bess as a Mentor

Ann Stock served as office manager and deputy press secretary for Walter Mondale, and later became White House social secretary during the Clinton administration. She recalled the help Bess gave her from the start.

ANN STOCK: In 1977 I had no job. One of my husband's friends worked for Senator Mondale at the time, about to become Vice President Mondale, and said, "You should turn in your resume because you're organized and they're looking for people in the press office." I thought, "Well, what do I know about this? Nothing." But I went ahead, put together a resume. The day before the inaugural, I had an interview with the press secretary and the deputy press secretary to become the office manager in the vice president's office.

I didn't get the job until a couple days after the inauguration and right as the vice president was getting ready to go around the world to meet all of our allies and tell them who Carter and Mondale were. The entire senior staff got on the plane with Mondale, and they literally went around the world. I was left in charge of the Mondale press office, and I had not one clue. Basically I was told to report to the White House because they were about to take off on this trip. So I reported to the White House, and I'm sitting in my office with my head in my hands, literally thinking, "I don't even know what to do next."

In walks Bess, who had the office directly across the hall from me. She was just wandering around, trying to figure out who was in what offices. I was in 279 and she was in 280 in the beautiful Old Executive Office Building, with high ceilings and gorgeous offices. She comes in and sits down and says, essentially, "Who are you and what are you doing here?" As she talked to me, she realized that I was brand new. I had not worked on the campaign. I did not know the staff. I was highly organized, and I thought I knew what I was doing, but the aura of the White House very quickly took over.

She realized that I was slightly terrified, and I was thinking at the time that I would probably use these next ten days to get to know what I was doing. She said, "Come talk to me." So I said, "Can I set up a meeting?" There was no Google in those days, so I called a couple people to ask, "What do you know about Bess Abell?" "You don't know who Bess Abell is?" they said. "Not really. I mean, I know she's here and she's Joan Mondale's key person, but tell me about her." That was when I found out that she had so much experience in the White House as social secretary for the Johnsons and she was now running Joan Mondale's office. She was essentially her chief of staff and she put everything together for Joan. So I made an appointment a day or two later, and I went in to see Bess. I had by then a couple days intervening to just kind of learn how to get across the street to the White House, learn how to go get lunch, learn where the East Room was located, and learn where the president and first lady lived.

I got put in charge of taking Vice President Mondale over to all the events, and that scared me. So I went to see Bess, and my first question was, "How do I learn my job and how do I learn about this place?" Literally, she saw that I was anxious and told me, "Don't be nervous. It's all going to come in due time." The sage advice that she gave me was take it one day at a time. Then she laughed and said—I will never forget this—"When you don't completely know what you're doing, always, always shut up and listen." I had a look of surprise on my face, and she laughed just this big, uproarious laugh. She was clear and direct, and she meant it.

Bess added, "If you listen, you'll pick up clues from everybody around you. You'll see in the conversation who are allies, who are enemies, what they're trying to do, who you can bring round the bend quickly, and who you can't." She talked a lot about communication and working with press because you have to know that everything you're saying could be quoted.

She was extremely helpful in giving me confidence that I could learn, even though I didn't know the White House, that I had a role model. She was supremely confident. She was very outgoing. She loved what she was doing.

The other question I asked her was, not having worked for Mondale in the campaign, I didn't know any of the staffers. What would that be like? She said, "That's a supreme advantage. Because you don't know who does what to whom. So you're starting with a clean slate. You're in an office that has to work with every other office in the place because you're in the press office, so everybody's got to be able to trust you." She said, "They've got to be able to trust that what your word is, goes. That you're open and honest and that you'll work with them and you'll try and figure out how to make sure that they're in the best light."

You alluded to the difference between Joan's personality and Bess's personality, and how Joan was—

ANN STOCK: Shy and quiet. I think Bess was able to take Joan's passion and shyness and reticence and, knowing what Bess knew about the arts, put together a schedule and projects taking Joan's passion and making it work. It was remarkable what the two of them got done. One was very shy and the other very outgoing, but they were a team the likes of which I think I haven't seen all that many times.

If you look at the years that they worked together, Joan changed and became more outgoing. I think a large part of that is due to being around Bess and watching her interact with people. I don't know that anybody would put their finger on that. Except to say that by the time the administration was over, Joan was much more confident and outgoing. Maybe she'd always been that way, but at the beginning of the administration, she was pretty shy and reticent, and to me it was almost all part of a package of what Bess was supremely good at, literally putting Joan in situations and events where she would shine. Bess knew how to do that because she was so supremely confident and outgoing. Joan got used to doing that more.

I'm not so sure before Joan was in this public position that Joan had spoken that much, had been out, and had a regular schedule where she was talking to people and imparting information and giving speeches. She had done lots of tours, and I think she was extremely confident when she was talking about the arts. But I think Bess brought out in her more of the passion and the confidence. It was like "Frick and Frack." They just melded together and did really good things. They came together in a way that did a lot of good for the arts and humanities and in ways that might not have been expected at the beginning. Both Joan and Bess had a lot of arts and humanities contacts, and when they melded it all together, they really made the place zing. They put a lot of focus on the arts and humanities that had never been on that area before, and changed the way that people thought about the arts and humanities, not taking it for granted. Having a second lady of the land step up and talk about it in a way that people understood and go into communities and pat artists on the back and look at their art and really enjoy it and get all types of people involved in the arts and humanities. It's what both women brought to the table. Both from different perspectives, but it came together in a way that was very beneficial.[16]

DEBORAH M. SALE: I was on the vice president's staff in that role [special assistant] for a couple of years, but working more and more closely with Bess and Joan and spending a lot more time with Bess. The role as the executive director of the Federal Council on the Arts and Humanities came open. Bess encouraged me to apply for that role. She convinced me, really, that I could do that. I think I might have been a little timid about taking it on. Bess was really an incredible mentor to me—certainly the best mentor I have ever had and among the few people I've considered to be mentors. She was exceptional and encouraged me in every way. So I applied to become the executive director of the Federal Council on the Arts and Humanities. And I think she really convinced Joe Duffey [head of the National Endowment for the Humanities] that I could do this job. I think there was less concern on the parts of others who were making this decision, but I do think she did convince Joe.[17]

In April 1978 Bess was recognized for her long support of the arts when she received the first North Carolina School of the Arts Honor Award. Georgia artist John Kehoe designed the award, a cast-iron butterfly on a marble base. Actress Helen Hays presented the award "in recognition of Mrs. Abell's years of effective, selfless, and dedicated service to the arts." Bess also received gifts from local artists, including an iron dogwood tree with butterflies. Still, Bess let people at the ceremony know that even though she was proud to receive the honor, they needed to know that in order to attend the event she had to miss her first Kentucky Derby in twelve years![18]

DEBORAH M. SALE: Bess, Joan, and I really did work together hand in glove from the point I joined the Federal Council forward. We spent quite a bit of time in North Carolina because the objectives that Joan had and that Bess helped her realize were to make it possible for people to be proud of the artists who lived in their communities, and for the artists themselves to feel like they could live and work in their communities and be appreciated—that everyone didn't have to go to the East Coast or the West Coast to be an artist in America.[19]

What can you say about the relationship between Joan Mondale and Rosalynn Carter?

MICHAEL S. BERMAN: There was never any arguments. They were very accommodating. The Mondales' entertainment style was different than the Carters because Carter did not permit alcohol and Mondale did. I remember the first time a group of congressmen came to the house for a party early on, once they'd moved in. The gates have moved now, but there was a gate about 40 or 50 feet from the front door of the house, and Joan and Fritz were greeting them at that gate. One fellow, Jack Brooks from Texas, broke away from the group immediately, came up onto the porch where I was standing, went inside, looked around, came out on the porch, put his hands together, and said, "They've got the hard stuff, it's okay, boys." The Mondales served hard liquor, except when Carter came.[20]

Ambassador to the Arts

Jimmy Carter appointed Joan Mondale honorary chair of the Federal Council on the Arts and Humanities. She had studied art in college, was an accomplished potter, and had worked in art galleries before coming to Washington. She turned the vice president's official residence into a showcase for American art, featuring the works of Robert Rauschenberg, Edward Hopper, Louise Nevelson, and Ansel Adams. As the *New York Times* noted, "It became an annual rite of spring for journalists to gather to see the new paintings, sculptures and crafts that Ms. Mondale had borrowed from American museums."[21]

As her chief of staff, Bess once more won notice for producing innovative events, sometimes on short notice, that promoted both art and the artists. Newspapers again called her the "Iron Butterfly." "Actually, neither title gives a true picture of Bess, whose quiet, fantastic efficiency is coupled with self-effacing modesty," wrote one reporter. "But under that soft, Southern exterior is a firmness that never falters."[22]

How did the notion of Joan of Art come about?

WALTER MONDALE: Well, that was Joan. Joan really wanted to be around the arts, this big community. She wanted to help build their interest in what the artists were producing. She always told me she wanted to provide an audience for the artists. She meant that deeply, and all her life, that's what she did. Bess understood that, and Joan would go anywhere, but she loved going to the arts community and she did a lot of that. Bess helped her on that as well.[23]

BESS ABELL: President Carter gave Joan a wonderful gift when he asked her to be his ambassador to artists and the cultural community. I think she picked up the ball and ran with it. One of the first things that she did was plan a working lunch in the vice president's house around that wonderful dining room table that was a gift from Nelson Rockefeller and had been in their house in New York for years. Joan wanted to gather a group of people that would help her and want to work with her. She called Claiborne Pell, who was "Mr. Arts" in the Senate, and she called Sid Yates, who filled that same spot in the House of Representatives. Then she had Liv Biddle [Chairman of the National Endowment for the Arts, 1977–1979] and Joe Duffey, who President Carter had nominated to head the National Endowment for the Humanities, and Lane Kirkland, who was a big labor leader and very interested in the arts. They were all playing on the same team, and I think that did a lot to get her started out on the right foot.

Her mailbox was always full. She was getting constant invitations. It was like they came over the transom. She would go and appear at places and open museums, art exhibits, and make various speeches, and she would always need to be introduced. People know what the First Lady is, but they got all mixed up in introducing Fritz's wife. They didn't know quite how to handle it and would get tongue tied. She was introduced as the First Wife of the vice president; once it was the Second Wife of the vice president. My personal favorite of all those introductions was when she was introduced at least twice as the Vice of the President. Meanwhile, tears would be rolling down my cheeks, and I would be holding myself, hoping I wouldn't laugh out loud like a madwoman.[24]

Were Joan's contributions to the arts in large part due to Bess's efforts?
JUDY WHITTLESEY: I'm sure that Joan would have been doing things anyway, but without Bess I don't know that she would have been doing them on the big stage in the way that she did. Because Bess knew government, crafts were displayed in the Renwick Gallery across from the OEOB [Old Executive Office Building], designating that as a craft museum. I don't think that would have happened. And lobbying for photographers to take the cabinet portraits for the administration. There were so many things like

this that I'm sure that Bess designed the strategy. She actually designed a little lunch for Joan to have lunch with the person that was the head of the [National] Portrait Gallery. They went to visit one of his favorite sculptures in Rock Creek Cemetery, Saint-Gaudens' *Grief* [the Adams Memorial]. It was a little lobbying plan to encourage him to go along with their idea of using photographs rather than paintings for the cabinet portraits, and this was in recognition of photographers as artists. And it happened, and they were exquisite photographs.[25]

DEBORAH M. SALE: After we got into the White House Bess had an initial conversation with Joan about the role she might play. It was basically to tell her that if she wanted to make a mark as the vice president's wife, then she should choose one thing to do. Mrs. Johnson had done that and had been very successful. Bess really knew and understood that you couldn't be all things to all people and have anyone ever recognize who you were. Mrs. Mondale said that, well, the thing that she'd cared most about was the arts, that she'd been an art history major, she was a ceramicist herself, and that she really cared about the arts in America. I think Bess knew that the National Council on the Arts and the arts and humanities existed as a legal entity because it had come about during the Johnson administration with the advent of the law that created the National Endowment for the Arts and the National Endowment for the Humanities. Its authority is within that same law. Initially it was active, and then it had sort of gone dormant over a number of different administrations after the Johnson administration. They decided to revive it and to sort of create from that a vehicle from which Joan Mondale could basically support the arts and the humanities in America.[26]

ANN STOCK: Joan loved crafts. She started collecting crafts. Crafts were throughout the house, so you could see the furniture, the crafts, and the art collection. Bess came up with this idea of putting in a new art collection every year. I think the first one was from Minneapolis. Joan had worked in the Minneapolis Institute of Art, and someone there helped put together that first collection. You start to see a pattern here, and you start to see Bess's fine hand, knowing what she would have known as social secretary and who she should work with. She had all the contacts, and she put them to extremely good use.[27]

I thought that Bess had gotten Joan to emphasize the crafts.
DEBORAH M. SALE: Joan was a craftsperson already because Joan was a potter by training. That's what she did. So she really did understand the

crafts. Now, Bess knew a lot about the crafts as well. Joan knew a lot about contemporary craft and the history of craft as well. But Bess knew also about places like Jugtown [Pottery] in North Carolina, which is where the whiskey jugs were made years and years ago. She knew about that specific history of craft and brought that knowledge, but Joan was a craftsman and, therefore, was very interested in that kind of work and very open to that kind of work. My feeling was that she and Bess had a tremendous sort of equality of conversation about crafts because they both had a keen interest and a strong knowledge in that arena. I think that would be probably more accurate.

Kentucky has an incredible craft tradition and has had forever. So my impression was that Bess had seen a lot of craft work, appreciated it, and also had a sense of where else it was being done. Bess was very strategic about where to go. And a lot of their decisions were based on what they would see there. This is the surrounding community. This is the political community in which they sit. And this is what we can achieve. I think that Bess had a greater understanding of the reach of these traditions in many ways.

I raised that question because the Mondales invited so many painters to their dinners.

DEBORAH M. SALE: Well, that's because of the art program in the vice president's residence. Joan and Bess, in determining how to showcase the arts from the beginning, decided to bring modern art into the vice president's residence. And much of that was painting and sculpture. A smidgen of that was craft, contemporary craft, because all the art was by working artists, people who were alive at the time. Joan was on the board of the Walker Art Center in Minnesota, and Martin Friedman was its head. So Joan asked Martin to curate the first art exhibition in the vice president's house.

The next year they decided to focus the art regionally. The next person they asked was Bob Buck, who was at that point at the Albright-Knox [Art Gallery] in Buffalo. There were dinners that those artists whose work was in the house were all invited to, to celebrate their art being there. So that's the reason that so many more visual artists were guests, because there were just fewer pieces of craft. But Bess, and Joan, and I, went to Jugtown, in North Carolina. We went to Penland, which was a big craft school in North Carolina. And we saw Dale Chihuly blow glass at Penland. He was teaching there at the time. We went to his studios on the West Coast as well. We just saw an incredible amount of craft.[28]

JUDY WHITTLESEY: The decision was made early on that each of the four years would feature an art collection in the vice president's residence that represented art from the museums of a particular region of the country. It did not mean artists. So this was a fine definition that you had to understand in order to appreciate the exhibit, because during the Northeastern Region exhibit, you wouldn't just find Northeastern artists, you would find art that came from museums in that region.

So there was a curator from a museum in a region each of those four years who curated the art that then hung in the vice president's residence, and Bess coordinated a reception to introduce the collection. It was a big deal each time the new collection went up, and then it would go down and a new collection would come in. They created a brochure about the house with the art that was produced for each of the collections. And there was also a piece of contemporary sculpture in front of the wonderful Victorian vice president's residence in the driveway that would also be selected by the museum director, who would be the curator. I think Harry Hopkins from the San Francisco Museum [of Modern Art] was the first curator, the first region. This gathered a lot of interest, attention, media attention. It focused attention on art from those museums. It was a plan that achieved so many of the goals that I think that Bess and Joan had in terms of kind of turning the lights on art in communities with the federal opportunity to spotlight artists.[29]

MICHAEL S. BERMAN: Joan was not an unsophisticated person, but she was pretty much socially unsophisticated in terms of Washington. What Bess provided for her, early on in particular, as we were taking over the vice president's residence and it was becoming a social place, she gave Joan a lot of security and comfort about what they were doing and how they were doing it. I remember one particular scene: Joan had her ideas about art. They were slightly different than my own. And I ended up with the job of trying to finance bringing the art in from various galleries around the country. I had to figure out how to do it as a 501(c)(3); there was no organization.

Bess, I remember, suggested to me, "Why don't you get one of the art galleries to be the collector. You could then finance them." It was a gallery out in California that we ended up using. That's what we did, so although the art never went through them, whatever art was picked by Joan and whoever else was working with her would be treated as if it was being lent to that gallery. That gallery was sending it to—quote-unquote—the vice president's house, and then all the costs went through them. That's what I raised the money for. There were no election laws in those days, as we know them now.

I do remember one conversation in which, as the arts started to come in, Bess and Joan were standing there—stuff was being unpacked—and I looked at it and I basically said something quite unkind about it. "Why are you bringing all this odd stuff in here?" Bess was laughing. Joan simply said, "Michael, as long as we're together, you raise the money, I'll pick the art."[30]

ANN STOCK: They used to maximum advantage the relationship with Jimmy Carter. Every time Joan was going over to see Jimmy Carter, Bess would always be running around, trying to get talking points and things together for her to think about exactly what she needed to say to him. President Carter, last year [2018], when it was Mondale's ninetieth birthday and everybody went out to Minnesota, said that he's never been lobbied so hard on arts funding as he was by Joan Mondale. He had over twenty meetings with her. The fine hand of Bess was all over that. You think of what they did. They got GSA [General Services Administration] to put crafts in the gift shops of their buildings. They got all the heads of the cabinet departments to hang art in the buildings. Everything they touched, Bess had a hand in it.

When I think of Bess, I think of her as the organizer, mastermind, majordomo, the person who made it work. Unlike the social secretary job, where she stepped out front and you knew who Bess was, you knew who Bess was in this job, but Joan was the principal with the arts. But you knew the power sat with Bess. She was the person that organized everything. She clearly made sure that the schedule focused on Joan's passion.

You have to step back and think about contemporary arts and artists who were just coming into being in the '70s and more so in the '80s. But again, if you look at what Bess did with Joan, every trip, and I think almost every single trip that Joan went anywhere, whether it was arts-related or not, usually she met with an artist like Louise Nevelson, Willem de Kooning, Richard Diebenkorn, Jasper Johns, Frank Stella, or Robert Rauschenberg.

What was Bess's relationship with the West Wing?
ANN STOCK: They were afraid of her! They liked her, she worked with everybody. I mean, she was an honest broker. You knew that if she said she was going to do something, she did it. You knew that you could go into a meeting, sit down, and I'd say I was going to do this, you'd say you were going to do that, she'd come back, and it'd be done. Nobody had to call Bess or anybody in her office fifteen times to see if they'd done what they said

they were going to do. You could count on her word. You can always count on Bess's word. I've never seen her not come through.[31]

Travels with Joan

BESS ABELL: President Carter, after naming her to be his liaison to the cultural community, did many wonderful things for Joan. One was he named her to head a delegation to Finland. It was in December. It was cold, colder than Minneapolis, and it was dark, I mean they are right up there by the Arctic Circle, and the sun shone a little bit kind of like twilight for about two and a half hours a day. The president of Finland, President Urho Kekkonen, had been in office there for years and years and years. He was president and also prime minister, but I don't think at the same time.

It was a major holiday in Finland, schools were closed, government buildings were closed, I think even shops were closed. People didn't have anything to do. It was dark outside. At that time they had one television channel, so people sat home in the dark and watched television. Joan got to be a really big star in Helsinki.

Each delegation was supposed to present a gift to President Kekkonen. So Joan said, "It's Christmas. Let's take him Christmas decorations." She had just finished decorating the tree at the vice president's house and had done it with pieces done by American craftspeople and American artists, and it was beautiful. She said, "Let's do the same thing. Let's give President Kekkonen the same thing." She found a wonderful clay box, and she went around and gathered up lots of interesting, fun, appropriate decorations to give to President Kekkonen. Then it was sent to the State Department. They took the gift and wrapped it up magnificently with seals and ribbons and so forth, and it went with us to Helsinki. Just before Joan and the American ambassador and I were going to go in to present this gift to President Kekkonen, Joan said, "This isn't going to work. He will never remember it, he will never remember it," and she began tearing off all this elegant wrapping. She said, "I will present it to him. I will get him to take the top off and then we will look at all the decorations." Well, that is what happened, and, of course, everybody in Helsinki was watching it on TV. She became a really big star.

Fritz had said when the trip was being put together, "Helsinki is so close to Leningrad, it would be great if Joan could go to Leningrad and to the Hermitage." I guess he and lots of other people began working on making that happen. In Washington, DC, you can find an expert on everything. I was looking for an expert that would help plan Joan's side trip if it turned out to be to Leningrad.

I found a man named Fred Starr at the Smithsonian, who was an expert on lots of things. I asked him, "What would you think would be of the most use and the most pleasure that Joan would gain from a trip to Leningrad?" He said, "Of course, she has to go to the Hermitage. Yes, yes. And then, from what I read about her, what she would most like to see are the paintings that are in the dusty basement of the Russian Museum by a Russian artist named Wassily Kandinsky. He is a persona non grata. So, they are hiding all his canvases in the dusty basement of the Russian Museum." I mentioned it to Joan. She replied, "A chance to see Kandinsky canvases? How wonderful if that could happen." So we had been meeting with the three members of the Soviet delegation throughout the time in Helsinki, and they invited us to tea. Of course, we went, and of course Joan was polite and gracious and wonderful and all smiles and said how much she was looking forward to being in Leningrad and seeing the Hermitage and added that she would also love to go to the Russian Museum and see paintings by the Russian artist Kandinsky.

They said, "No, no, not possible, not, not, possible." She kept saying in that sweet, pleasant, nonconfrontational way what she hoped would happen. We wound up our tea party and left and went back, and we didn't know what would happen, but, by golly, when we got to the Russian Museum, we were taken down to the dusty basement, and they did pull out some canvases that were not as dusty probably when we saw them as they had been before.[32]

Writer Mary Lynn Kotz recalled traveling with Joan Mondale and Bess Abell on one of their art excursions.

MARY LYNN KOTZ: Bess was the executive director for Joan Mondale, and I was doing a piece on her called "Joan of Art" for *ARTnews*. Joan Mondale, who is an art historian, had written a book on art in politics with a Rauschenberg on the cover. They had planned a trip, looking at the state art commissions, and Bess invited me to go with them. I was the only reporter who was invited on that trip. Bess said to me, "You'll have to dress so that you can carry your own suitcase because we're going with just us and a couple of secret servicemen, and they do not carry luggage. They carry guns."

It was just the three of us. The first stop was in Chicago where Claes Oldenburg had the great Bat Tower [*Batcolumn*]. Then we went from there to St. Louis and finally wound up in New Mexico. The New Mexico art people were just terrific. They had two things going: the Hispanic history and art, and Native American history and art. Joan was so excited. She got an audience with Georgia O'Keeffe. Bess and I were not invited in. Georgia just wanted to meet Joan Mondale, who was appreciative of her art. So she went in for thirty minutes for an afternoon tea way back at her Ghost Ranch, and we sat out in the car in front with the motor running. The one secret serviceman was with her inside, and the other was running the car, wondering if we were going to run out of gas. But she was there for only thirty minutes. When she came back, Joan was very enthusiastic about everything. She said to us, "Oh, I didn't even know she was still alive, and she's just turning ninety, and she's going blind." And I thought, "Ding, ding, ding, ding. That's a story for *ARTnews*."

As soon as I got back, I wrote O'Keeffe a letter asking if I might come and speak to her in October, because she said that was a good time. I went back, and she said, "Oh, I liked Joan Mondale." Georgia O'Keeffe had the best sense of humor, and her mind could just flash back from 1913 to two weeks ago to four months ago, and it was a great thing. So I'm sorry that the Georgia O'Keeffe story put off Joan Mondale's story for a month in *ARTnews*. But that was another great gift from Bess in my career, and she was just so generous with her ideas, and her ideas were always so smashing. She was such a creative and, at the same time, very organized person. Creative and knowledgeable and organized and a very loyal friend. I just love her.[33]

The 1980 Presidential Election

The Iranian hostage crisis overshadowed the 1980 election. President Carter staved off a challenge from Senator Edward M. Kennedy to win the Democratic nomination, but he limited his campaigning while trying to win release of the American captives. Consequently, the Mondales campaigned in the Carters' absence. Carter and Mondale lost the election to the Republican ticket of Ronald Reagan and George H. W. Bush.

WALTER MONDALE: Bess was a trooper. She didn't pull punches at all, and she was experienced politically, and Joan needed that advice and that help. So, when the campaign started, they hit the trail. They went everywhere, and she was the perfect aid for Joan because Joan was not as strategic in her thinking. She could get it, but she needed somebody like Bess to see the larger political picture and how you might affect it, and she was great at that.

That was a grueling campaign in 1980.
WALTER MONDALE: Oh, it was awful. I was doing six, seven speeches a day, covering a lot of space between each of them. It was a painful period

because it was clear that we could lose. That was miserable, and poor Joan had to go out and try to make a difference, as I did, as Rosalynn and everybody did, but we couldn't get people to buy us again. You could feel it through the audiences. The audiences were nice, but you look at their eyes and they're just flat. I know Joan went through a lot of that with Bess, and we were both dispirited by it.

Bess was always positive. Every day was a great day, and she would see things that she'd feel good about, and she could pump Joan up in a wonderful way. No, no. That was one of her great gifts she brought to us. She was not a downer. She was an upper all the time.[34]

MICHAEL S. BERMAN: It was a hard campaign, and Joan was out a lot and Fritz was obviously out full time. Carter wasn't campaigning, so we were very busy. We carried the load. Not we, but he did and therefore our staff did, to a degree that probably has never been repeated since then for the obvious reasons.[35]

NEAL P. GILLEN: Bess would reach out to people. When she was working for Mrs. Mondale, she called me, wanting to know if I had any ideas about the forthcoming 1980 Democratic convention in New York. I told her that a good idea would be a poster. I didn't remember if there was one for Carter's '76 convention in New York. She thought it was a good idea and arranged for the well-known artist Frank Stella to do a poster. The posters were signed and numbered and given to campaign contributors. It was a good and thoughtful souvenir. Bess had an artistic side—it was sort of contradictory because she is a very well-organized person—but she also had an artistic side to come up with that design.[36]

Did Bess participate in the 1980 campaign for reelection?

ANN STOCK: They had some of their own schedule. Remember, Jimmy Carter didn't travel in '80. So Mondale was the person. I mean, we spent a couple months in Iowa, and I think Joan was probably on the road a lot more than they might have been had President Carter been out campaigning. But President Carter didn't campaign at all in '80.

What was Bess like on the road?

ANN STOCK: Fun. You always wanted to be on a Bess Abell trip and a Joan Mondale trip because they did things that were fun. Substantive, but fun.

And Bess would always be the one that would gather the troops up at the end of the day and say, "Let's have a drink," or "Let's go out to dinner."

ANN STOCK: Always. Always. But again, that's her congenial, convivial nature. Like she's a person that brings people together. They debrief from the day. They talk about what's going to happen the next day. They think about what they've learned, what they need to think about for the next day. She was always bringing people together.[37]

What was the time from November to January like for you all?

WALTER MONDALE: A really depressing thing. We were going back to private life. We were moving back to our old home in DC, and the home was in shambles. I don't know how it got as bad as it did, but I remember walking into that house first time we went there after the election, and boy was it in desperate need of repair and improvement. Bess helped Joan sort that stuff out. I distinctly remember Bess was over there I think trying to perk up Joan and help her get on the path of leaving the vice president's house and going home. It wasn't as bad as it sounds. Being vice president is tough. You've got all the responsibility, but you're not the principal and you're also isolated.

The vice president's house is a beautiful house, but you are isolated. There's nobody around there, and you don't have neighbors to come and see you. You could invite people, but the normal ebb and flow of people that you would have in your neighbors, but that's not there in the vice president's house. I think both Joan and I looked forward to being in a more normal neighborhood and community where we could be with friends. So, we were kind of half wanting to go back home, and Bess really tried to make it as pleasant as possible.[38]

MICHAEL S. BERMAN: It was tough because you're unwinding everything. They still had their home on Lowell Street, which they had rented out during this time. But happily the lease—I'd set it up basically so that if something happened, they'd be able to get back in there. So they're moving back there. It was just a difficult time. I was the last person on the Mondale staff to leave the White House on the day that Reagan had his inaugural. And I left [at] exactly 12:01 a.m., walked out of my office and walked across the street because we had a transition out office on Jackson Place.[39]

DEBORAH M. SALE: Toward the end of the Carter-Mondale administration, after President Carter lost, Bess asked me if I was going to stay, and I said, "No." I was going to go back to New York. She said, "Well, that's good." She said, "We always want to continue to be friends." But she said, "I've seen many people try to stay after the administration in which they were so active, and they thought they would be invited to the same dinner parties. And that's not the way Washington works." It was very good advice. She knew that it was the right decision not to stay.[40]

TYLER ABELL: Bess had grown to be such a friend of Joan's that they continued their friendship for the rest of her life. When she died, Bess was asked to speak at Mrs. Mondale's funeral service. And Bess gave a somewhat amusing talk about some of her days with Mrs. Mondale. Fritz came up to Bess after the service and told Bess how great her talk was. He just loved it. And he said, "The best part about it was that it loosened Jimmy Carter up, so Jimmy gave a much better speech after your speech."[41]

Do you remember when it was no longer Mr. Vice President and Mrs. Mondale, it was Joan and Fritz?

WALTER MONDALE: Right, and that's the way we wanted it. We didn't want to go around with titles when it was over. Bess knew that and was all for that. One of the tough questions we had to deal with is whether we remained in Washington, where we'd lived for over twenty years, now that we were out of public office, and I do remember this. Bess said to Joan, "You know, there's only so many places at that table, and when you're no longer in public office, they give that place to someone else," and that was correct. Kind of hard to accept, but on the other hand, we accepted that. That didn't bother me, and I asked Joan if we could go home. She said sure. So, Bess had something to do with that by giving us that sage advice. Bess meant so much to Joan and to me. She was a big, big person in our lives.[42]

11

Life after the White House

A newspaper account in 1975 recorded the end of the old era of Washington party-giving, epitomized by Perle Mesta, the hostess of lavish formal parties for Washington's political and social elites during the Truman and Eisenhower eras. Reporter Ann Wood noted that in the rise of a new age of more free-spirited public party-giving, "when an event can raise political funds, push a good cause or sell a book, people in the know turn to Bess Abell, who can dream up an idea, invite the right people, and create a party that everyone will talk about." Between working for the Johnsons and the Mondales, Bess had turned her skills into a public-relations operation, organizing initiatives and events ranging from planning a Lyndon B. Johnson memorial grove beside the Potomac River to fundraisers for political candidates and the National Committee of the Democratic Party. "Her system is to explore party possibilities for the happy union of party and party-giver, like a matchmaker, once the would-be host puts himself in her hands."

Among the events Bess Abell Enterprises organized was a book party given by Simon and Schuster for the publication of *All the President's Men*. The Washington press noted: "The publishing house wanted to launch the book here where they didn't know the scene. She arranged a cocktail party in the big tree-shaded garden in the back of the Textile Museum, a mansion in an elegant embassy area off Connecticut Ave. The guests were chic, literate, and literary. The food was superb, and it lasted until the sun set, when all the guests went home. And that was as Bess had planned, because there were no lights in the garden. Knowing when to end a party is a gift, too."[1]

TYLER ABELL: When Bess left the Johnson White House, she wasn't sure what she wanted to do. She decided to call her new business Bess Abell Enterprises. I told her that whatever she did, she shouldn't call her new business Bess Abell and Associates. I said, "In the first place, everybody who does that, they don't have any associates. That's just a name. Call yourself something that shows some activity. So Bess Abell Enterprises would be a good way to go, and you can do anything that's enterprising." She would give parties and that was probably the biggest thing.

When the Johnsons went back to Texas, she stayed here. She was frequently asked to plan a party that would publicize an event of some sort or another. She did a book party for the book that I was doing, editing volume one of the Drew Pearson diaries [Tyler Abell, ed., *Drew Pearson Diaries, 1949–1959* (1974)]. The party was better than the book. It was spectacular.

For the publication of *All the President's Men*, they got her to do a book party for them, which, again, was a big success. And Mary Lynn Kotz—Bess suggested to Mary Lynn Kotz a book that Mary Lynn did, called *Upstairs at the White House*. She was a terrific help to Mary Lynn in getting that book done. She introduced Mary Lynn to the usher at the White House and the head waiter, John Ficklin. Mary Lynn gives Bess terrific credit for not only helping her to put the book together but then publicizing the book so effectively with the big party that she did.

I first met Bob Strauss at the 1960 Democratic convention, but we did not have any real further contact until after President Johnson left the White House. Bob came to Washington and opened a law firm and then became treasurer of the Democratic National Committee. Around 1969 Bob and Helen Strauss invited Bess and me to go to the horse races with them. Later, in April 1971, Bob asked Bess to manage a big Democratic fundraising dinner at the Hilton Hotel in Washington.

Bess agreed to do the complete dinner, including seating, menu, table decorations, music, and lighting for $5,000. I told Bess that I thought that she should charge Strauss more. She finally decided that she would and wrote the contract with him so that she would be paid $5,000, and if the dinner was a big success, she would get $10,000. The dinner was a huge success against all kinds of odds because of different squabbles amongst Democrats that tried to trip it up and make it go wrong. Nevertheless, the dinner was a sellout. The Hilton had the largest ballroom in Washington, so it was the biggest crowd you could have.

When the time came to tell Bob Strauss that he should pay her $10,000, Bess became really worried. She thought, "The press is going to get ahold of this, and then it'll be a huge controversy." I told Bess, "Well, I think you did your job, and that was the agreement. You should just tell him that you believe that you are entitled to the $10,000." So Bess did, and just as she predicted, it did come out in the press with a big picture of her: "Bess Abell paid $10,000 for Democratic fundraiser." When Strauss was asked about it, far from complaining, he rose to Bess's defense. She was so happy because he said, "Absolutely, we paid $10,000, and she was worth more than that. We were lucky to get Bess Abell for that, and we could not have done it without her." Strauss became a very important person in Bess's life. She thought the world of him.

In 1972, prior to the Democratic National Convention in Miami, Bob and Bess teamed up again for a large event. John Y. Brown Jr., who would later become governor of Kentucky, convinced Strauss to do a telethon. Bess was the main organizer of a party for the big donors that served as the kickoff of the twenty-four-hour telethon.

Many of us thought Strauss should be chairman of the Democratic National Committee. And he did become chairman following George McGovern's nomination, which turned into a political disaster. McGovern could not even carry his own state of South Dakota. He did carry Massachusetts and the District of Columbia.

After the 1972 campaign Bess worked on and off at the Democratic National Committee, becoming the staff person who worked most closely with the Democratic Governors' Conference. She worked in New York City prior to the Democratic Convention, organizing it, and was there when Joan Mondale called her and invited her to manage Joan's work in the 1976 campaign.

Another important person in Bess's life was Edward Bennett Williams [Washington attorney and owner of the Washington Redskins and Baltimore Orioles]. It was Bess who introduced him to Lyndon Johnson. I remember Bess coming home one day and saying that she thought that the president would really enjoy meeting Ed Williams, and she was going to invite him to a stag dinner. Williams and Johnson really did enjoy each other. Bess was there at the dinner, of course. Bess made sure that Williams was seated either across from Johnson or next to Johnson. Williams was so appreciative that he invited Bess to join him in his box at the Washington Redskins football game.[2]

CAROL CARLYLE: When we left the White House, Bess was hired by Robert Strauss to run this huge fundraising event. Robert Strauss called me up himself and said he wanted me to come to work for him. Bess had signed on to work and fundraise. The Democratic Committee, at that point, was about $8 million in debt. So this was our first event to tackle that and try to get uprighted before the next four years. We had a 2,000-person, a $1,000 a person, dinner at the Hilton Hotel. That was execution under fire. Every table was set for ten people, and we had to internally seat everybody. That meant there were place cards for 2,000 people. How did we accomplish that? When I look back, we had no computers. Everything was on 3×5 cards and was done by hand. Bess was our engineer, everything from the decorations to the menu to who sat where.

There you are in the middle of the night, seating a 2,000-person dinner, doing all these floor charts, and moving people around, and you would be in an uproar. "Well, I can't get this done because somebody else hasn't moved along," and she would just calmly move it along so you could get your job done. She had a very easy, take-hold, but it didn't show, method of making it all work.[3]

The Democratic National Convention took place in Miami Beach in July 1972. Bess's friend, Bob Hartnett, served in the Florida state legislature and at her request hosted a reception at his home for the Young Democrats attending the convention. Harnett recalled that the convention was "a series of disorganized procedures" that resulted in the nomination of Senator George McGovern, who was not Bess's favorite candidate. But what he remembered most was Bess's reaction to the Watergate burglary that had taken place a month earlier.

BOB HARTNETT: The following day, by previous invitation, the Abells joined us to be our guests at a resort in Naples, Florida, in which I was a partner. While driving across the Tamiami Trail crossing through the Florida Everglades we were speculating about the chances of the Democratic nominee's possible success in the coming November election. During that ongoing discussion there was a newscast about the break-in. It announced that the burglary of the Watergate offices of the Democratic Party had been traced to men working on behalf of the Committee to Re-elect the President, aka President Richard M. Nixon. The story implicated the entire campaign staff and others. To most, it sort of sounded like a "minor story" in the campaign, which was about to get underway.

But not to Bess Abell! We could see her natural-born political instincts spring to life! As the radio announcer finished up the "small item," Bess said, "If we, the Democrats, had a decently qualified candidate for president, he would wrap that story right around Nixon's head and beat him with it!" Well, George McGovern didn't do that. On November 7, 1972, Richard Nixon carried forty-nine of the fifty states. However, Bess's sixth sense of politics came to fruition almost exactly two years to that date, when Nixon resigned the presidency. Over the prior two years, the Democrats wrapped the Watergate burglary around Nixon's neck, and he left town, just as Bess had predicted.[4]

The Counter-Gridiron

As more women reporters began covering the news from Washington, they objected to their exclusion from the prestigious Gridiron Club, a century-old institution that invited the president and other political leaders to an annual white-tie dinner. In the 1970s, women reporters picketed the dinners and encouraged its famous guests not to attend. These efforts proved unproductive.[5]

Women journalists credited Bess Abell with dreaming up the carnival format for their hugely successful Counter-Gridiron party, held on the same night as the Gridiron and attracting its own celebrities. She "roamed through the evening in blue jeans and a T-shirt emblazoned, 'Trust in God, SHE will provide.' She plans a party, organizes it, and follows through, taking care of all the hundreds of details that make a success."[6]

Eileen Shanahan, who covered politics from the Washington bureau of the *New York Times*, recalled the background of the movement.

EILEEN SHANAHAN: First of all, I'll explain why the Gridiron Club was important. It was the way that Washington bureau chiefs, mainly, really made their editors feel important. This was a dinner with a club that had fifty white male members. It was like a fraternity, with self-perpetuating membership. They selected their own successors, and they had just this one gigantic dinner a year (they had a smaller dinner, too, but it didn't amount to anything), which virtually every president went to, every Cabinet member, every Supreme Court justice, every you-name-it. And their editors just loved it because they had guests and a head table. But most of all these big-name guests were scattered through the audience so your editor from back home got to sit next to the secretary of the treasury or whomever, and the editors loved it. And it made the bureau chiefs more important in the eyes of their own employers. It also cemented contacts, much more than it would do today, the press corps has gotten so large.

But it was very important. All the top officials—male officials—and editors loved to go to the Gridiron dinner. First of all, it was an entertaining evening. They did all this satirical singing, taking popular songs and writing new satirical lyrics to them. It was a fun evening. I got to go several times, after women were finally admitted.

Well, anyway, there was a group of journalists, including a lot of the younger journalists, younger than my generation, mostly women, but some men, who really started to try and force the Gridiron to admit women members. It was ultimately successful after eight years.[7]

TYLER ABELL: Organizing the White House country fairs led to, several years later, an event to get women into the Gridiron Club. The Gridiron Club was a very stuffy men's club that does not even have a clubhouse. They held a dinner once a year and only invited men because that was the way it started. It was limited to fifty men of the top echelon of newspaper reporters and correspondents in Washington. The ladies said, "Well, this is not fair."

The women's movement got stronger and stronger. They said, "We want to have at least the opportunity to join the Gridiron Club," because the Gridiron Club, basically, made news. If you were a member of the Gridiron Club, you could invite guests to the Gridiron Club's once-a-year dinner. That marked you for some distinction and also gave you the opportunity to talk to people or where you could show how good you were, and help you get better stories or better assignments to cover better stories. The women, I think with a certain amount of justification, thought that they should be included because women had decided that they should be allowed to climb up out of just doing the social pages. And you ought to be able to be a member of the most distinguished press club.

They tried protesting, but that didn't get them anywhere. So Bess decided that they should do a Counter-Gridiron party where they would invite the same type of people who would do things at the party. She said, "We'll do it like a fair." She got a lot of these distinguished newspaper ladies to help, and they ran a country fair, like the White House country fair, but they did it in the evening. They called it the Counter-Gridiron Fair. They did it the same night as the Gridiron Club, which was always on a Saturday night. And they got a lot of people out there doing interesting things. Dan Rather sold kisses. Martha Mitchell, the wife of the Attorney General, would make phone calls for you. They set up a special telephone out there so that you would come on and you would pay, and Martha Mitchell would call anybody you wanted her to because Martha had gotten the reputation of calling people in the middle of the night. They had somebody that told fortunes. There was a little bit of prize money passed out, and it was made to be fun and you could buy drinks. They made a couple thousand dollars, which they contributed to an outfit called Journalists for Professional Equality. And they got lots of press!

They did that three times, in 1974, 1975, and 1976, until the Gridiron Club finally invited Helen Thomas to be a member. So it worked. Ann

Wood worked with Bess on that. And Ann Wood has a big notebook with all the details of how that Counter-Gridiron was run. But Bess just had the ability to pull people together. They invited dignitaries like Ed Muskie, Dan Rather, William Cohen, and Martha Mitchell. Then Bess orchestrated the whole thing. She rented space at Mount Vernon Seminary and College on Foxhall Road. She was not able to talk them into donating the grounds, but they did supply the space for a fairly reasonable price. I do not believe they would have done it except Bess talked them into it.[8]

Bess enlisted White House and later Senate Curator James Ketchum for her organizing committee.

JAMES R. KETCHUM: Counter-Gridiron was a group made up of mostly women who were covering Washington and some of their editors as well, who organized an event that was held the same weekend as the Gridiron Club dinner itself. They brought together many interesting people—it was like a giant carnival. I remember the one that was held soon after the Saturday Night Massacre in the Nixon administration where [former Attorney General] Elliot Richardson was signing pardons. And Martha Mitchell, who had been known to make these midnight calls to Helen Thomas, about what John Mitchell was really doing, Martha became a telephone operator. You would go up and plunk down five bucks a minute and she would call your family.

One booth was selling flower seed left over from the '60s' beautification days. It was an effort to gain as much publicity as possible. Instead of doing nothing but picket lines to really have something that people could come to and be reminded.

Some of these things were taken rather seriously, although those of us who were kind of in on trying to make them saleable didn't take them seriously at all, except for the proceeds that would come from them. But within a handful of years, the Gridiron finally admitted women.[9]

Merry-Go-Round Farm

In the 1980s, Bess and Tyler devoted their attention to converting Drew Pearson's money-losing farm in Maryland into a successful real estate venture. They devised a plan to subdivide part of the farm into lots for homes while retaining portions of the land as a horse farm, and turned to a landscape architect who had worked on Lady Bird Johnson's beautification program. Their desire was that the property "undergo the transformation from farm to estate while preserving the qualities and conditions" that originally attracted people to the rural area outside of Washington, DC.[10]

TYLER ABELL: Bess was phenomenal at dealing with contractors on all the house work that she did. She'd always get the right contractor and always have him work and work well. She had a way of knowing how to deal with people. She said, "You have to just show them that you're interested in them and then they don't think that you're looking down on them. They think that you're working with them." She was just masterful with that. Which was the type of thing her father did too. She didn't say that she learned that from her father, but for sure that is where that approach to life came from.

One of the best things that Bess ever did was to make Merry-Go-Round Farm work. She really was terrific and played a great role in many, many different respects. She went into the business of planting more trees, the overall landscaping for the whole development, and planting I don't know how many thousands of daffodil bulbs, certainly ten or fifteen thousand. A lot of it was actually putting the stake in the ground and dropping the bulb, physical work. She always worked with the guys that she was telling where to plant the bulbs, so she didn't plant them all by herself. But she would go along and plant while they were planting. They were part of the family, and they appreciated being thought of as part of the family.

She thought up the idea and carried it off to give a party. It started out as a Christmas party for the people who were boarding horses out here and people who had bought lots. And that started as a wreath-making party, which was really great. It gave somebody something to do and it has to do with Christmas, and it all pulls a party together instead of just standing around talking and drinking. But finally, the place got too big to do wreath-making, so she shifted to other things. Since it was a horse community, one was having horse races. She would do horse racing, the kind where you have fake horses. You roll the dice and, with a roll of the dice, one horse gets ahead of the other. If you've got the winning horse, you won a prize, which would have been a wreath or some Christmas-type prize.

One year, she had everybody get their picture taken and make a Christmas card. She had some of her pals that were painters, and designers, and calligraphers at the White House do this huge screen where faces could be shown through it. She had a photographer, and the screen was there, then the guests would stand up behind the screen with their faces out, then get their picture taken and then that would be your Christmas card.

As time went on, she did "Merry-Go-Round Farm Musings," a newsletter that talked about the production of houses here at Merry-Go-Round Farm and who was buying and that sort of thing. We went through a real bad financial bump on the road. We almost didn't make it. And the only reason we did make it is Bess's work convinced the banker that we would make it. He took me aside and said, "Tyler, the only reason we renewed this loan is because of Bess. And I didn't think you were going to make it. But when I saw the work that she was doing, in particular, with that newspaper, I realized that that was going to sell lots and so we renewed the loan."

Then much, much later, out here at the farm, she was very good at gardening and joined the Hoe'n Hope Garden Club. I had never heard of the Hoe'n Hope Garden Club, and I do not know how she came across it, but it was an all-ladies garden club, and they did not do much gardening. Now, Bess got them to actually do some gardening. She said, "Well, we'll plant at some of these places that need some landscaping." So she planted at the Glen Echo Fire Department and the children's garden at the Children's National Hospital. And then she became the president of the garden club for a couple years. And everybody thought she was the best president they ever had. I imagine she was.[11]

SHIRLEY JAMES: I once went home with Bess for a visit. That was my first time to be at the farm and, oh wow, I just loved it. I had Luvie's [Pearson] room, overlooking the river. That was my chance to get to know Farmer Bess and Farmer Tyler. One day we went to pick strawberries, and it was like hunting Easter eggs. There were loads of strawberries. We came home and made strawberry jam. And of course, roaming around and the horses, it's just wonderful waking up there.

I was there when Bess set up her beehives. She was very concerned about the bees because the environment has gotten very bad for the bees with all the insecticides and everything. So she went and learned what she should do and how to do it. Finally, the day came when Bess had her hives, and they were set up just below where the garden was, not far off the road. Tyler and I went up there, and Tyler really kept his distance. He didn't want to be stung, and I didn't either, but it was so fascinating. I kept getting in closer. She was very intense about what she was doing, very calm but intense. She had her beekeeper's hat that she had made, a god-awful thing, and the gloves and veil to cover her face. It was really fascinating to watch. Then several years later, I started getting honey. All their friends got honey. I'm still getting honey every Christmas from those bees.

And of course, sitting out on that terrace, looking over the river, having real bourbon. I won't call it a lecture, but there is a spiel you get about what is truly bourbon and where it has to come from. I'm sure you've heard it. But anyway, we were having real, serious bourbon. It's good stuff, and it was a great time.[12]

Teaching Class at the Johnson Ranch

As an alumna of the Johnson White House, Bess served on the board of the National Archives Foundation and maintained close connections with the Lyndon B. Johnson Presidential Library. The library's longtime director, Harry Middleton, taught a spring semester course at the University of Texas called "The Johnson Years" and invited Bess each year to speak to his students at the Johnson ranch.

TYLER ABELL: Harry Middleton became a big guy in Bess's life. We hardly knew him at all when he was in the White House. But after he became director of the library, I got to know him a little bit because the Drew Pearson papers went to the library. That meant a fair amount of interaction between me and Harry. Then, Harry decided to give an undergraduate course about LBJ at the University of Texas. Harry conducted it by giving two talks a week for the semester.

Bess described it as helping Harry paint the fence like Tom Sawyer did, by talking his friends into the joys of painting the fence. Harry would talk people like Bess, and later me, into giving a talk for it. You would talk about your relationship with Lyndon Johnson when he was president. So the students were getting modern history told by people who were making it. Most young people thought of Johnson as the president who fought the Vietnamese war, whereas there was an awful lot more to Johnson than that. Bess would tell these wonderful stories about Johnson that just brought down the house. It showed a little piece of the president that, if you had not heard Bess tell the story, you would not have thought that that was even possible.[13]

SHIRLEY JAMES: Harry Middleton started teaching a class on the presidency of Lyndon Johnson. Mrs. Johnson wanted to attend some of Harry's classes, but Mrs. Johnson was not an early riser during that time. As she got older, she slept later and later. So it was my suggestion that Harry bring his class to the ranch. Harry, who always had such brilliant ideas, decided that Bess and Tyler should come to speak. They both spoke to Harry's honors students. Tyler spoke to the kids in the library, and then Bess would speak to them out at the ranch. Mrs. Johnson would give a luncheon for them.

It was just wonderful. Bess loved interacting with the students, and they loved it. I would give a tour of the house. And then Bess would speak. I remember how she talked about the White House and the weddings and told so many wonderful stories. She pretty much gave the same talk year after year. It couldn't have been improved on, and they loved hearing about all of that. After Mrs. Johnson died, Bess and Tyler still came each year until Harry retired from teaching. Bess talked about the weddings. She talked about being at the ranch the day that Kennedy was assassinated. She talked about the whistle-stop trip through the South and having to send an empty engine ahead on the track because there had been bomb threats. How gutsy it must have been to live in those times. I call those the glory days.

How did the students react to Bess's presentations?

SHIRLEY JAMES: Oh, they took notes and listened intently, asked questions, lots of questions. When the classes were over, I would ask the students, "Who is your favorite person that has talked to you?" They would always say, Bess.[14]

Reflections on the Iron Butterfly

LUCI BAINES JOHNSON: If you asked me to try to sum up Bess in a few words, it would be difficult because she was a woman of many attributes. But one of them that stands out was she instinctively did her homework for herself and for those she was working for or with so that there were as few surprises that were negative as possible. And Mother believed in doing her homework. And Bess would come up with the most creative diversity of folks. She'd choose everybody from Robert Merrill to the Christy Minstrels to entertain. All on the same stage. I mean, saying there's a richness that's far beyond.[15]

LYNDA JOHNSON ROBB: I don't know how Bess knew as much as she did. Did she just read every Amy Vanderbilt, every protocol book? One, of course, I think she came from a genteel family. I mean, Daddy was rough and ready. He didn't care a whit whether you used the right fork, or whether we had the oyster bowls—none of that stuff was his interest. And Mother was not all that interested, either. So you had to have somebody who did things right.

She was the dean of the social secretaries, and they would get together and swap stories and have lunch, because they had so much in common.

And social secretaries were not mean people. You have plenty of people in administration that just have to be mean because that's the job they have. They have to be the no, no, no's and the gruff people. But social secretaries, they're social secretaries, they're supposed to be sociable.[16]

Would she survive as a social secretary in today's world, do you think?

PATRICIA PERKINS ANDRINGA: First of all, I believe Bess could survive anywhere. So the issue is more, would she have been happy? Would she have enjoyed it as a job? It's hard to say. Each first lady selects somebody whom they feel will represent them well, and they usually know, although sometimes they don't. So I think that she and Mrs. Johnson had a very special relationship which enabled her to bring out the best in both of them. It's very hard to speculate. Bess would survive and do a very good job. And perhaps might even be able to make the office a better place to be than it is probably right now. I doubt it would change her.[17]

From your perspective, what kind of a life did Bess Abell carve for herself?

ANN STOCK: I think if you ask her, she carved out the love of her life, two fabulous kids, a career that she did on her own terms that was fulfilling, satisfying, and wonderfully creative. But I think at the center of her life were her husband and her kids. And that she would say she lived a life well. And to the fullest extent. Bess always made sure that she didn't leave any stone unturned.

And what do you consider her legacy to be?

ANN STOCK: That she trained so many people to not be afraid of politics, not be afraid of events, to succeed and be confident in what they do by the example that she led. She was a role model before we knew what role models were. Just the example that she set and the way that she went about her business was extraordinary. It's an extraordinary example for all of us to emulate and follow. She has been the center of all of these social secretary lunches because of how she comported herself and led her life. And she was fun. It was fun, and it was a happy time for her. All kinds of challenges to it, but I think Bess is one of these people that chooses to look at what makes the glasses half full, not half empty. Extraordinary woman.[18]

If Bess had been born in the 1980s, what do you think her career path could have been?

DEBORAH M. SALE: Well, she probably could have been easily chief of staff to the President or Vice President Mondale. It wouldn't have been assumed that she should work for the wife if she had been born later because she had every quality that you would need to be a major player and figure. And she was, in her way. But she probably would have assumed that was not available to her. In the Johnson administration obviously she was very young, but could she have been the White House Chief of Staff if she were a few years older? Sure. Absolutely. At a later time, she could have easily succeeded her father if she had wanted to do that because she had all of the political skills that it would take to do that.

There's no doubt that Bess could have done anything, particularly anything that was related to government and politics, because it was just so much a part of her. It was so easy for her. And she really did have a strategic policy sense too. She knew how to create a construct to determine what should be done. And then she knew, also, how to follow up and make sure that everything got done that was supposed to be done. But I think she could have done anything that came her way.

I think we were taught not to ask for something. I think that was true of Bess. It certainly was true of me growing up. But I think that in some way, in today's culture, she would have stepped up and been recognized because she would have felt permission to say, "I can do that and I'd like to," whereas I suspect that she did the things that came her way, which is true of many women. Most women in life, until fairly recently, didn't go after things. They did the things that came to them. But her abilities were so great that she could have done, I think, anything that came her way. And anything that she did do was done beautifully, extremely beautifully, thoughtfully, with just enormous capacity.[19]

What were the values that she instilled in you?

CAROL CARLYLE: I think the work ethic. We worked hard and long, put everything we had into it. You can always make it work. You can always get it done.

From my vantage point, I never, ever saw where Bess's relationships weren't harmonious. As I said, she was an iron butterfly. If they didn't think it was right or their opinion on how to do something was different, she worked it out, and usually she came out on top with her calm but forceful demeanor and polite demeanor.[20]

Can you describe the skill set?

LINDA JANE HOLDEN: Oh, a confident imagination, a willingness to make things fun and interesting and delightful, and always looking for the humorous side of it, that unexpected, delightful surprise—like in their kitchen there's some invitations and things that she devised through the years for different events. They're just so fun. I often thought, "Gosh, she's just so lighthearted." She didn't get down in the dumps, at least that was never my impression of her. But she was extremely creative and imaginative, but she didn't second-guess herself. She just dove right in and went for it, and everybody loved it. It just, I think, put everybody at ease and made everything a lot more fun and enjoyable and successful, too, depending on whatever she was trying to achieve.[21]

What do you think her standing should be in the sort of lineup of former social secretaries? Where does she stand in that group?

JAMES R. JONES: She was as good as there was. She knew what you're supposed to get out of a function, and it was not just to have a good time, but it was other reasons: to help the president, to help Mrs. Johnson, etc. And she pulled it off with great aplomb. So I don't know of any social secretary that I have followed in any way that would be better than Bess. No. I think she was as good as they got.

If there was a function, it had all the moving parts to it thought out and anticipated where something might have gone wrong to correct. It was just well-organized, and there was the warmth to it, which emanated from the Johnsons and their staffs that made you feel at home when you came to the White House or some function they had. So I think that was the main thing. Those things that end up looking good or looking like they're well thought out, they are well thought out. There were a lot of details that go into all of those things. And they're not just who stands where, but what kind of a tent do you have, and where is the tent located, and who moves when and where. And Bess had all that down. We didn't have to worry about that and didn't have to interfere in any way.[22]

NEAL P. GILLEN: The thing that stands out in my mind, getting to know Bess over the years, she was a kind and a generous person, very generous with her time, which was very precious. She was loved by the White House press corps, men and women. I never heard a bad word uttered about her from anyone.

She was intuitive. She was a quick judge of people. And she was also inquisitive, but in a nice, charming, sort of Southern way. She was not pushy in that regard. And also, she was determined too. If it was something that she thought had to be done or should be done, she would nudge you on that, nudge in a nice way. In that regard, she was resourceful and very well-organized, had to be well-organized, and she reciprocated.

Bess set the standard that they all tried to meet, and that says a lot. If you look at those who became social secretary, they're all physically attractive. They're articulate. They're well-mannered. They're considerate. They're nice. They're friendly. They're well-organized. I mean, it's all the Bess Abell standard that's been carried on down.

It takes a lot of patience, especially when you have a guy like Johnson. He's so demanding and what have you. I know there were times when President Johnson made demands on Bess and pushed Bess as he did his other staff members. Mrs. Johnson was not the type of person to do that. So she really had two bosses, I would say, at the White House because Johnson considered everyone inside that fence one of his gofers, and that's how he treated them.[23]

TYLER ABELL: Bess was very good at knowing how people worked. I think that is one of the reasons she got along with the Johnsons because they were very people-oriented. President Johnson doesn't get much credit for being a great personality, but he absolutely was. He could play it any way he wanted to, and he recognized that Bess was good at that as well.[24]

Almost everything Bess did was a success, and mostly it just came to her naturally. I think because of her father's interest in cooking and entertaining, that field came easily to her. As social secretary, she had to exercise her party-giving skills. And, of course, the more you exercise a skill, the better you get at it.[25]

JAMES R. KETCHUM: After leaving the White House, Bess never stopped being the shoulder to lean on and the helping hand.[26]

Epilogue

Lyndon Johnson once called Bess Abell the most efficient person working in his White House. "She should be in the cabinet," he raved. Had she been born at a later time she might well have achieved that distinction. Had she been a son, her father, Earle Clements, would undoubtedly have groomed her for a career in Kentucky politics. Had she accepted her father's offer to help financially to attend law school in 1956, when her husband Tyler went to George Washington University's law school, she might have served in any number of government positions. But she came to maturity in an era before the women's movement had redefined women's aspirations and expectations.

Instead, Bess carved out a career in the social and cultural milieu of Washington, DC, which is enveloped in politics. Her standing became formalized at the White House from 1963 to 1969. During that turbulent era, when protesters often spilled into the streets outside, Bess created an atmosphere of conviviality within the White House, planning dinners, receptions, weddings, and countless other social and cultural gatherings that made the Johnson years somewhat less stressful.

Bess tapped so many singers, musicians, dancers, and poets to perform at social events that colleagues began referring to her as an impresario. She juggled entertainment with proper protocol, assuring that everything was appropriate and that all guests—from heads of state to her friends from Kentucky—felt comfortable in that imposing setting. Most of all, she helped to divert attention from the national and international challenges that encroached daily on the White House, enabling the Johnsons to fulfill their social obligations in relative peace.

As the Vietnam War intensified, Bess shrewdly kept track of those who signed petitions opposing the president's foreign policies in order to avoid inviting them to perform at White House events. Only occasionally did the antiwar protests slip by her and disrupt the functions that she so carefully planned. She handled the unexpected as resolutely and discreetly as possible. Not for nothing did she acquire the label Iron Butterfly.

Her story has a timeless quality to it. Long after the turbulent 1960s, the White House has remained a political, diplomatic, and social stage and a target for demonstrators. Efforts to maintain a peaceful atmosphere within its walls in no way diminish the legitimacy or the urgency of those protests. Presidential administrations must attempt to carry on while coping with dissent. "A number of people thought we should have gone to the days of World War II when there was absolutely no entertaining in the White House at all," she recalled in her oral history to the Johnson Library. "I didn't agree with that, and I don't think it was purely because I wouldn't have had anything to do if we had traveled that route." Devoted wholeheartedly to her post, she drew the line against only one thing: "I didn't see any need in giving a forum to people who were going to embarrass the president."[1]

Like many women of her time, Bess demonstrated her professional capabilities largely outside the reach of the general public. Her many skills and contributions were known more to those within the White House walls than to those without. But her years as social secretary, and later as chief of staff to Joan Mondale, and even later as a social consultant offered a window on how Washington really works.

While Bess's profile eventually became very public, her family life meant everything to her. The young couple who ran off to marry on New Year's Eve stood beside each other through good times and bad for over six decades. Tyler could not be prouder of Bess's accomplishments. Her sons remember a loving mother who just happened to work at a rather fascinating place. Her grandchildren each experienced the "Kentucky tour" meant to remind them of their roots, taking them back to Bess's hometown, to the college she attended, and to the capital where her father had governed.

As a hostess in her own home she picked up on a rule set by Lyndon Johnson and insisted that, no matter how many people were seated at the table, there would be just one conversation. Moreover, she had no qualms about guiding the topics for that one conversation. With her inquisitive mind, Bess was known for asking very pointed questions of her dinner guests. Her intent was not to embarrass; she really wanted to know. Like her father, she could be sweet, warm, and firm in one sentence. She did not suffer fools or those with no real opinions well.

Reflecting her political upbringing, Bess never let a good story go unused and perhaps at times even embellished. Although her voice has now been stilled, this account of her career has drawn from her own compelling narrative. As Bess did throughout her career, she speaks for herself.

The Interviewees

ABELL, BESS [ELIZABETH HUGHES CLEMENTS ABELL]: White House social secretary during the Johnson administration, chief of staff to Joan Mondale, and director of Bess Abell Enterprises.

ABELL, DAN TYLER: Older son of Bess and Tyler Abell.

ABELL, LYNDON: Younger son of Bess and Tyler Abell.

ABELL, TYLER: Bess's husband, a lawyer, assistant postmaster general, and chief of protocol during the Johnson administration.

ANDRINGA, PATRICIA PERKINS: As a student at Mount Holyoke College, she interned with Bess Abell at the White House social secretary's office.

ARNOLD, JANE DYER, AND J. P.: Jane was a childhood friend of Bess's from Morganfield, Kentucky.

BAKER, BOBBY [ROBERT GENE BAKER]: Secretary for the majority during Lyndon Johnson's tenure as Senate Democratic majority leader.

BERMAN, MICHAEL S.: Washington lawyer and lobbyist, who served as White House counsel to Vice President Walter Mondale.

BOGGS, LINDY [MARIE CORINNE MORRISON CLAIBORNE BOGGS]: Wife of Louisiana representative Hale Boggs; she was elected to Congress after his death in 1971 and served until 1991.

CARLYLE, CAROL: Assistant to Tyler Abell at the US Post Office Department, then detailed to the White House as Bess Abell's secretary.

CARPENTER, LIZ [MARY ELIZABETH SUTHERLAND CARPENTER]: Washington correspondent for Texas newspapers who became Lady Bird Johnson's press secretary.

CATER, DOUGLASS [SILAS DOUGLASS CATER JR.]: Editor of *The Reporter* magazine and special assistant to President Johnson.

CLEMENTS, EARLE C.: Bess Clements Abell's father, who served as US representative (1945–1947), governor of Kentucky (1947–1950), and senator from Kentucky (1951–1957), later becoming executive director of the Senate Democratic Campaign Committee.

DUNETZ, MARTA: Assistant to Liz Carpenter, Lady Bird Johnson's press secretary.

DURR, VIRGINIA FOSTER: Civil rights activist and founding member of the Southern Conference for Human Welfare.

GILLEN, NEAL P.: Lawyer, lobbyist, and author, who served as an advance man for both Lyndon and Lady Bird Johnson during the 1964 presidential campaign.

HOLDEN, LINDA JANE [HOYT]: Author of "The Lady Bird Special: The Power of a Whistle-stop Campaign" in *White House History* (Spring 2017), *Presidents' Gardens* (2013), and *The Gardens of Bunny Mellon* (2018).

JAMES, SHIRLEY: Luci Baines Johnson's assistant, beginning in 1974, and later Lady Bird Johnson's executive assistant from 1992 to 2007.

JOHNSON, LADY BIRD [CLAUDIA ALTA TAYLOR JOHNSON]: Wife of Lyndon B. Johnson, mother of Lynda Johnson Robb and Luci Baines Johnson, and first lady from 1963 to 1969.

JOHNSON, LUCI BAINES: Younger daughter of Lyndon and Lady Bird Johnson. She married Patrick Nugent at the National Shrine of the Immaculate Conception on August 6, 1966. That marriage was later annulled, and she married Ian Turpin in 1984.

JONES, JAMES R.: Legislative aide to Congressman Ed Edmondson. He worked as an advance man on the Lady Bird Special before joining the

White House staff in 1965 and becoming the president's appointments secretary (the equivalent of chief of staff) in 1968. He later served in the House of Representatives from Oklahoma from 1973 to 1987.

KETCHUM, JAMES R.: White House curator during the Kennedy, Johnson, and Nixon administrations, 1963–1970, and later US Senate curator, 1970–1995.

KITT, EARTHA: Broadway and Hollywood singer, actress, and activist. After her White House incident in 1968 she could find no work as a performer in the United States and lived abroad for the next decade.

KOTZ, MARY LYNN: A volunteer with Bess Abell at the White House and later coauthor, with J. B. West, of *Upstairs at the White House.* Her husband, Nick Kotz, covered the White House for the *Des Moines Register.*

LAMB, BRIAN: Social aide at the White House, 1966–1967, while a naval officer. After serving in the White House Office of Telecommunications Policy, he founded C-SPAN, which began broadcasting in 1979.

MONDALE, WALTER: Senator from Minnesota, 1964–1976; vice president of the United States, 1977–1981; Democratic presidential candidate in 1984; and husband of Joan Mondale.

ROBB, LYNDA JOHNSON: Older daughter of Lyndon and Lady Bird Johnson. She was married at the White House on December 9, 1967, to Marine Captain Charles Robb, who later served as governor of Virginia, 1982–1986, and senator from Virginia, 1989–2001.

RUSHING, MARGARET FORD: Childhood friend of Bess's from Morganfield, Kentucky.

SALE, DEBORAH M.: Special assistant to Vice President Walter Mondale and executive director of the Federal Council on the Arts and the Humanities in the Carter administration.

SHANAHAN, EILEEN: Washington correspondent for the *New York Times,* 1962–1977, and assistant secretary for public affairs in the Health, Education and Welfare Department during the Carter administration.

STOCK, ANN: A Pan American flight attendant who became deputy press secretary to Vice President Walter Mondale in 1980. She later served as White House social secretary during the Clinton administration and assistant secretary of state for educational and cultural affairs during the Obama administration.

WHITTLESEY, JUDY: Served on the staff of Vice President Walter Mondale and on the campaign and transition staffs of several Democratic presidential and vice presidential candidates.

Acknowledgments

Bess Clements Abell loved to talk about her busy and colorful life. Whether addressing a large crowd in an auditorium, a small gathering of guests around a dinner table, or a lone oral historian, she could amuse, inform, and inspire her listeners. Although Bess never wrote a memoir, she left an abundance of recorded memories that we have tapped for this book.

Tyler Abell not only encouraged us to write about his wife of sixty-five years but arranged for Brien Williams, a skilled oral historian, to interview many of her family, friends, and colleagues. We were also able to draw upon interviews conducted by the Lyndon B. Johnson Presidential Library, the Louie B. Nunn Center for Oral History at the University of Kentucky Libraries, the Gerald R. Ford Presidential Museum, the Clinton Presidential Center, the George W. Bush Presidential Center, and the White House Historical Association. These provide a rich source of recent American history through their diligent and systematic interviewing.

Richard Norton Smith, who wrote the foreword, interviewed Bess Abell on several occasions. Also included in this book are interviews that we did, either for this book or as part of our other professional activities. We want to thank all who contributed their memories and insights. It seems that everyone who knew Bess had compelling stories about her that they were willing to share. That says a lot about her.

Christy Thrailkill, assistant to Tyler Abell, provided invaluable help during every step of the project. Janice Elias Birdwhistell read every chapter multiple times and helped locate and secure photographs. Kopana Terry and Doug Boyd, Nunn Center for Oral History, provided important support for the project. Jason Flahardy, UK Libraries audiovisual archivist, assisted with photographs from the Earle C. Clements Collection. *Louisville Courier-Journal* senior photographer Pat McDonogh helped secure many of the photographs for the book.

And, of course, we are grateful to Ashley Runyon, director of the University Press of Kentucky, Victoria Robinson, assistant to the director and Acquisitions, and the entire UPK staff for guiding the book to publication.

Notes

Introduction

1. Bess Clements Abell interviewed by Terry L. Birdwhistell, September 26, 2007, Louie B. Nunn Center for Oral History, University of Kentucky Libraries Special Collections Research Center, Lexington, Kentucky (hereafter UKLSCRC).

2. Lady Bird Johnson interviewed by Terry L. Birdwhistell, October 19, 1976, Louie B. Nunn Center for Oral History, UKLSCRC.

1. The Governor's Daughter

1. With the exception of note 8, all of the quotations from Bess Clements Abell in this chapter are drawn from a September 26, 2007 interview conducted by Terry L. Birdwhistell for the Earle C. Clements Oral History Project, Louie B. Nunn Center for Oral History, UKLSCRC.

2. Tyler Abell interviewed by Brien Williams, May 29, 2018, Louie B. Nunn Center for Oral History, UKLSCRC.

3. Willard Rouse Jillson, "Earle C. Clements: A Biographical Sketch," *Register of the Kentucky Historical Society* 46, no. 154 (January 1948): 375–383; Thomas Syvertsen, "Earle Chester Clements and the Democratic Party, 1920–1950" (PhD diss., University of Kentucky, 1982); *Louisville Courier-Journal*, May 31, 1913.

4. Earle C. Clements interviewed by James W. Hammack Jr. and Forrest C. Pogue, July 29, 1974, Louie B. Nunn Center for Oral History, UKLSCRC.

5. Following his time in prison, Baldwin Clements disappeared, but Lucy Clements Scull must have thought he was in Chicago. She ran a personal advertisement in the *Chicago Tribune*: "Father passed away in Kentucky, wife granted divorce, Mother would love to see you, Lucy." *Chicago Tribune*, March 15, 1925.

6. Margaret Ford Rushing interviewed by Terry L. Birdwhistell, September 10, 2019, Louie B. Nunn Center for Oral History, UKLSCRC.

7. Tyler Abell interview.

8. Bess Abell Oral History Interview 1, May 28, 1969, by T. H. Baker, LBJ Library, Austin, Texas, pp. 1–2 (online, pp. 1–2): http://www.lbjlibrary.net/assets/documents/archives/oral_histories/abell_b/ABELL01.PDF.

9. Ann Wood, "The Newest 'Mostest' Hostess, *New York Daily News*, March 16, 1975.

10. Bess Abell, remarks at the 2016 Earle C. Clements Innovation in Education Award Ceremony, August 22, 2016, YouTube, https://www.youtube.com/watch?v=emUbwWlsbLI.

11. Jane Dyer Arnold and J. P. Arnold interviewed by Terry L. Birdwhistell, May 18, 1977, Louie B. Nunn Center for Oral History, UKLSCRC.

12. Margaret Ford Rushing interview, September 10, 2019.

13. Tyler Abell interview, May 29, 2018.

2. The Johnson Orbit

1. Bess Abell Oral History Interview 1, May 28, 1969, by T. H. Baker, LBJ Library, Austin, Texas, pp. 1–2 (online, pp. 2–3): http://www.lbjlibrary.net/assets/documents /archives/oral_histories/abell_b/ABELL01.PDF.

2. Earle C. Clements Oral History Interview 1, October 24, 1974, by Michael L. Gillette, pp. 2–3, Internet Copy, LBJ Library: http://www.lbjlibrary.net/assets/documents /archives/oral_histories/clements_e/Clements-E1.pdf.

3. Lady Bird Johnson Interview 36, August 1994, by Harry Middleton, LBJ Library, p. 23: http://www.lbjlibrary.net/assets/documents/archives/oral_histories/johnson_c /CTJ%2036.pdf; also cited in Michael L. Gillette, *Lady Bird Johnson: An Oral History* (New York: Oxford University Press, 2012), p. 247.

4. Lady Bird Johnson interviewed by Terry L. Birdwhistell, October 19, 1976, Louie B. Nunn Center for Oral History, UKLSCRC.

5. Lynda Johnson Robb interviewed by Donald A. Ritchie, October 11, 2019, Louie B. Nunn Center for Oral History, UKLSCRC.

6. Tyler Abell interviewed by Brien Williams, May 29, 2018, Louie B. Nunn Center for Oral History, UKLSCRC.

7. *Louisville Courier-Journal,* January 3, 1955.

8. Tyler Abell interview, May 29, 2018.

9. Ibid.

10. Bess Abell Interview 1, May 28, 1969, pp. 2–3.

11. Marie McNair, "The Johnsons Honor Young Couple," *Washington Post,* March 26, 1955.

12. Lady Bird Johnson Interview 36, August 1994, pp. 22–23.

13. Lynda Johnson Robb interview, October 11, 2019.

14. Judith Axler, "The Couple Who Now Reign over Official Society in the Capital," *New York Times,* October 1, 1968.

15. Tyler Abell Interview 1, May 8, 1969, by T. H. Baker, LBJ Library, pp. 3–5, https:// discoverlbj.org/item/oh-abellt-19690508-1-00-23.

16. Lady Bird Johnson interview, October 19, 1976.

17. Robert G. [Bobby] Baker interviewed by Donald A. Ritchie, June 1, 2009, US Senate Historical Office, Washington, DC, p. 54.

18. Tyler Abell Interview 1, May 8, 1969, pp. 5, 8–12, 26.

19. Neal P. Gillen interviewed by Brien Williams, October 3, 2019, Louie B. Nunn Center for Oral History, UKLSCRC.

20. Tyler Abell Interview 1, May 8, 1969, pp. 5, 8–12, 26.

21. Ibid.

22. Bess Abell interviewed by Capricia Penavic Marshall for "Role of the First Lady," June 4, 2014, Clinton Presidential Center, C-SPAN Video Archive, https://www.c-span.org/video/?319588-1/panel-discussion-role-lady.

23. Tyler Abell interview, May 29, 2018.

24. Bess Abell interviewed by Capricia Penavic Marshall for "Role of the First Lady," June 4, 2014.

25. Bess Abell Interview 1, May 28, 1969, p. 4.

26. Bess Abell interviewed by Richard Norton Smith, January 29, 2008, White House Historical Association, Washington, DC, p. 2.

27. Tyler Abell interview, May 29, 2018.

28. Bess Abell interview, January 29, 2008.

29. Tyler Abell interview, May 29, 2018.

30. Bess Abell Interview 1, May 28, 1969, pp. 3–5.

3. A Part-Time Job

1. Michael Dobbin, "A 'Part-Time' Job and What It Grew Into," *Baltimore Sun*, August 7, 1966.

2. Lady Bird Johnson interviewed by Terry L. Birdwhistell, October 19, 1976, Louie B. Nunn Center for Oral History, UKLSCRC.

3. Bess Abell video interview, October 22, 2003, LBJ Library, Austin, Texas, https://www.youtube.com/watch?v=E3RJ5Kd-Qhs.

4. Michael L. Gillette, *Lady Bird Johnson: An Oral History* (New York: Oxford University Press, 2012), pp. 338–339.

5. Tyler Abell Interview 1, May 8, 1969, by T. H. Baker, LBJ Library, p. 26, https://discoverlbj.org/item/oh-abellt-19690508-1-00-23.

6. Bess Abell Interview 1, May 28, 1969, by T. H. Baker, LBJ Library, p. 5, http://www.lbjlibrary.net/assets/documents/archives/oral_histories/abell_b/ABELL01.PDF.

7. Bess Abell interviewed by Richard Norton Smith, January 29, 2008, White House Historical Association, Washington, DC.

8. Liz Carpenter Interview 1, December 3, 1968, by Joe B. Frantz, LBJ Library, pp. 21–22, 36–37, https://discoverlbj.org/item/oh-carpenterl-19681203-1-74-193-a.

9. Tyler Abell Interview 1, May 8, 1969, p. 26.

10. James R. Ketchum interviewed by Brien Williams, July 18, 2018, Louie B. Nunn Center for Oral History, UKLSCRC.

11. Shirley James interviewed by Michael L. Gillette, August 20, 2020, Louie B. Nunn Center for Oral History, UKLSCRC.

12. Lynda Johnson Robb interviewed by Donald A. Ritchie, October 11, 2019, Louie B. Nunn Center for Oral History, UKLSCRC.

13. Luci Baines Johnson interviewed by Michael L. Gillette, October 18, 2019, Louie B. Nunn Center for Oral History, UKLSCRC.

14. Lady Bird Johnson Interview 44, January 26, 1996, by Harry Middleton, LBJ Library, http://www.lbjlibrary.net/assets/documents/archives/oral_histories/johnson_c/CTJ%2044.pdf.

15. Mike Feinsilber, "The First Aide to the Second Lady," UPI story in the *Boca Raton News*, July 19, 1978.

16. Bess Abell Interview 1, May 28, 1969, p. 5.

17. Bess Abell interview, January 29, 2008.

18. Tyler Abell interviewed by Brien Williams, May 29, 2018, Louie B. Nunn Center for Oral History, UKLSCRC.

19. Luci Baines Johnson interview, October 18, 2019.

20. Bess Abell Interview 1, May 28, 1969, pp. 5–8.

21. Ibid.

22. Tyler Abell to authors, April 2020.

23. Bess Abell interview, January 29, 2008.

24. Tyler Abell Interview 1, May 8, 1969, pp. 26–29.

25. Bess Abell Interview 1, May 28, 1969, p. 16.

26. Tyler Abell interview, May 29, 2018.

27. Bess Abell Interview 1, May 28, 1969, pp. 17–20.

28. Bess Abell interviewed by Capricia Penavic Marshall for "Role of the First Lady," June 4, 2014, Clinton Presidential Center, C-SPAN Video Archives, https://www.c-span.org/video/?319588-1/panel-discussion-role-lady.

29. Bess Abell interview, January 29, 2008.

30. Dorothy McCardle, "White House Aide Knows the Ropes," *Washington Post*, December 13, 1963.

4. White House Social Secretary

1. J. B. West with Mary Lynn Kotz, *Upstairs at the White House: My Life with the First Ladies* (New York: Coward, McCann & Geoghegan, 1973), pp. 284–285.

2. Ibid., p. 294; Jack Valenti, *A Very Human President* (New York: W. W. Norton & Co., 1975), p. 304.

3. Lady Bird Johnson, *A White House Diary* (New York: Holt, Rinehart and Winston, 1970), p. 19.

4. West, *Upstairs at the White House*, p. 342.

5. Bess Abell interviewed by Capricia Penavic Marshall for "Role of the First Lady," June 4, 2014, Clinton Presidential Center, C-SPAN Video Archive, https://www.c-span.org/video/?319588-1/panel-discussion-role-lady.

6. Bess Abell video interview, October 22, 2003, LBJ Library, Austin, Texas, https://www.youtube.com/watch?v=E3RJ5Kd-Qhs.

7. James R. Jones interviewed by Brien Williams, October 9, 2019, Louie B. Nunn Center for Oral History, UKLSCRC.

8. Bess Abell Interview 1, May 28, 1969, by T. H. Baker, LBJ Library, Austin, Texas, pp. 20–23, http://www.lbjlibrary.net/assets/documents/archives/oral_histories/abell_b/ABELL01.PDF.

9. Bess Abell video interview, October 22, 2003.

10. Bess Abell Interview 1, May 28, 1969, pp. 2–14.

11. Lynda Johnson Robb interviewed by Donald A. Ritchie, October 11, 2019, Louie B. Nunn Center for Oral History, UKLSCRC.

12. Neal P. Gillen interviewed by Brien Williams, October 3, 2019, Louie B. Nunn Center for Oral History, UKLSCRC.

13. Johnson, *A White House Diary*, p. 487.

14. West, *Upstairs at the White House*, pp. 341–342.

15. Bess Abell Interview 1, May 28, 1969, pp. 25–26.

16. James R. Ketchum interviewed by Brien Williams, July 18, 2018, Louie B. Nunn Center for Oral History, UKLSCRC.

17. Marta Dunetz interviewed by Brien Williams, February 8, 2020, Louie B. Nunn Center for Oral History, UKLSCRC.

18. Lyndon Abell interviewed by Terry L. Birdwhistell, January 27, 2020, Louie B. Nunn Center for Oral History, UKLSCRC.

19. Dan Abell interviewed by Terry L. Birdwhistell, February 3, 2020, Louie B. Nunn Center for Oral History, UKLSCRC.

20. Lyndon Abell interview, January 27, 2020.

21. Dan Abell interview, February 3, 2020.

22. Lyndon Abell interview, January 27, 2020.

23. Dan Abell interview, February 3, 2020.

24. Marta Dunetz interview, February 8, 2020.

25. West, *Upstairs at the White House*, p. 340.

26. Bess Abell Interview 1, May 28, 1969, pp. 8–10.

27. Ibid.

28. Bess Abell interviewed by Richard Norton Smith for "Behind the Scenes in the East Wing: Social Secretaries to First Ladies," March 5, 2012, George W. Bush Presidential Center, C-SPAN Video Archive, https://www.c-span.org/video/?305012-1/scenes-east-wing-social-secretaries-ladies.

29. Lynda Johnson Robb interview, October 11, 2019.

30. Bess Abell Interview 3, July 1, 1969, by T. H. Baker, pp. 1–5, http://www.lbjlibrary.net/assets/documents/archives/oral_histories/abell_b/ABELL03.PDF.

31. Lynda Johnson Robb interview, October 11, 2019.

32. Brian Lamb interviewed by Donald A. Ritchie, February 20, 2020, Louie B. Nunn Center for Oral History, UKLSCRC.

33. Bess Abell Interview 3, July 1, 1969, pp. 21–22.

34. West, *Upstairs at the White House*, pp. 336–337.

35. Notes provided by Tyler Abell.

36. Bess Abell interviewed by Richard Norton Smith, January 29, 2008, White House Historical Association, Washington, DC.

5. White House Impresario

1. J. B. West with Mary Lynn Kotz, *Upstairs at the White House: My Life with the First Ladies* (New York: Coward, McCann & Geoghegan, 1973), p. 340.

2. Bess Abell Interview 3, July 1, 1969, by T. H. Baker, LBJ Library, Austin, Texas, pp. 11–12, http://www.lbjlibrary.net/assets/documents/archives/oral_histories/abell_b/ABELL03.PDF.

3. Carol Carlyle interviewed by Brien Williams, October 16, 2019, Louie B. Nunn Center for Oral History, UKLSCRC.

4. Tyler Abell interviewed by Brien Williams, June 15, 2018, Louie B. Nunn Center for Oral History, UKLSCRC.

5. Bess Abell Interview 3, July 1, 1969, pp. 11–15.

6. Bess Abell interviewed by Rick Albin, "Insiders Look at the White House," April 8, 2009, Gerald R. Ford Presidential Museum, Grand Rapids, Michigan, YouTube, https://www.youtube.com/watch?v=k4bsDiRaf6g&t=3928s.

7. Bess Abell Interview 3, July 1, 1969, pp. 11–15.

8. Bess Abell interviewed by Richard Norton Smith, January 29, 2008, White House Historical Association, Washington, DC.

9. Bess Abell interviewed by Richard Norton Smith, February 19, 2007, "Remembering LBJ," George Mason University, Fairfax, Virginia, C-SPAN Video Archive, https://www.c-span.org/video/?196703-1/remembering-lbj.

10. Bess Abell Interview 3, July 1, 1969, pp. 19–22.

11. Bess Abell interview, January 29, 2008.

12. Jack Valenti, *A Very Human President* (New York: W. W. Norton & Co., 1975), p. 78.

13. West, *Upstairs at the White House*, p. 335.

14. Bess Abell Interview 3, July 1, 1969, p. 20.

15. Bess Abell interview, January 29, 2008.

16. Lyndon Abell interviewed by Terry L. Birdwhistell, January 27, 2020, Louie B. Nunn Center for Oral History, UKLSCRC.

17. Ann Wood, "The Newest 'Mostest' Hostess," *New York Daily News*, March 16, 1975.

18. Bess Abell interviewed by Richard Norton Smith for "Behind the Scenes in the East Wing: Social Secretaries to First Ladies," March 5, 2012, George W. Bush Presidential Center, Dallas, Texas, C-SPAN Video Archive, https://www.c-span.org/video/?305012-1 /scenes-east-wing-social-secretaries-ladies&event=305012&playEvent.

19. Liz Carpenter, *Ruffles and Flourishes* (Garden City, NY: Doubleday & Co., 1970), p. 193.

20. Barbara Gamarekian, "Tales of a Black-Tie Town," *New York Times*, November 24, 1987.

21. Bess Abell interviewed by Steve Scully, "US-Mexico State Dinner," October 10, 1995, C-SPAN Video Archive, https://www.c-span.org/video/?67555-1/us-mexico-state -dinner.

22. Bess Abell Interview 3, July 1, 1969, pp. 2–10.

23. Carol Carlyle interview, October 16, 2019.

6. The Lady Bird Special

1. Bess Abell Interview 2, June 13, 1969, by T. H. Baker, LBJ Library, Austin, Texas, pp. 1–4, https://discoverlbj.org/item/oh-abellb-19690613-2-84-29. Lady Bird Johnson did give speeches in LBJ's 1941 and 1948 Senate campaigns, but her schedule was never as intense as it would be on the whistle-stop trip.

2. Tyler Abell interviewed by Brien Williams, June 5, 2018, Louie B. Nunn Center for Oral History, UKLSCRC.

3. Bess Abell Interview 2, June 13, 1969, pp. 8–9.

4. Linda Jane Holden, "The Lady Bird Special: The Power of a Whistle-stop Campaign," *White House History* 45 (Spring 2017): 18–29.

5. Linda Jane Holden interviewed by Brien Williams, February 23, 2019, Louie B. Nunn Center for Oral History, UKLSCRC.

6. Liz Carpenter Interview 1, December 3, 1968, by Joe B. Frantz, LBJ Library, pp. 9–10, https://discoverlbj.org/item/oh-carpenterl-19681203-1-74-193-a.

7. Bess Abell Interview 2, June 13, 1969, pp. 9–10.

8. Bess Abell interviewed by Richard Norton Smith, January 29, 2008, White House Historical Association, Washington, DC.

9. Tyler Abell interview, June 5, 2018.

10. Liz Carpenter Interview 1, December 3, 1968, pp. 11–12.

11. Bess Abell Interview 2, June 13, 1969, p. 11.

12. Liz Carpenter Interview 1, December 3, 1968, pp. 15–16.

13. Luci Baines Johnson interviewed by Michael L. Gillette, October 18, 2019, Louie B. Nunn Center for Oral History, UKLSCRC.

14. Bess Abell Interview 2, June 13, 1969, p. 13.

15. Liz Carpenter Interview 3, May 15, 1969, by Joe B. Frantz, LBJ Library, p. 18, https://discoverlbj.org/item/oh-carpenterl-19690515-3-74-193-c.

16. Neal P. Gillen interviewed by Brien Williams, October 3, 2019, Louie B. Nunn Center for Oral History, UKLSCRC.

17. Liz Carpenter Interview 1, December 3, 1968, pp. 6–17.

18. Linda Jane Holden interviewed by Brien Williams, February 23, 2019, Louie B. Nunn Center for Oral History, UKLSCRC.

19. Liz Carpenter, *Ruffles and Flourishes* (Garden City, NY: Doubleday & Co., 1970), p. 145. See also Nancy Beck Young, *Two Suns of the Southwest: Lyndon Johnson, Barry Goldwater, and the 1964 Battle between Liberalism and Conservatism* (Lawrence: University Press of Kansas, 2019), pp. 185–187.

20. Bess Abell Interview 2, June 13, 1969, p. 13.

21. Liz Carpenter Interview 1, December 3, 1968, p 12.

22. Bess Abell Interview 2, June 13, 1969, pp. 12–14.

23. Bess Abell interview, January 29, 2008.

24. Lindy Boggs interviewed by Michael L. Gillette, February 15, 1977, LBJ Library, pp. 11–15.

25. Virginia Foster Durr interviewed by Mary Walton Livingston, October 17, 1967, LBJ Library, pp. 26–29.

26. Linda Jane Holden interview, February 23, 2019; "Crude and rude fundamental violations of elementary etiquette have no place in South Carolina politics," editorial, "A Disgrace," *Greenwood (SC) Index-Journal*, October 9, 1964.

27. James R. Jones interviewed by Brien Williams, October 9, 2019, Louie B. Nunn Center for Oral History, UKLSCRC.

28. Robert David Johnson, *All the Way with LBJ: The 1964 Presidential Election* (New York: Cambridge University Press, 2009), pp. 271–275.

29. Bess Abell Interview 2, June 13, 1969, p. 13.

30. Bess Abell interviewed by Mark Updegrove, "Tribute to Lady Bird Johnson," December 6, 2012, National Archives, C-SPAN Video Archive, https://www.c-span.org/video/?309829-1/tribute-lady-bird-johnson.

31. Bess Abell Interview 2, June 13, 1969, pp. 14–15.

32. Liz Carpenter Interview 1, December 3, 1968, pp. 12–13, 18.

33. Lindy Boggs interview, February 15, 1977, p. 15.

34. Bess Abell Interview 2, June 13, 1969, pp. 16–17.

35. Tyler Abell interview, June 5, 2018.

36. Neal P. Gillen interview, October 3, 2019.

7. White House Weddings

1. Bess Abell Interview 2, June 13, 1969, by T. H. Baker, LBJ Library, Austin, Texas, pp. 5–8, https://discoverlbj.org/item/oh-abellb-19690613-2-84-29.

2. Lynda Johnson Robb interviewed by Donald A. Ritchie, November 26, 2019, Louie B. Nunn Center for Oral History, UKLSCRC.

3. Luci Baines Johnson interviewed by Michael L. Gillette, October 18, 2019, Louie B. Nunn Center for Oral History, UKLSCRC.

4. Bess Abell Interview 2, June 13, 1969, pp. 5–7.

5. Lynda Johnson Robb interview, November 26, 2019.

6. Bess Abell Interview 2, June 13, 1969, pp. 7–8.

7. Bess Abell interviewed by Richard Norton Smith, January 29, 2008, White House Historical Association, Washington, DC.

8. James R. Ketchum interviewed by Brien Williams, July 18, 2018, Louie B. Nunn Center for Oral History, UKLSCRC.

9. Linda Jane Holden interviewed by Brien Williams, February 23, 2019, Louie B. Nunn Center for Oral History, UKLSCRC.

10. J. B. West with Mary Lynn Kotz, *Upstairs at the White House: My Life with the First Ladies* (New York: Coward, McCann & Geoghegan, 1973), pp. 346–347.

11. Bess Abell interview, January 29, 2008.

12. Bess Abell Interview 2, June 13, 1969, p. 9.

13. Bess Abell interview, January 29, 2008.

14. Luci Baines Johnson interview, October 18, 2019.

15. Bess Abell Interview 2, June 13, 1969, p. 9.

16. Bess Abell interview, January 29, 2008.

17. Liz Carpenter Interview 4, August 27, 1969, by Joe B. Frantz, LBJ Library, pp. 21–22, https://www.discoverlbj.org/item/oh-carpenterl-19690827-4-74-193-d.

18. Liz Carpenter, *Ruffles and Flourishes* (Garden City, NY: Doubleday & Co., 1970), p. 267.

19. Bess Abell Interview 2, June 13, 1969, pp. 9–10.

20. Brian Lamb interviewed by Donald A. Ritchie, February 20, 2020, Louie B. Nunn Center for Oral History, UKLSCRC.

21. Bess Abell interview, January 29, 2008.

22. Bess Abell Interview 3, July 1, 1969, by T. H. Baker, LBJ Library, Austin, Texas, pp. 8–10, https://discoverlbj.org/item/oh-abellb-19690701-3-84-30.

23. Luci Baines Johnson interview, October 18, 2019.

24. Lady Bird Johnson, *A White House Diary* (New York: Holt, Rinehart and Winston, 1970), p. 407.

25. Luci Baines Johnson interview, October 18, 2019.

26. Johnson, *A White House Diary*, p. 599.

27. Bess Abell Interview 2, June 13, 1969, pp. 5–8.

28. James R. Ketchum interviewed by Donald A. Ritchie, November 30, 2004, US Senate Historical Office, Washington, DC. See also "Lynda Johnson Tells the Story behind Her Engagement," *McCall's* (November 1967), 80–81.

29. Lynda Johnson Robb interviewed by Harry Middleton, August 23, 2004, C-SPAN Video Archive, https://www.c-span.org/video/?316276-1/lynda-johnson-robb-interview.

30. Lynda Johnson Robb interview, November 26, 2019.

31. Lynda Johnson Robb interview, August 23, 2004.

32. Lynda Johnson Robb interview, November 26, 2019.

33. Lynda Johnson Robb interview, August 23, 2004. Willie Day Taylor, a longtime LBJ staff member, essentially functioned as a surrogate mother to young Lynda and Luci whenever Lady Bird Johnson had to be away.

34. Bess Abell interviewed by Capricia Penavic Marshall for "Role of the First Lady," June 4, 2014, C-SPAN Video Archive, https://www.c-span.org/video/?319588-1/panel -discussion-role-lady.

35. Bess Abell interview, January 29, 2008.

36. Ibid.

37. Lynda Johnson Robb interview, November 26, 2019.

38. Carol Carlyle interviewed by Brien Williams, October 16, 2019, Louie B. Nunn Center for Oral History, UKLSCRC.

39. Brian Lamb interview, February 20, 2020.

8. In Time of War and Protest

1. Jack Valenti, *A Very Human President* (New York: W. W. Norton & Co., 1975), p. 78.

2. Bess Abell interviewed by Richard Norton Smith, "Behind the Scenes in the East Wing: Social Secretaries to First Ladies," March 5, 2012, C-SPAN Video Archive, https://www.c-span.org/video/?319588-1/panel-discussion-role-lady.

3. "Eric F. Goldman Dies at 73; Historian Was Johnson Aide," *Washington Post*, February 21, 1989.

4. Liz Carpenter, *Ruffles and Flourishes* (Garden City, NY: Doubleday & Co., 1970), p. 209.

5. Eric F. Goldman, *The Tragedy of Lyndon Johnson* (New York: Alfred A. Knopf, 1969), pp. 419, 457–475; Tevi Troy, *Intellectuals and the American Presidency: Philosophers, Jesters, or Technicians?* (Lanham, MD: Rowman and Littlefield, 2002), pp. 68–73.

6. James R. Ketchum interviewed by Donald A. Ritchie, November 30, 2004, US Senate Historical Office, Washington, DC, pp. 122–123.

7. Bess Abell interview March 5, 2012.

8. Bess Abell Interview 3, July 1, 1969, by T. H. Baker, LBJ Library, Austin, Texas, pp. 15–19, https://discoverlbj.org/item/oh-abellb-19690701-3-84-30.

9. James R. Ketchum interview, November 30, 2004, p. 156.

10. Douglass Cater interviewed by David G. Macomb, May 8, 1969, LBJ Library, p. 7, https://www.discoverlbj.org/item/oh-caters-19690508-2-72-19-b.

11. Lady Bird Johnson, *A White House Diary* (New York: Holt, Rinehart and Winston, 1970), p. 287.

12. Bess Abell interviewed by Richard Norton Smith, January 29, 2008, White House Historical Association, Washington, DC.

13. Bess Abell interview, "Behind the Scenes in the East Wing," March 5, 2012.

14. Carol Carlyle interviewed by Brien Williams, October 16, 2019, Louie B. Nunn Center for Oral History, UKLSCRC.

15. Bess Abell interview, January 29, 2008.

16. Johnson, *A White House Diary*, pp. 620–624.

17. Bess Abell Interview 3, July 1, 1969, pp. 15–19.

18. Liz Carpenter Interview 2, April 4, 1969, by Joe B. Frantz, LBJ Library, pp. 34–35, https://www.discoverlbj.org/item/oh-carpenterl-19690404-2-74-193-b.

19. Bess Abell interview, March 5, 2012.

20. Bess Abell interview, January 29, 2008.

21. Liz Carpenter Interview 2, April 4, 1969, p. 35.

22. Eartha Kitt interviewed by Renee Poussaint, June 7, 2006, the National Visionary Leadership Project, https://www.youtube.com/watch?v=5JrtRhsxWyY.

23. Liz Carpenter Interview 2, April 4, 1969, p. 36.

24. James R. Ketchum interview, November 30, 2004, p. 158.

25. Liz Carpenter Interview 4, August 27, 1969, by Joe B. Frantz, LBJ Library, pp. 28–30, https://www.discoverlbj.org/item/oh-carpenterl-19690827-4-74-193-d.

26. Johnson, *A White House Diary*, p. 655.

27. Patricia Perkins Andringa interviewed by Brien Williams, September 20, 2019, Louie B. Nunn Center for Oral History, UKLSCRC.

28. Tyler Abell interviewed by Brien Williams, June 15, 2018, Louie B. Nunn Center for Oral History, UKLSCRC.

9. Part of the Family

1. Bess Abell interviewed by Rick Albin, "Insiders Look at the White House," April 8, 2009, Gerald R. Ford Presidential Museum, https://www.youtube.com/watch?v=k4bsDiRaf6g.

2. Lyndon B. Johnson recorded telephone conversation with Bess Abell, April 17, 1964, Miller Center, University of Virginia, https://millercenter.org/the-presidency/secret-white-house-tapes/conversation-bess-abell-and-juanita-roberts-april-17-1964.

3. Tyler Abell interviewed by Brien Williams, May 29, 2018, Louie B. Nunn Center for Oral History, UKLSCRC.

4. Bess Abell Interview 2, June 13, 1969, by T. H. Baker, LBJ Library, Austin, Texas, pp. 4–5.

5. Mary Lynn Kotz interviewed by Brien Williams, July 11, 2018, Louie B. Nunn Center for Oral History, UKLSCRC.

6. J. B. West with Mary Lynn Kotz, *Upstairs at the White House: My Life with the First Ladies* (New York: Coward, McCann & Geoghegan, 1973), p. 310.

7. James R. Ketchum interviewed by Donald A. Ritchie, November 30, 2004, US Senate Historical Office, Washington, DC, p. 165.

8. James R. Ketchum interviewed by Brien Williams, July 18, 2018, Louie B. Nunn Center for Oral History, UKLSCRC.

9. Barbara Gamarekian, "All the President's Wines," *New York Times*, January 15, 1986.

10. C. Thomas Bendorf, aide to Senator Claire Engle and Governor Pat Brown, Director of Government Relations for Lockheed Corporation.

11. Tyler Abell interviewed by Brien Williams, June 15, 2018, Louie B. Nunn Center for Oral History, UKLSCRC.

12. Frederick. J. Ryan Jr., *Wine and the White House: A History* (Washington, DC: White House Historical Association, 2020), p. 74.

13. Carol Carlyle interviewed by Brien Williams, October 16, 2019, Louie B. Nunn Center for Oral History, UKLSCRC.

14. Patricia Perkins Andringa interviewed by Brien Williams, September 20, 2019, Louie B. Nunn Center for Oral History, UKLSCRC.

15. Bess Abell interviewed by Capricia Penavic Marshall for "Role of the First Lady," June 4, 2014, Clinton Presidential Center, C-SPAN Video Archive. https://www.c-span .org/video/?319588-1/panel-discussion-role-lady.

16. Richard Tanner Johnson, *Managing the White House: An Intimate Study of the Presidency* (New York: Harper & Row, 1974), p. 176.

17. Tyler Abell interview, June 15, 2018.

18. James R. Jones interviewed by Brien Williams, October 9, 2019, Louie B. Nunn Center for Oral History, UKLSCRC.

19. Bess Abell video interview, October 22, 2003, LBJ Library, https://www.youtube .com/watch?v=E3RJ5Kd-Qhs.

20. Patricia Perkins Andringa interview, September 20, 2019.

21. Tyler Abell Interview 2, May 29, 1969, by T. H. Baker, LBJ Library, pp. 27–39.

22. Luci Baines Johnson interviewed by Michael L. Gillette, October 18, 2019, Louie B. Nunn Center for Oral History, UKLSCRC.

23. Carol Carlyle interview, October 16, 2019.

24. James R. Ketchum interview, November 30, 2004, p. 165.

25. West, *Upstairs at the White House*, p. 345.

26. Bess Abell interviewed by Mark Updegrove, December 6, 2012, "Tribute to Lady Bird Johnson," National Archives, C-SPAN Video Archive, https://www.c-span.org /video/?309829-1/tribute-lady-bird-johnson.

27. Lynda Johnson Robb interviewed by Donald A. Ritchie, November 26, 2019, Louie B. Nunn Center for Oral History, UKLSCRC.

28. Linda Jane Holden, *The Gardens of Bunny Mellon* (New York: Vendome, 2018).

29. Linda Jane Holden interviewed by Brien Williams, February 23, 2019, Louie B. Nunn Center for Oral History, UKLSCRC.

30. Bess Abell interviewed by Capricia Penavic Marshall for "Role of the First Lady," June 4, 2014.

31. Bess Abell interviewed by Richard Norton Smith, January 29, 2008, White House Historical Association, Washington, DC.

10. Joan of Art

1. Bess Abell interviewed by Richard Norton Smith, January 29, 2008, White House Historical Association, Washington, DC.

2. Tyler Abell interviewed by Brien Williams, June 5, 2018, Louie B. Nunn Center for Oral History, UKLSCRC.

3. Walter Mondale interviewed by Brien Williams, August 22, 2018, Louie B. Nunn Center for Oral History, UKLSCRC.

4. Michael S. Berman interviewed by Brien Williams, July 20, 2018, Louie B. Nunn Center for Oral History, UKLSCRC.

5. Bess Abell eulogy at Joan Mondale's Memorial Service, Minneapolis, Minnesota, February 8, 2014, Tyler Abell Papers, Potomac, Maryland.

6. Bess Abell, "Favorite Traveling Companion," Tyler Abell Papers.

7. Walter Mondale interview, August 22, 2018.

8. Judy Whittlesey interviewed by Brien Williams, July 15, 2018, Louie B. Nunn Center for Oral History, UKLSCRC.

9. Tyler Abell interview, June 5, 2018.

10. Deborah M. Sale interviewed by Brien Williams, August 24, 2018, Louie B. Nunn Center for Oral History, UKLSCRC.

11. Walter F. Mondale with David Hage, *The Good Fight: A Life in Liberal Politics* (New York: Scribner, 2010), p. 184.

12. Walter Mondale interview, August 22, 2018.

13. Michael S. Berman interview, July 20, 2018.

14. Bess Abell interviewed by Terry L. Birdwhistell, September 26, 2007, Louie B. Nunn Center for Oral History, UKLSCRC.

15. Judy Whittlesey interview, July 15, 2018.

16. Ann Stock interviewed by Brien Williams, January 23, 2019, Louie B. Nunn Center for Oral History, UKLSCRC.

17. Deborah M. Sale interview, August 24, 2018.

18. *Louisville Courier-Journal*, May 7, 1978.

19. Deborah M. Sale interview, August 24, 2018.

20. Michael S. Berman interview, July 20, 2018.

21. Anita Gates, "Joan Mondale, Who Merged Politics with Art, Dies at 83," *New York Times*, February 3, 2014.

22. Betty Beale, "It's Bess Abell's Turn to Be Honored," *Cincinnati Enquirer*, April 2, 1978.

23. Walter Mondale interview, August 22, 2018.

24. Bess Abell eulogy at Joan Mondale's Memorial Service, February 8, 2014.

25. Judy Whittlesey interview, July 15, 2018.

26. Deborah M. Sale interview, August 24, 2018.

27. Ann Stock interview, January 23, 2019.

28. Deborah M. Sale interview, August 24, 2018.

29. Judy Whittlesey interview, July 15, 2018.

30. Michael S. Berman interview, July 20, 2018.

31. Ann Stock interview, January 23, 2019.

32. Bess Abell eulogy at Joan Mondale's Memorial Service, February 8, 2014.

33. Mary Lynn Kotz interviewed by Brien Williams, July 11, 2018, Louie B. Nunn Center for Oral History, UKLSCRC.

34. Walter Mondale interview, August 22, 2018.

35. Michael S. Berman interview, July 20, 2018.

36. Neal P. Gillen interviewed by Brien Williams, October 3, 2019, Louie B. Nunn Center for Oral History, UKLSCRC.

37. Ann Stock interview, January 23, 2019.

38. Walter Mondale interview, August 22, 2018.

39. Michael S. Berman interview, July 20, 2018.

40. Deborah M. Sale interview, August 24, 2018.

41. Tyler Abell interviewed by Brien Williams, June 15, 2018, Louie B. Nunn Center for Oral History, UKLSCRC.

42. Walter Mondale interview, August 22, 2018.

11. Life after the White House

1. Ann Wood, "The Newest 'Mostest' Hostess," *New York Daily News*, March 16, 1975.

2. Tyler Abell interviewed by Brien Williams, June 15, 2018, Louie B. Nunn Center for Oral History, UKLSCRC. See also See Kathryn J. McGarr, *The Whole Damn Deal: Robert Strauss and the Art of Politics* (New York: Public Affairs, 2011), pp. 95–100.

3. Carol Carlyle interviewed by Brien Williams, October 16, 2019, Louie B. Nunn Center for Oral History, UKLSCRC.

4. Bob Hartnett letter to Tyler Abell, November 2020, Tyler Abell Papers, Potomac, Maryland.

5. Donald A. Ritchie, *Reporting from Washington: The History of the Washington Press Corps* (New York: Oxford University Press, 2005), pp. 179–182.

6. Wood, "The Newest 'Mostest' Hostess." See also Jeannette Smyth, "Party Instead of Picketing," *Washington Post*, April 6, 1974.

7. Eileen Shanahan interviewed by Mary Marshall Clark, June 6, 1993, Washington Press Club Foundation, Washington, DC, http://beta.wpcf.org/oralhistory/shan9.html.

8. Tyler Abell interview, June 15, 2018.

9. James R. Ketchum interviewed by Donald A. Ritchie, November 30, 2004, US Senate Historical Office, Washington, DC, pp. 146–149.

10. Katrina Mason, "Architects Find a Dream Come True at Potomac's Merry-Go-Round Farm," *Washington Post*, March 18, 2000. See also Sarah Booth Conroy, "A Muckraker's Heaven," *Washington Post*, October 29, 1989.

11. Tyler Abell interview, June 15, 2018.

12. Shirley James interviewed by Michael L. Gillette, January 24, 2020, Louie B. Nunn Center for Oral History, UKLSCRC.

13. Tyler Abell interview, June 15, 2018.

14. Shirley James interview, January 24, 2020.

15. Luci Baines Johnson interviewed by Michael L. Gillette, October 18, 2019, Louie B. Nunn Center for Oral History, UKLSCRC.

16. Lynda Johnson Robb interviewed by Donald A. Ritchie, October 11, 2019, Louie B. Nunn Center for Oral History, UKLSCRC.

17. Patricia Perkins Andringa interviewed by Brien Williams, September 20, 2019, Louie B. Nunn Center for Oral History, UKLSCRC.

18. Ann Stock interviewed by Brien Williams, January 23, 2019, Louie B. Nunn Center for Oral History, UKLSCRC.

19. Deborah M. Sale interviewed by Brien Williams, August 24, 2018, Louie B. Nunn Center for Oral History, UKLSCRC.

20. Carol Carlyle interview, October 16, 2019.

21. Linda Jane Holden interviewed by Brien Williams, February 23, 2019, Louie B. Nunn Center for Oral History, UKLSCRC.

22. James R. Jones interviewed by Brien Williams, October 9, 2019, Louie B. Nunn Center for Oral History, UKLSCRC.

23. Neal P. Gillen interviewed by Brien Williams, October 3, 2019, Louie B. Nunn Center for Oral History, UKLSCRC.

24. Tyler Abell interviewed by Brien Williams, May 29, 2018, Louie B. Nunn Center for Oral History, UKLSCRC.

25. Tyler Abell interview, June 15, 2018.

26. James R. Ketchum interviewed by Brien Williams, July 18, 2018, Louie B. Nunn Center for Oral History, UKLSCRC.

Epilogue

1. Bess Abell Interview 3, July 1, 1969, by T. H. Baker, LBJ Library, Austin, Texas, pp. 16–18, https://www.discoverlbj.org/item/oh-abellb-19690701-3-84-30.

Index

Kentucky Remembered:
An Oral History Series

James C. Klotter, Terry L. Birdwhistell, and Douglas A. Boyd, Series Editors

Books in the Series

About the Authors

Donald A. Ritchie is Historian Emeritus of the US Senate. He served as president of the Oral History Association and on the council of the American Historical Association. His books include *Press Gallery: Congress and the Washington Correspondents*; *Reporting from Washington: The History of the Washington Press Corps*; *The Columnist: Leaks, Lies, and Libel in Drew Pearson's Washington*; *The U.S. Congress: A Very Short Introduction*; and *Doing Oral History*.

Terry L. Birdwhistell is senior oral historian and founding director of the Louie B. Nunn Center for Oral History at the University of Kentucky Libraries and previously served as Dean of Libraries. A former president of the Oral History Association, he is coauthor of *Our Rightful Place: Women at the University of Kentucky, 1880–1945*, co–general editor of *Kentucky Remembered: An Oral History Series*, and editor of *Engineering Corporate Success: A Memoir*, by James Hardymon.